W9-BII-844

WHAT CAN I DO WITH A MAJOR IN... ?

How To *Choose* and *Use* Your College Major

- Careers graduates of the 21 most popular majors have entered from 1960 to the present

- Strategies for choosing your college major and planning your career

Lawrence R. Malnig, Ph.D.

Director/Counseling Center
SAINT PETER'S COLLEGE
With
Anita Malnig

With a Foreword by
Robert Hoppock, Ph.D.

Emeritus Professor
of Counselor Education
NEW YORK UNIVERSITY

Abbott Press   **Box 433**   **Ridgefield, N.J. 07657**

Printed and Published By

ABBOTT PRESS
P.O. BOX 433
RIDGEFIELD, N.J. 07657

Library of Congress Number: 83-73269

ISBN: Cloth: 0-9612678-1-X

ISBN: Paper: 0-9612678-0-1

Designed and Illustrated By Elizabeth Case
PRINTED IN THE UNITED STATES OF AMERICA

WHAT CAN I DO WITH A MAJOR IN . . . ?

HOW TO *CHOOSE* AND *USE* YOUR COLLEGE MAJOR

ALL-NEW SELF-HELP FEATURES

- ✓ A personal self-assessment plan
- ✓ Selecting jobs that fit your personality
- ✓ Entry jobs for men/Entry jobs for women
- ✓ Avoiding the stereotyped major-to-job rut
- ✓ Expanding horizons — before and *after* college

Get happiness out of your work or you may never know what happiness is.
— *Elbert Hubbard*

To my family —
Laura, Anita, and Julie.

To my dear friend
— James A. Pegolotti —
who with care, compassion, and
respect for each one's individuality
helps students dare to be their best.

To the men and women graduates
of Saint Peter's College — whose
achievements made this book possible.

— ADEQUACY —

The spider spins his tapestries
With grey-blue threads of strength
And gives each silky filigree
Its necessary length.

So let me weave my sum of days
With fibers of strong thought
And give to every task of mine
The depth and breadth I ought.

ANTHONY NAVARRA

FOREWORD

A number of colleges have published follow-up reports on the jobs their seniors got after graduating. Some institutions have related this information to the respective college majors. These colleges deserve thanks and commendations from students, counselors, and parents for their institutional integrity in reporting what really happens to their product.

Malnig has gone much further. He has followed up alumni/alumnae for more than two decades, has reported entry-level jobs, and has then gone on to identify the career-jobs they subsequently moved into. In addition, the Holland Occupational Codes and Worker Functions Ratings he has associated with each job, in this completely new edition, will help readers expand their career prospects and identify the positions that are likely to match their personal needs and preferences. In doing that, he has provided a much-needed document that students, parents, and counselors all over the United States can use once again — this time even more specifically —to find out what a college graduate can do with his or her major in . . .

ROBERT HOPPOCK

ACKNOWLEDGMENTS

We thank the many colleagues and counselors across the country who so generously volunteered their suggestions for this new edition. We also appreciate the information we received from Robert Hoppock (New York University), John L. Holland (Johns Hopkins University), Jean Britton (University of Utah), Jo-Ida C. Hansen (University of Minnesota), Mildred Barker and Elaine Levy (New York State Department of Labor), Edward V. Collins, James J. Harrison, William A. Huebner, Eugene R. King, Martin H. Rosenbluth, Grace W. Schut and Richard D. Tetreau (Saint Peter's College), Marcia L. Mentkowski (Alverno College), Timothy Welles (Drew University), Bruce Riesenberg (University of California/Irvine), Henry Campbell (Jersey City State College), Robert Stump (Marymount College/Virginia), David H. Wilder (Bucknell University), Howard E. Mitchell (Wharton School, University of Pennsylvania), Heather Becker (University of Texas/Austin) and Robert Calvert (Garrett Park Press).

We also thank Eugene J. Kennedy, Lawrence R. Tormey, Michael M. Brown, Joan A. Malloy, and William K. Stoms, Jr. who helped in collecting our data; Gene N. Corbo and Barbara P. Mansfield for processing the results; and Peter M. Gotlieb for reviewing our manuscript. In the Counseling Center, our colleagues Lona Whitmarsh and Donald J. Marotto for their advice and moral support; Elizabeth Clossey, whose secretarial skills and constant good cheer make her a precious asset.

PREFACE

How people choose careers, prepare for them, and eventually prosper in them concerns most of us, directly or indirectly, throughout our lives. Helping students of all ages reach their goal of gainful employment involves those of us who teach, counsel, and train them, as well as those of us who foot the bill.

At one time or another, the list of individuals who find themselves caught up in career-planning includes, naturally enough, students in high school and college — both part-time and full-time. But it also takes into account, increasingly in our era, men and women planning to resume studies or even start college after years of life experience elsewhere.

Then there are career-changers, and those who are nearing retirement but want to go on putting their skills and insights to work in other fields of endeavor.

And professionally engaged in this intricate process of career-planning are high-school counselors and college counselors, placement officers, psychologists, social workers, clergy, psychiatrists, librarians, teachers and administrators at all educational levels, employment interviewers, campus recruiters, personnel managers, training and development officers, school trustees and legislators.

This list also includes those who have a personal interest in how career-planning turns out: husbands, wives, relatives, and parents.

This new, enlarged, and updated edition of *"What Can I Do With A Major In . . . ?"* brings together some of the most recent tools that career specialists, test-developers, and government agencies have devised to help people decide what they want to study and where they want to work.

In **Part One**, we explain the meaning of the numbers and letter-codes we use throughout this book to identify and classify jobs. Then we show how this ingenious system of numbers — taken from the United States Employment Service's *Dictionary of Occupational Titles* — and the letter codes, developed by John L. Holland to represent personality types, can help you relate your interests and personal preferences to satisfying, rewarding careers. We have also illustrated ways you can use these tools to help you make important educational decisions.

Part Two suggests how you can describe your interests and aptitudes in ways that enable you to identify those educational and career possibilities that may be open to *you* in particular. It also points out the pitfalls to avoid so you can make a positive, constructive evaluation of yourself.

Then in **Part Three**, we show how you can select from the later sections under each major — course descriptions, career leads, hiring institutions — whatever *you* may need to put *your* plans in focus.

In **Part Four**, each of the 21 majors we cover includes a list of the jobs that graduates of that major now hold, and separate columns for men and women showing the *beginning* jobs they got right after graduation.

And **Part Five** of *"What Can I Do With A Major In . . . ?"* lists in alphabetical order, for easy reference, the jobs that graduates currently hold. Then it shows how many *different* majors each occupation draws on to fill its ranks.

In other words, we show you:

1. how to identify your personal skills and interests;

2. how to match your assets with jobs that require those assets;

3. the current trends in hiring people with your training; and,

4. how to put all this information to work for *you.*

While we suggest some ways to use our information and to assess your personal characteristics, we have not used up *all* the possibilities open to you by any means. You can put your imagination and ingenuity to work expanding those possibilities, without limit. You can begin, for example, by asking your best friends to predict your future career and to give you reasons for their choice — or you can experiment with your own combination of the number and letter codes we describe in Part One of this book.

We wish you well in this rewarding adventure. Like others, *you* too can make it — whatever your goal.

CONTENTS

v   FOREWORD BY ROBERT HOPPOCK
vi   ACKNOWLEDGMENTS
vii PREFACE
1-4 INTRODUCTION

5 PART ONE
Meaning of Number and Letter Codes

27 PART TWO
Guide to Self-Assessment

37 PART THREE
How to Use:

    39 Description of Major
    41 Career Leads
    44 Hiring Institutions
    46 Current Occupations of Graduates
    47 Index: Major of Graduates by Occupation

51 PART FOUR
Careers by Departmental Major:

53 ACCOUNTANCY

59 ART HISTORY

63 BIOLOGY

71 CHEMISTRY

77 CLASSICS

81 ECONOMICS

91 EDUCATION

97 ENGLISH

105 HISTORY

113 MANAGEMENT

121 MARKETING

129 MATHEMATICS/COMPUTER SCIENCE

135 MODERN LANGUAGES

141 NATURAL SCIENCE

147 PHILOSOPHY

153 PHYSICS

159 POLITICAL SCIENCE

165 PSYCHOLOGY

171 SOCIOLOGY

177 URBAN STUDIES

183 PART FIVE
Index: Major of Graduates by Occupation

INTRODUCTION

T his book has been 15 years in the making. It began with an attempt to answer the most nagging question students at Saint Peter's College asked us:

- "What can I do with my major in . . . ?"

In our search for answers to this question, we raised some of our own:

- "Do graduates actually get the jobs we told them were available?"

- "What other jobs do they find?"

- "What are the more common beginning jobs?"

To get answers to these questions, we surveyed our alumni and, in 1968, we first reported the results in a mimeographed list showing the jobs that graduates of each major got. The results were quite unforeseen: Graduates were not landing the jobs one might reasonably expect. Yet the positive response we received from educators who said the well-worn copies of our report had captured considerable student interest, encouraged us to continue our research and to update our information. Seven years later we issued our first book-form edition of *"What Can I Do With A Major In . . . ?"* for national distribution.

In that 1975 Edition, we had occupations carry the numbers assigned to them in *The Dictionary of Occupational Titles* (DOT). We also had one listing, by major, for jobs alumni secured within five years after graduation, and another for occupations they held six to 25 years after leaving college.

We have expanded this current edition to include some of the suggestions counselors and other professional practitioners, nationwide, have sent us. Some liked particularly the research-based findings which confirm that liberal arts majors enter a wide variety of occupations; others said our factual data helped dispel stereotyped ideas about majors and careers. We have updated both categories of information in this, our 1984 Edition.

One of the helpful new touches in this Edition is a separate listing for the beginning jobs men and women got within five years after graduating. Another is the addition of DOT Worker Functions Ratings for each occupation. These ratings show the degree to which each job involves contact with *data, people,* and *things.*

We have also given each job a three-letter designation. This is the Holland Job Code which indicates the personality-type of people in that occupation. Holland uses the same code to describe the qualities of the work-environment because the surroundings reflect the personalities of the people who work there.

The meaning and uses of these classifications appear in the chapters that follow. But to put it briefly, by following the directions we have provided, readers can develop a personal letter-code that represents the kinds of activities and work environments they prefer. Then they can select careers listed under a major, or in the Index, which have the same letters as their personal three-letter code. The occupations the readers get by this matching process will identify those jobs that are likely to satisfy their needs.

The most surprising thing about our findings was the fact — which surfaced so consistently we couldn't help but be impressed by it — that regardless of their major, college graduates *enter a wide range of occupations, many of them seemingly unrelated to undergraduate studies.* These findings have forced us to conclude that *any* major, apparently, equips students with knowledge and skills that they can apply to a wide range of jobs in many diverse fields.

We have not been able to come up with easy explanations for this unexpected relationship between majors and careers. But that doesn't mean it's not important to develop accurate occupational information and to help students with careful academic planning. Quite the contrary. Besides information about the training and skill a job calls for, students need to know about the qualities that lead to success in a whole galaxy of occupations and how they can develop those qualities in a particular course of study, be it mathematics, psychology, or history. And they need to be aware of their personality traits and learn about the kinds of jobs that can accommodate those traits.

As we continued our research, we discovered that we were not alone in our findings about majors and careers. Colleges and universities across the country — CUNY, Mount Holyoke, Bucknell, Drew, Indiana, Utah, and California-Irvine — came up with similar results. This diversity of alumni jobs so impressed the authors of the Placement Office's Study at Indiana University that they titled their 1979 publication, *You Can Do Just About Anything.*

Another study now in progress seeks to discover which skills lead to career success and how one can incorporate them in college majors. This is taking place at Alverno College in Milwaukee, Wisconsin. Marcia L. Mentkowski and Austin Doherty issued an interim report on it in 1980 titled *Careering After College: Establishing the Validity of Abilities Learned in College for Later Success.* Their research aims to develop a competence model based on specific behaviors which make for success on a job. The investigators then plan to compare this model with the one they currently use at Alverno College and to suggest appropriate improvements.

The Wharton School of Finance at the University of Pennsylvania published in 1980 another pertinent study under the direction of Dr. Howard E. Mitchell, titled *The Extent and Nature of Vocational Change Among College Graduates: 1964-65 to 1977.* This investigation found that even technically-trained college graduates have many skills that transfer readily, and that the professional and technical skills we often associate with certain occupations are not so unique after all. The authors point out that "there appears to be a high degree of commonality of tasks as well as prerequisite skills between many seemingly different occupations which make transfers possible without major investments in formal education or training."

These studies support what we maintain here:

That students have a broad array of career opportunities open to them regardless of their major.

Nevertheless, planning a course of studies that will provide both immediately-marketable and long-range career skills is a difficult task for students today because of rising educational costs, uncertain economic conditions, and pressures from well-meaning parents and relatives to take "practical" courses. To accomplish this planning, besides examining all the objective data they have about careers, students also need to evaluate themselves:

- Do they like competitive or cooperative work situations?

- Are they happier working independently or in a structured environment?

- Do they prefer to speak and write, or to delve into facts and figures?

Our book offers several ways students can get this information and learn more about themselves, and then apply that information in choosing a compatible major, as well as in uncovering diverse career possibilities. A further bonus will be the discovery that, whichever major they've picked, the career possibilities under that major are surprisingly varied and virtually unlimited. Of course, this approach, as with any other, cannot guarantee job success. But as a method based on accurate information about jobs and ways to increase self-awareness, it will enable readers to move ahead with greater confidence and a heightened sense of direction.

We hope our research will serve as a useful guide for both students and the counselors who always look for better ways to help them. We wish those students fulfillment and success in the choices they make. We know from experience that counselors will get *their* fulfillment from seeing how they had a hand in helping their students achieve their goals.

L.R.M.

PART ONE
MEANING OF NUMBER AND LETTER CODES

The test of a vocation is the love of the drudgery it involves.
— Logan Pearsall Smith

PART ONE
MEANING OF NUMBER
AND LETTER CODES

Each of the occupations you will find listed in this book has the same six-digit number as the one the United States Government Publication *The Dictionary of Occupational Titles* (DOT) assigns to it. The Dictionary's Fourth and current Edition (1977) contains extensive definitions of some 20,000 jobs. This numerical classification system gives each occupation its own separate and distinct number. This arrangement makes it possible for the reader to get a complete picture of any occupation we mention in this book by looking up the number the DOT assigns to that job.

Each occupation we have listed has two sets of three-digit numbers separated by a decimal — for example, Accountant *160.167.* The first three numbers classify the job. The second three indicate how much it involves contact with *data, people,* and *things.* We'll have more to say about that later.

Besides these numbers, each occupation has a three-*letter* code. This code is from a classification system which John L. Holland, the noted vocational psychologist, originated.

Holland's letters follow the DOT's numerical designation like this: Accountant 160.167 *CES.* His letters indicate, in descending order, the more pronounced characteristics of both the people who hold those jobs and the environment where they do the work. Take the Accountant's letters, for example: The "C" stands for Conventional (orderly), which is the most common trait of people in this occupation. The work environment also reflects this orderliness. Next comes "E" for Enterprising — a prevalent but less common trait in accountants. And "S" for Social, a quality fewer accountants possess compared to the first two. The letters do not mean you will need these traits to be an accountant. They show only which of the six traits in this classification system accountants are most likely to have.

Below you will find other examples. We also explain in more detail the numbering system itself, and the meaning of the six letters which make up Holland's Summary Occupational Code.

Numerical Classification

The three digits in front of the decimal classify 1) the job's broad *category*, 2) its *subdivisions*, and 3) the specific *group* the job belongs to. For example, the number for Food Chemist is 022. The first digit, ZERO, tells you it comes under the heading of Professional, Technical, and Managerial positions. The second digit, TWO, narrows it down to occupations in Mathematics and the Physical Sciences. And the third number, also a TWO in this case, tells us that this occupation is in the more precise subgroup of Jobs in Chemistry.

In *The Dictionary Of Occupational Titles*, nine broad first-digit categories classify most occupations. These categories are:

0 and 1. Professional, Technical, Managerial

2. Clerical and Sales

3. Service

4. Agricultural, Fishery, Forestry, and Related

5. Processing

6. Machine Trades

7. Benchwork

8. Structural Work

9. Miscellaneous

These nine categories break down into 82 subdivisions by adding a second digit. Take the number 07. The first number 0 indicates a Professional, Technical or Managerial occupation, and the second number 7 shows it's in the subdivision of Medicine and Health. Then, by adding a third digit, you can expand these 82 subdivisions into 559 smaller, homogeneous groups. In the number 075, for instance, the five would further indicate that *Registered Nurses* constitute a subgroup of occupations in Medicine and Health.

Since only college graduates hold the jobs we list in this book, you can expect that most of those jobs will fall under the first category of Professional, Technical and Managerial occupations. When this category splits up into the narrower subdivisions we have illustrated above, the number of the different occupational groups under this heading expands to 100. We have listed those 100 three-digit subgroups below.

We have also listed the 60 three-digit subgroups that appear under Clerical and Sales Occupations, because it is in this area that many college graduates have found both beginning jobs and, eventually, careers such as Computer Operations Supervisor (213), Insurance Claims Adjuster (241) and Pharmaceutical Detailer (262), to name just a few.

THREE-DIGIT OCCUPATIONAL GROUPS
The Dictionary of Occupational Titles p. xxxvi

PROFESSIONAL, TECHNICAL, AND MANAGERIAL OCCUPATIONS

00/01
Occupations in architecture, engineering, and surveying

001	Architectural occupations
002	Aeronautical engineering occupations
003	Electrical/electronics engineering occupations
005	Civil engineering occupations
006	Ceramic engineering occupations
007	Mechanical engineering occupations
008	Chemical engineering occupations
010	Mining and petroleum engineering occupations
011	Metallurgy and metallurgical occupations
012	Industrial engineering occupations
013	Agricultural engineering occupations
014	Marine engineering occupations
015	Nuclear engineering occupations
017	Drafters, n.e.c.*
018	Surveying/cartographic occupations

*Not elsewhere classified

019   Occupations in architecture, engineering, and surveying, n.e.c.

02
Occupations in mathematics and physical sciences

020   Occupations in mathematics

021   Occupations in astronomy

022   Occupations in chemistry

023   Occupations in physics

024   Occupations in geology

025   Occupations in meteorology

029   Occupations in mathematics and physical sciences, n.e.c.

04
Occupations in life sciences

040   Occupations in agricultural sciences

041   Occupations in biological sciences

045   Occupations in psychology

049   Occupations in life sciences, n.e.c.

05
Occupations in social sciences

050   Occupations in economics

051   Occupations in political science

052   Occupations in history

054   Occupations in sociology

055   Occupations in anthropology

059   Occupations in social sciences, n.e.c.

07
Occupations in medicine and health

070   Physicians and surgeons

071   Osteopaths

072   Dentists

073   Veterinarians

074   Pharmacists

075   Registered nurses

076   Therapists

077   Dietitians

078   Occupations in medical and dental technology

079   Occupations in medicine and health, n.e.c.

09
Occupations in education

090   Occupations in college and university education

091   Occupations in secondary school education

092   Occupations in preschool, primary school, and kindergarten education

094   Occupations in education of the handicapped

096   Home economists and farm advisers

097 Occupations in vocational education, n.e.c.

099 Occupations in education, n.e.c.

**10
Occupations in museum, library, and archival sciences**

100 Librarians

101 Archivists

102 Museum curators and related occupations

109 Occupations in museum, library, and archival sciences, n.e.c.

**11
Occupations in law and jurisprudence**

110 Lawyers

111 Judges

119 Occupations in law and jurisprudence, n.e.c.

**12
Occupations in religion and theology**

120 Clergy

129 Occupations in religion and theology, n.e.c.

**13
Occupations in writing**

131 Writers

132 Editors: publication, broadcast, and script

137 Interpreters and translators

139 Occupations in writing, n.e.c.

**14
Occupations in art**

141 Commercial artists: designers and illustrators, graphic arts

142 Environmental, product, and related designers

143 Occupations in photography

144 Fine artists: painters, sculptors, and related occupations

149 Occupations in art, n.e.c.

**15
Occupations in entertainment and recreation**

150 Occupations in dramatics

151 Occupations in dancing

152 Occupations in music

153 Occupations in athletics and sports

159 Occupations in entertainment and recreation, n.e.c.

**16
Occupations in administrative specializations**

160 Accountants and auditors

161 Budget and management systems analysis occupations

162 Purchasing management occupations

163 Sales and distribution management occupations

164 Advertising management occupations

165 Public relations management occupations

166 Personnel administration occupations

168 Inspectors and investigators, managerial and public service

169 Occupations in administrative specializations, n.e.c.

18
Managers and officials, n.e.c.

180 Agriculture, forestry, and fishing industry managers and officials

181 Mining industry managers and officials

182 Construction industry managers and officials

183 Manufacturing industry managers and officials

184 Transportation, communication, and utilities industry managers and officials

185 Wholesale and retail trade managers and officials

186 Finance, insurance, and real estate managers and officials

187 Service industry managers and officials

188 Public administration managers and officials

189 Miscellaneous managers and officials, n.e.c.

19
Miscellaneous professional, technical, and managerial occupations

191 Agents and appraisers, n.e.c.

193 Radio operators

194 Sound, film, and videotape recording, and reproduction occupations

195 Occupations in social and welfare work

196 Airplane pilots and navigators

197 Ship captains, mates, pilots and engineers

198 Railroad conductors

199 Miscellaneous professional, technical, and managerial occupations, n.e.c.

CLERICAL AND SALES OCCUPATIONS

20
Stenography, typing, filing and related occupations

201 Secretaries

202 Stenographers

203 Typists and typewriting-machine operators

205 Interviewing clerks

206 File clerks

207   Duplicating-machine operators and tenders

208   Mailing and miscellaneous office machine operators

209   Stenography, typing, filing, and related occupations

21
Computing and account-recording occupations

210   Bookkeepers and bookkeeping-machine operators

211   Cashiers and tellers

213   Electronic and electro-mechanical data processors

214   Billing and rate clerks

215   Payroll, timekeeping, and duty-roster clerks

216   Accounting and statistical clerks

217   Account-recording-machine operators, n.e.c.

219   Computing and account-recording occupations, n.e.c.

22
Production and stock clerks and related occupations

221   Production clerks

222   Shipping, receiving, stock, and related clerical occupations

229   Production and stock clerks and related occupations, n.e.c.

23
Information and message distribution occupations

230   Hand delivery and distribution occupations

235   Telephone operators

236   Telegraph operators

237   Information and reception clerks

238   Accommodation clerks and gate and ticket agents

239   Information and message distribution occupations, n.e.c.

24
Miscellaneous clerical occupations

241   Investigators, adjusters, and related occupations

243   Government service clerks, n.e.c.

245   Medical service clerks, n.e.c.

247   Advertising-service clerks, n.e.c.

248   Transportation-service clerks, n.e.c.

249   Miscellaneous clerical occupations, n.e.c.

25
Sales occupations, services

250   Sales occupations, real estate and insurance

251   Sales occupations, business and financial services

252   Sales occupations, transportation services

253 Sales occupations, utilities

254 Sales occupations, printing and advertising

259 Sales occupations, services, n.e.c.

26
Sales occupations, consumable commodities

260 Sales occupations, agricultural and food products

261 Sales occupations, textile products, apparel, and notions

262 Sales occupations, chemicals, drugs, and sundries

269 Sales occupations, miscellaneous consumable commodities, n.e.c.

27
Sales occupations, commodities, n.e.c.

270 Sales occupations, home furniture, furnishings, and appliances

271 Sales occupations, electrical goods, except home appliances

272 Sales occupations, farm and gardening equipment and supplies

273 Sales occupations, transportation equipment, parts, and supplies

274 Sales occupations, industrial and related equipment and supplies

275 Sales occupations, business and commercial equipment and supplies

276 Sales occupations, medical and scientific equipment and supplies

277 Sales occupations, sporting, hobby, stationery, and related goods

279 Sales occupations, miscellaneous commodities, n.e.c.

29
Miscellaneous sales occupations

290 Sales clerks

291 Vending and door to door selling occupations

292 Route sales and delivery occupations

293 Solicitors

294 Auctioneers

295 Rental clerks

296 Shoppers

297 Sales promotion occupations

298 Merchandise displayers

299 Miscellaneous sales occupations, n.e.c.

We have not listed the subdivisions of the other seven categories because not many college graduates find jobs in them. Those who do establish careers in the service occupations, for instance, go in mostly for the Protective Services, 373-376, such as Firefighter, Special Agent, etc. Those in the remaining categories usually enter the Skilled Trades.

An important thing to keep in mind is that the 100 listings under Professional, Technical and Managerial occupations refer to *groups* of occupations rather than to the *number* of individual jobs. For example, the group 024, Occupations in Geology, contains all the individual occupations that have something to do with the earth's crust. It includes jobs such as Hydrologist, Mineralogist, Seismologist, and even Prospector — 17 in all. But the number of jobs for each group varies. The 070 group, Physicians and Surgeons, contains 26 specific jobs while 055, Anthropology, has only five. When we add all the individual jobs these 100 groups list, we get a total of some 1,500 separate titles for the Professional, Technical, and Managerial category.

When numerous occupations have the same three-digit designation, the DOT lists them according to how much the job involves contact with *data, people,* and *things.* The second set of three digits indicates that, and we explain how it does so in the next section.

For example, under the three-digit group 160, the DOT lists 17 different jobs for Accountants and Auditors. The one at the head of the list, Tax Accountant 160.*162,* involves the most direct contact with *data, people,* and *things,* while the one at the bottom — Estimator 160.*267* — involves the least.

Worker Functions Ratings

The second set of three digits, separated from the first set by a decimal, indicates, as we have said, how much someone in that job has to deal with *data, people,* and *things.*

The first number after the decimal refers to *data,* the second to *people,* and the third to *things.* These numbers range from 0 to 8. The lower numbers indicate the more complex functions —those that call for a higher degree of responsibility and judgment.

For instance, under Data, Analyzing bears a TWO. But Copying is a less complicated function, so it bears a FIVE.

Here are the three categories, together with the specific functions the DOT lists for them in descending order of complexity:

Data	People	Things
0 Synthesizing	0 Mentoring	0 Setting Up
1 Coordinating	1 Negotiating	1 Precision Work
2 Analyzing	2 Instructing	2 Operating, Controlling
3 Compiling	3 Supervising	3 Driving/Operating
4 Computing	4 Diverting	4 Manipulating
5 Copying	5 Persuading	5 Tending
6 Comparing	6 Speaking/ Signaling	6 Feeding/Offbearing
	7 Serving	7 Handling
	8 Taking Instruction/Helping	

DATA

The first category, *Data*, refers to all types of information: words, numbers, ideas, concepts — known or assumed — from which one draws conclusions. Each of the six terms under this category tells the way one can work with data or information. Here are the definitions and some illustrations of those terms:

0 Synthesizing: Understanding, utilizing, and assimilating data to uncover, discover, perform certain tasks, and develop and create new ideas, concepts, etc.

Example: A *Safety Engineer* — 010.061 — for mines and quarries synthesizes vital information. He must inspect mines, and if he finds that anything is not up to safety standards, he must use principles of mining-engineering to correct the situation.

1 Coordinating: Determining time, place, and sequence of operations or action to be taken on the basis of analysis of data; executing that determination and/or reporting on events.

> Example: A *Radio, TV, or Movie Producer* — 159.117 — coordinates data. This person selects script-writers, equipment, and staff to take care of costumes, props, music. The producer reviews scripts and coordinates sound, script, photography, and other elements of production.

2 Analyzing: Examining and evaluating data. Presenting alternative actions in relation to the evaluation.

> Example: A *Police Officer* — 375.263 — especially on patrol, must size up an accident or a crime in progress and take appropriate steps.

3 Compiling: Gathering, collating, or classifying information. Reporting and/or carrying out a prescribed action in relation to that information.

> Example: A *Teller* — 211.362 — receives and pays out money, verifies amounts, and examines checks for endorsements. Keeps records of money, computes service charges, and issues receipts.

Here are the definitions of the remaining functions in this category:

4 Computing: Performing arithmetic operations and reporting on and/or carrying out a prescribed action in relation to them.

5 Copying: Transcribing, entering, or posting data.

6 Comparing: Examining the characteristics of data, people, or things to find out how they differ and what they have in common.

PEOPLE

This second category, *People*, describes the type of roles involved in working with people. It also includes dealing with animals on an individual basis as if they were humans, i.e., the way veterinarians do.

0 Mentoring: Giving advice and counsel to people for problems that may require legal, scientific, clinical, spiritual, or professional principles for their solution.

> Example: A *Criminal Lawyer* — 110.107 — deals with offenses against the state or society (theft, murder, arson). Such a lawyer interviews clients and witnesses to ascertain facts, prosecutes or defends the accused against charges, summarizes case to jury.

1 Negotiating: Exchanging ideas and information with others to formulate policies and jointly to arrive at decisions, conclusions, solutions.

> Example: The *Head Coach* of an athletic team — 153.117 —must evaluate players' skills and assign team positions accordingly; the coach also helps decide on trades and recruiting.

2 Instructing: Teaching, informing, educating by showing, lecturing, or guiding someone's performance.

> Example: A *Home Economist* — 096.121 —advises consumers, community groups, or homemakers on matters of nutrition, clothing, and other household concerns. This person may teach in schools, do research, or write instructive articles.

3 Supervising: Being in charge of a staff, assigning specific duties to them, maintaining harmonious relations among them, and promoting efficiency.

> Example: A *Recreation Supervisor* — 187.137 — coordinates and takes charge of many

types of recreational facilities. This person develops the recreational programs, hires personnel for activities, and oversees the entire process.

The definitions of the other functions in this category are as follows:

4 Diverting: Amusing others, usually on stage, television, in movies, on radio.

5 Persuading: Influencing others in favor of a product, service, or point of view.

6 Speaking/Signaling: Talking to people to give or receive information; also giving assignments or directions to helpers and assistants.

7 Serving: Taking care of the needs of people or animals, usually with immediate response.

8 Taking Instruction/Helping: Acting directly on instructions from a supervisor, with no responsibility involved.

THINGS

The last category, *Things*, lists the ways people can interact with inanimate objects in a work situation. Inanimate objects include tools, machines, equipment, and goods.

0 Setting Up: Altering and fixing equipment so that it is ready to do the job it was designed to do.

Example: A *Photo-Optics Technician* — 029.280 — sets and uses photo-optical equipment to photograph data for scientists and engineers. This involves doing detailed work according to specific diagrams and already-established procedures.

1 Precision Working: Manually using tools and/or equipment to bring about a specific end, and using skill and judgement in building the tools and equipment.

Example: A *Stained Glass Artist* — 142.061 — prepares and cuts glass to render a particular picture or design. The work involves cutting, waxing, painting, firing, and sometimes installing the finished window.

2 Operating and Controlling: Starting, stopping, and controlling the movement of machines or equipment. The operator of the equipment also sets up the machines and controls temperature, speed, pressure, etc.

Example: A *Telegrapher* — 236.562 — works the telegraph key and teletype machines to give and receive train orders, and keeps track of time, dates, and locations.

3 Driving/Operating: Steering and guiding the movement of equipment that fabricates things or moves people. The operator must watch dials and gauges, and judge distances.

Example: An *Airplane Pilot* — 196.263 — directs changes in fuel, load, and route; reads dials; makes sure all equipment is operating to assure maximum safety; runs through pre-flight checklist, etc.

And here are the definitions of all the other functions under this category.

4 Manipulating: Using one's body or tools to move, guide, or locate objects. Involves some judgment, but someone else usually lays out the work.

5 Tending: Starting, stopping, and adjusting controls of machines — e.g., flipping switches, turning dials — without having to exercise critical judgment in making those adjustments.

6 Feeding/Offbearing: Placing, throwing, or putting objects or materials into equipment which other operators run or which is automatic.

7 Handling: Handling involves only small contact with things. One might use one's body or simple tools to move or carry objects.

Let us return to the Food Chemist (022.061) for one last specific example of Worker Functions Ratings. In the full number following the decimal, the ZERO tells us that someone in this position *synthesizes* data; the second number, SIX, indicates a relatively minimal interaction with people, *speaking and signaling*; and the last number, ONE, shows that the job involves exercising considerable judgment and responsibility in dealing with things — *operating and controlling.*

What's especially interesting about the Worker Functions Ratings is that a particular pattern can be present in a variety of different occupations, as well as within related ones. Consequently, it's helpful in exploring occupations to have an idea of how much and in what capacity you would like to work with *data, people,* and *things.* It can be quite enlightening to see how the same second set of digits can accompany very different occupations. For instance, while the first three digits for Camp Director, 195, and Credit Manager, 168, are quite different, the second set of digits, 167, is the same for each. This means that while Credit Manager is mainly a business occupation and a Camp Director works in a social environment, both occupations involve the same degree of contact with *data, people,* and *things.* This kind of knowledge may open up new occupational possibilities for the reader to consider.

OCCUPATIONAL CODES

In addition to the six DOT numbers, each occupation in this book has a three-letter designation. These letters, as we have mentioned, indicate the personality characteristics most typical of people in that occupation, as well as the dominant features of the environment in which these people do their work. Personality and work environments resemble one another, according to Holland's theory, because people seek out work surroundings that please them. And once in the job, workers tend to modify that environment in ways that reflect their personalities.

For instance, a person scoring high on the social scale may derive satisfaction from helping others, as would a Licensed Practical Nurse. While taking care of others, this same person will help to create caring, nurturing conditions within the work situation.

John L. Holland, the vocational psychologist who originated this theory, reasoned that people in our culture could be classified under six broad categories which he labeled Realistic, Investigative, Artistic, Social, Enterprising, and Conventional (RIASEC). Each person, according to this theory, can be classified by a combination of these six types. For practical purposes, however, only the three letters representing the most pronounced traits are used to classify an occupation. For instance, a motion picture director would have the letter code AES: Artistic first of all, Enterprising next, and Social third.

The traits represented by these six types often develop from a person's long-term interests and experiences. For example, someone who as a child had chemistry sets, did scientific experiments, and won prizes at science fairs might very well carry over that interest into adult life. Holland would theorize that this person who had a strong scientific leaning —which Holland labels investigative — would probably function well in a work environment requiring this trait.

No one person possesses *only* the characteristics of one type, any more than we can say there are *only* six distinct types of people. People are complex, naturally enough, and display interesting combinations of these traits. Moreover, these personality definitions, described below, represent the *extreme* tendencies of a type, in order to emphasize how each personality description is different from the next.

But, these six categories can help you think constructively about your own tendencies: The classifications may help sharpen your focus on specific traits you possess and lead you to ways to use them best. For instance, you may become aware that your high rating on the social scale, based on your knack of making friends easily, is an ability you can use well in teaching or sales occupations.

Here is a listing of the six categories, with some of the

personal qualities related to each, and examples of the occupations that include people with these traits.

Realistic:

Realistic people prefer physical work and therefore are often physically strong and rugged. They also enjoy working with their hands, using tools and machines; frequently enough, this work takes them outdoors. Some occupations in which you'll find this type of person are: mechanical and construction jobs, technical laboratory jobs, agricultural/wildlife occupations, police work, skilled trades.

Here are some adjectives describing realistic people: stable, frank, genuine, practical, persistent, thrifty, natural. Some specific examples:

> **Ship Pilot** — 197.133, *REI* — Realistic first, Enterprising next, Investigative third.

> **Firefighter** — 373.364, *RSE* — Realistic first, Social second, Enterprising last.

Investigative:

The investigative person likes to observe, analyze, and solve problems, particularly in scientific and mathematical areas. This person probably is a creative thinker who would enjoy working with ideas, words and symbols, and might also like doing this work alone.

Some occupations in which you'd find this type of person are: psychologist, biologist, meteorologist, chemist.

Here are some descriptive adjectives associated with this theme: analytical, curious, independent, intellectual, precise, rational. Some specific examples:

> **Pharmacist** — 074.161, *IES* — Investigative first, Enterprising second, Social last.

> **Computer Programer** — 020.187, *IAS* — Investigative first, Artistic second, Social third.

Artistic:

The artistic person is likely to be unconventional and original in outlook and does self-expressive, creative work in any of the arts. Use of imagination is important to these people.

Artistic professions include artist, author, singer, dancer, poet, and music conductor.

Some of the adjectives describing artistic people are: expressive, imaginative, intuitive, introspective, original, non-conforming. And some specific examples are:

> **Music Conductor** — 152.047, *ASI* — Artistic first, Social second, Investigative last.

> **Dancing Teacher** — 151.027, *ASE* — Artistic first, Social second, Enterprising third.

Social:

Social people enjoy working with other people and are generally responsible, popular, and concerned about the well-being of others. These people also like to inform, train, and cure, and handle problems by talking about and examining relationships and feelings.

Social occupations include family counselors, sociologists, parole officers, camp directors.

Some of the adjectives associated with this theme are: cooperative, friendly, generous, helpful, idealistic, insightful, kind, and understanding. Some specific occupations are:

> **Clergy member** — 120.007, *SAI* — Social first, Artistic second, Investigative last.

> **Bartender** — 312.474, *SEC* — Social first, Enterprising next, Conventional third.

Enterprising:

The enterprising person, like the social person, also enjoys working with people. In this capacity, however, it is to influence, to persuade, to manage — and very often for economic gain. Such people are energetic and adventurous and often like material success, power, and status.

Enterprising occupations include stockbroker, television producer, salesperson, politician.

Some adjectives describing these people are: adventurous, ambitious, energetic, optimistic, self-confident, sociable, talkative. Specific examples are:

> **Commissary Manager** — 185.167, *ESI* — Enterprising first, Social second, Investigative last.

> **Building Contractor** — 182.167 *ERI* — Enterprising first, Realistic next, Investigative third.

Conventional:

Conventional people like working with data and often have good clerical and mechanical skills. They tend to work well in large organizations, following through on others' instructions and carrying out details.

Conventional professions include: auditor, proofreader, bank teller, statistician, bursar.

Adjectives describing conventional people are: conscientious, careful, orderly, persistent, practical, calm. Specific examples are:

> **Budget Accountant** — 160.167, *CES* — Conventional first, Enterprising second, Social last.

> **Secretary** — 201.362, *CSA* — Conventional first, Social second, Artistic last.

These numbers and letter codes can help you narrow down the work areas that attract you most and which you may want to examine more carefully.

The worker-functions ratings will enable you to identify those jobs within your area of interest which involve the degree of contact with *data, people,* and *things* you would find agreeable.

In addition, by examining the descriptions of the letter codes you can decide on the two or three which most closely describe you as you see yourself. Then, by putting these letters in order of rank to get your personal theme or code, you can see how closely it matches the code of the occupations you had selected on the basis of the DOT numbers.

In the next section, on self-assessment, you will find some more detailed guidelines for career exploration, as well as information about tests and counseling services that can assist you.

PART TWO

GUIDE TO
SELF-ASSESSMENT

Millionaires are successful because they do what they like and they do it well. — *Malcolm Forbes*

PART TWO
GUIDE TO SELF-ASSESSMENT

Now that you have an idea of how the mechanics of this book work, you'll want to go on and get a better idea about yourself and how you can use this information to your advantage in planning a career. Just where do you begin this search for career fulfillment?

The best place to start is with **yourself**.

Begin your career search by taking a long, accurate — and positive — look at yourself. Your quest is to discover interests and abilities which will be your tools for carving out your career. But self-assessment, like any other kind of self-confrontation, is easier said than done.

"Why does it seem so difficult to figure out what I'm interested in?" you might ask.

Why? Because we've often found that people struggle to measure up to unreasonable expectations they've set for themselves or that others have set for them, usually without realizing it. Some people get nervous at the thought of listing their skills and strong points. "Do I really have any?"

Others avoid any kind of self-examination because they fear they'll find out for sure that they indeed have all the shortcomings they suspect they do.

Still others hesitate to look at themselves because, unlike the self-doubters, they don't want to believe they have even a single flaw. The slightest imperfection, they feel, would make them worthless!

Both types of person hold back from this self-examination, often without knowing the underlying reason why.

Even if you don't fall directly into one of these more extreme groups, this kind of thinking may keep you from taking that important first step: accepting yourself as you are.

Once you allow yourself to become tolerant and realistic about yourself, you'll find self-assessment to be an interesting process, full of surprises. If you accept your strengths and your weaknesses, your assets *as well as* your liabilities, you'll begin to move.

Dwelling on faults and failures can only make you over-look the *positive* qualities you've developed. Whether you're an 18-year-old freshman trying to select a major, a 35-year-old homemaker trying to get up the nerve to enroll in college, or someone considering retirement, the human tendency to play down one's assets haunts each one of us.

When we ask students how they feel about the person they see in the mirror each day, we often hear a long list of faults. But when we ask them about their good qualities, they lose their tongues. Then they look puzzled and surprised when we tell them their records show they persevered long enough to complete elementary and high school, their performance sur-passed that of half the students in their graduating class, they made friends easily, and they had notable talents in verbal and linguistic subjects. All these positive pieces of information just from a transcript!

Homemakers over 30 or 35, away from school for a long time, also have trouble identifying their assets. They do not always see how their achievements in the home and community sprang from talents they can now further develop by coming back to school. They don't always understand that their ability to organize and schedule family activities, for instance, or to carry out a successful fund-raising campaign for the local church, or to teach arts and crafts to club members add up to aptitudes and abilities they can use in furthering their college studies. For instance, if you're the one who takes care of the family's finances, you might want to extend that talent to the study of accounting or economics. The old song "Accentuate the Positive" still holds true. Emphasizing the negative only short-circuits your awareness of qualities that can help you look ahead with purpose and self-confidence.

Even so, it's not so easy to dismiss negative myths about oneself. When we point out a skill in solving computa-tional problems or learning a new language, for instance, stu-dents will say it doesn't count because they did not have to try very hard. In other words, if you don't struggle over something it can't be worthwhile. They do not see that the task that comes easily to them may be difficult for someone else, and that their ability to do it with ease shows they have an aptitude they can build on.

This self-belittling behavior should not come as a surprise in the face of child-rearing and educational practices of parents and teachers that still devote more attention to detecting faults than to discovering and developing one's unique gifts and talents. Drawing attention to what someone has done well — what psychologists call positive reinforcement — is not a common practice, unfortunately, either in the classroom or on the job.

Another reason for this tendency we all have to be excessively self-critical is that we have let ourselves become conditioned to trying to measure up to what others expect of us. That way, without realizing it, we make other people's goals our own. For instance, we might believe we have to be the kind of doctor or lawyer our parents talk about so glowingly, or that we must at least match the income of cousin Phil or Rachel, or live in a fancy neighborhood with a Mercedes-Benz in the driveway. Under such pressures, it becomes impossible to define our own values, so we become unable to recognize, let alone question, the demands we unwittingly impose on ourselves. And, if we fail to live up to these unquestioned and unarticulated expectations, we begin to develop feelings of depression and futility, but with no idea where they are coming from.

So, it's vitally important to take stock, to get to know your likings and limitations, and to accept a realistic evaluation of yourself. Once you get beyond this web of negativity, of unreal expectations and exaggerated deficits, and begin to add up your true assets and interests, you will begin to experience a dramatic change in your attitude about yourself.

How to discover those assets and interests? Here's one way to begin your personal audit: List everything you did the day before — at home, at work, at play, at school. You eased an unyielding door. Did you really enjoy it? You shopped for a coat, read the paper, paid the bills, translated your French assignment and sketched your teacher's face in your notebook. How did you enjoy each activity? How did you feel when each was finished? Which ones did you do particularly well? Keep your list going. These activities can be physical, social, intellectual. They can involve speaking, writing, using your hands, thinking, or just imaginative daydreaming. These lists will start you thinking of yourself in a positive way as you focus on your accomplishments and capabilities.

Once you put your mind to it, you will find many other ways to tune in on your interests. For example, when you read a daily paper or a newsmagazine, which section do you go to first? And in what order do you read the other sections? Do you scour the Financial Section first, pick through the Book Reviews, and then skim over national and international news? Or do you spend most of your reading time absorbing new discoveries in science and technology, and devote what time remains to working out quizzes and puzzles?

Note, also, how deeply you plunge into any subject you like. Which ones do you talk about to your friends or go to the library to look up in greater detail? Do you actively seek out people who share your liking for, say, opera, politics, or space exploration? These are all good indicators of the nature and strength of your interests.

In your search, it is also important to pay attention to those areas of human endeavor you generally tend to ignore. This is a case where your negatives can have positive value for you. If you notice, for instance, that you would never know the difference if the Business or Travel Sections of your Sunday *Times* were missing, you can be sure that these subjects do not hold much educational or career interest for you. In other words, *it is equally useful to be aware of what you dislike* intensely and do poorly. This kind of information can save you the time you would waste following fruitless leads.

At this point, you might want to refer back to the description of number and letter codes. Suppose you've discovered that you spend some of your most enjoyable time with people —working in clubs, organizing groups, even giving parties. Review in detail the People Section under Worker Functions

Ratings to get an idea of all the ways you can interact with people in a work situation.

Then, in the section on the Holland Letter Codes, read about the Social Theme. How do these descriptions fit in with your own personality assessment? Are you getting a clearer picture of yourself?

If you follow the suggestions we have made, at this point you should have a rather detailed summary of your current preferences and leanings as they relate to most academic and vocational areas.

Now the question is — how do you go about linking this knowledge to a suitable course of study or the choice of a future career? How can you know if your attraction to mathematics, or writing, for example, will continue, or if you have the ability to succeed in either of these fields of study?

Don't fret. Just keep ferreting out everything you know about yourself. Look at your past history: school activities, summer jobs, leisure-time pursuits, hobbies and community activities. Which kind of tasks held your interest consistently over a long period of time? What skills did you use most, and which ones were superior compared to those of people around you?

In school, for example, which homework assignments did you like to do first? And in what subjects did answers come to you quickly? While you may not have paid particular attention to it at the time, you probably were aware that in classes you looked forward to attending because you did so well, there were some students who dreaded being there and had to struggle to get passing grades. These are the indicators that will point out your most prominent skills and interests, the ones that have endured. They are the best predictors of what you will *continue* to like and do well.

Whether your skills are verbal or computational, you are not likely to lose them later on, nor are they likely to atrophy because you have been away from school for a long period of time. What you've done now has been to catalog your current interests and find out if you have the drive and the abilities you will need to sustain those interests.

Strengthened by this knowledge, you can now tackle the task of finding suitable educational and career objectives with greater assurance and a firmer sense of direction.

Whether you are in school, at home, or holding down a job in business, there is another route you can follow in doing your career audit. You can take a "test" or interest inventory, either by yourself or with the assistance of a counselor. Simply contact the high school, college, United States Employment Service or community agency nearest you to get the help you need.

One interest inventory you can score and evaluate yourself is the Self-Directed Search (SDS) by John L. Holland, the vocational psychologist whose Occupational Letter code we've described for you. The advantage of this inventory is that it enables you to do your own scoring, profiling, and interpretation so you can get immediate results. Holland also has a companion booklet titled *The Occupations Finder* which lists occupations according to their letter codes.

If you've worked out your personality letter-code, you can see what occupations are listed under that code in *The Occupations Finder*. In addition, each of the 500 occupations that Holland lists in his booklet under the different combinations of three-letter codes is accompanied by the six-digit code it carries in the DOT. This makes it possible for you to go to *The Dictionary of Occupational Titles* to look up additional jobs under the DOT numbers that appear most frequently under your letter code.

The Strong-Campbell Interest Inventory (SCII) is another "test" you can take to help you in your career search. This Inventory calls for the services of a professional counselor to interpret the results, which require machine scoring.

The results of your Interest Inventory appear in a profile which has 162 occupational scales arranged under the six general occupational themes based on Holland's personality types. From this profile, you can obtain your own occupational letter-code as well as an indication of how closely your career interests resemble those of people who like the job they hold.

Since this profile has separate norms for men and

women, in most jobs you can compare your scores with those of members of your own sex. Each of these aids can increase your prospects of finding a satisfying course of study or a career.

If you use both these inventories you will note that in some instances the SDS and the SCII assign different letter codes to the same occupation. Holland explains that these letter codes can be useful but that they are *changeable* approximations that will constantly undergo revision as research continues. When discrepancies do occur, Holland advises that you read the job and code descriptions and then use your own judgment in arriving at a letter code for the occupation.

There are also other interest inventories available to you through the agencies we have mentioned. These two inventories, however, are the most popular and rest on solid research that has been going on for many years. But bear in mind that no test or inventory can perform magic. Carefully think things through for yourself first. That way, inventories can give you good leads to explore your future career possibilities.

PART THREE

HOW TO USE —
- Description of Major
- Career Leads
- Hiring Institutions
- Current Occupations of Graduates
- Major of Graduates by Occupation

A new principle is an inexhaustible source of new views.
— *Vauvenargues*

PART THREE
DESCRIPTION OF MAJOR

S tudents often have the wrong idea about the meaning and subject matter of the curriculum in which they plan to major. Time after time, students change majors or drop out of school because they did not foresee that accounting, for example, would require more than basic numerical computations, that physics would have so much mathematics, or that nursing brings you so much into contact with sick people.

To help you avoid making such mistakes, we have provided a short, clear definition of each discipline or major. These definitions identify the key characteristics of a major that distinguish it from all the others. We have emphasized *differences* rather than similarities to help you avoid confusion.

If you favor a particular major, you can use these definitions to detect possible errors in your notions about it. By contrasting the definition of *your* major with the descriptions of the others, you can sharpen your understanding of your discipline and see how it relates to those others. This information can help you select a minor as well as electives that can give you the flexibility you may be seeking in your studies.

Students frequently ask about the advantages and disadvantages of certain majors for securing a job. It would take half the pages in this book to cover the many aspects of this question — and the answer still would not be adequate. The personal factors that make a major suitable for you are much more important than the *current* market for jobs related to it.

Yes, we can say that Computer Science is the fastest growing major in colleges. It is also true that today it offers some of the highest starting salaries. But all this means little if you do not have the temperament, the interest, and the aptitudes that this field requires. If you don't possess the necessary attributes for computer science, you may have difficulty finding satisfactory work. And even if you do land a job, you may wind up unhappy and make little progress in it.

After all, your college major does not train you for one specific job. It seeks to develop your aptitudes and abilities so that you can use them with satisfaction and profit *in the broadest variety of careers*. That's why it is so important to choose a major which allows *your* individual talents to flourish. More people than you may realize find themselves trapped in well-paying jobs they would like to leave but can't, because their financial commitments do not permit them to take a more satisfying position that would at first pay a lot less money.

Even if we tried to evaluate majors in terms of today's market, it would be risky business. Choosing a major this way calls for predictions of what lies three to four years ahead. Who can predict that far ahead when even our most respected economists cannot agree whether interest rates will rise or fall in the next three months? Just a few years ago the prospects for engineering and teaching seemed dismal. Today engineers are in short supply and we are seeing reports of teacher shortages, at least in science, mathematics, and special education at this time.

This is not to say you can disregard the career implications of the studies you undertake and pay no attention to the ways you might improve the immediate marketability of your skills, no matter what major you choose. Whatever courses in computer science, management or accounting you can fit into your schedule will stand you in good stead. What's more, you will never regret any special efforts you make to develop your writing and speaking skills. Executives put these skills at the head of the list when they enumerate the qualities you need to succeed in business.

Especially when the economy is sluggish the best advice is to make your studies as flexible and wide-ranging as you can. This means that enlightened self-fulfillment is the best road to a reasonably happy existence. And the object is to achieve this fulfillment in a way that will also bring you the greatest financial reward.

Ultimately, what pays off is how well you appraise yourself and find ways to discover, develop, and use your skills and capabilities. The most important thing about your education is how well it suits *you* and what *you* creatively do with it.

CAREER LEADS

Each specific major in this book has a section that lists *Career Leads*. These leads include some of the occupations graduates of that major went into, as well as other jobs related to that area of study. You can use these leads to expand your knowledge of the range of jobs connected to your major field, and to get a better grasp of your own likes and dislikes regarding occupations.

In almost every profession, there is room for people whose interest patterns and personalities vary. But job seekers often don't take so wide a view of occupations as they might, and sometimes fail to look beyond common stereotypes. For example, a common image of a lawyer is that of an outgoing, talkative person who enjoys addressing a jury. Many students do not realize that there are also lawyers who limit themselves to research, who write, or who hold full-time executive positions. Nor do people always recognize the value of an undergraduate major in pre-med, classics, or physics, as background for law studies. For instance, the study of anatomy can facilitate an attorney's grasp of a malpractice suit; classics gives one an understanding of the origins of a legal system; and physics can be helpful in the practice of patent law or litigations between large scientific corporations.

Other possibilities that students do not immediately think of for chemistry, accounting, or almost any other major, are jobs as editors of technical books and periodicals; art history majors seldom realize that banks and other financial institutions may need their skills to design brochures and other printed materials.

Using the Career Leads section, you can start your evaluation of career interests related to your major by checking off the occupations that appeal to you. List those careers with their six-digit numbers alongside. Then, underline the first three digits preceding the decimal which appear most often. These three digits will identify the occupational division you prefer. For example, if the first three numbers are 052, they indicate you prefer occupations in history; if 072, dentistry; if 143, occupations in photography.

Say, for example, that as an art history major you come up with 102 and 141 as the first three digits of the careers you prefer. For 102, you will find three listings under Career Leads, and for 141 you will find six. If you are interested in learning about additional careers in these two groups, you can then go to *The Dictionary of Occupational Titles*. There, under 102 — Museum Curators and Related Occupations — you will find a description of these eight different occupations:

102.017	Curator (museum)
102.117	Supervisor, historic sites
102.167	Art Conservator
102.261	Conservation Technician
102.261	Paintings Restorer
102.361	Restorer, Lace and Textiles (museum)
102.367	Fine Arts Packer
102.381	Museum Technician

In the same manner, under 141 — Commercial Artists: Designers and Illustrators, Graphic Arts — you will find 11 listings. This will enable you to see the much broader scope of options within the groups that attract you.

The Career Leads section of a particular major will sometimes point out a seemingly unrelated connection you might easily overlook. For instance, since you find a Dramatic Arts Historian under 052 — Occupations in History — in *The Dictionary of Occupational Titles*, it may lead you to explore additional occupations not only in history but also other fields such as anthropology, archeology, and ethnology in which your art history training might apply.

Once you have identified some of the jobs you like, you can make some finer distinctions about your preferences by referring to the second set of three numbers following the decimal.

As we explained in the section on the Meaning of Number and Letter Codes, these numbers tell you the degree to which a job requires you to work with data, people, and things. With this information, you can find which jobs are more compatible with your disposition. Assume, for example, that as an art history major you are interested in the 141 group of occupations, and you select the following two of the 11 listed in the DOT.

	Data	People	Things
Illustrator 141.	0	6	1
Art Director 141.	0	3	1

You would find that an Illustrator is just as much involved as the Art Director with Data (0) and Things (1), but that the Art Director has a much higher degree of direct involvement with People, as the lower number indicates. This knowledge could help you decide which job you might wish to seek out first.

The last item of information related to the title of an occupation under Career Leads is the three-letter occupational code which we have also previously described under Meaning of Number and Letter Codes. This letter code gives you some idea of the personality traits of people in a particular job, as well as the outstanding features of its work environment. As you recall, there are six personality types: Realistic, Investigative, Artistic, Social, Enterprising, and Conventional (RIASEC).

In the above example, Illustrator and Art Director, the letter codes for both are AIS. This information allows you to look up all other AIS occupations found in this book — even if listed under other majors. This may help you discover not only new career leads but also supplementary courses that could assist you in rounding out your background.

Also, remember that these letter codes are not ironclad measures. They are merely *estimates* of the qualities they represent. For this reason, you may be able to locate other promising careers by looking for occupations that have various combinations of your letter code.

Whatever leads you decide to pursue, it will be worth your time to check out the precise nature of the work in *The Dictionary of Occupational Titles* and the *Occupational Outlook Handbook*, both of which are published by the United States Department of Labor. The DOT gives precise descriptions of each job, while the OOH gives some current assessment of the job market. Checking these books will help you avoid romantic illusions about a job that may in the end disappoint you. It will also prevent you from turning down a job on the basis of false notions you may have acquired about it. Frequently jobs you fear will "chain you to a desk," or jobs you want because you "like to work with people," turn out to be quite different from what you'd expected.

There is no quick or foolproof way of finding the right job for *you*. But whatever combination or sequence of methods you use, you are sure to increase your knowledge about careers and gain an awareness of *your* interests and needs. These insights can help you face your future with increasing self-assurance.

HIRING INSTITUTIONS

Here we present a variety of establishments that can use the training you acquired in your major field of study. Once you discover the wide range of fields available to you, this information will make you aware of the types of potential employers you might consider when looking for a job.

Some organizations identify so strongly with a particular product or service that we sometimes neglect to investigate the many other kinds of jobs they offer. For example, labor unions and corporations such as IBM need teachers for the many training and educational programs they conduct on their own premises. Hospitals, besides needing nurses and doctors, require social workers, librarians, and finance officers. Department stores use art history and English majors to design and write their many manuals and advertising copy.

Also, regardless of what they produce, the largest corporations employ almost every conceivable type of college graduate and professional. True, a high school may hire more teachers than the phone company, and the Internal Revenue Service may hire more accountants than a health club, but remember: You can fill only one job whether there are two or 22 openings. The trick is to be the best applicant for the one job you really want.

To get that one job which is best for you, once again, it will pay you to work hard at the self-assessment we have suggested for you. By doing this, you can find out which leads will be most profitable in meeting *your* needs and help you avoid chasing down blind alleys. You will have an edge if, as is likely, you discover unusual connections that take you off the beaten track.

In the course of evaluating your skills and interests, take account of the nature of the institutions and the details of jobs that interest you. Remember that hiring institutions — work environments — have their own personality traits just as you do. Determine those features which for you would be advantages or disadvantages.

For example, one job may require extensive travel and another may entail relocation to a Sunbelt State. If you like to travel, the first job would present an advantage. If you need a more stable and structured environment to function effectively, you might consider travel as a disadvantage. In the same way, the Sunbelt is a plus if you enjoy tanning yourself, but a minus if warm weather drains you, or if you like snow and ski slopes.

Other factors worth thinking about are the products or data you will handle and the types of people with whom you would have contact. As a sporting goods salesperson, for instance, you would spend much time in country clubs, health spas, or college recreation centers, while medical detailing for a pharmaceutical firm will take you to doctors' offices and hospitals. As an accountant, your social contacts would vary substantially if you worked for NBC-TV, the Carnegie Foundation, or the FBI. Nurses would have equally varied interpersonal experiences if they worked in a hospital, aboard a cruise ship, or at the Kennedy Space Center.

Since your work environment can have a profound influence on your social life, it will be helpful to know how pleasant conditions are likely to be for you. As a personnel officer who loves music but has a limited interest in sports, you would certainly be happier working for the Metropolitan Opera Company than at Madison Square Garden.

Finally, the size and the type of control that an employment establishment exercises can have consequences important for you to know about. For example, in a large corporation such as GE or IBM, there would be more opportunity to move up the ladder in your specialty. On the other hand, in a smaller corporation you can get a more diversified experience, which can broaden your options regarding areas to specialize in for the future.

Also, note how employment conditions differ in private industry, in government, and various kinds of non-profit organizations. Jobs with municipal, State, and Federal agencies tend to have more security than jobs in private industry, but at the same time are likely to be more rigid and bureaucratic. Then, too, government jobs, at all levels, unless they're on a civil service track, will last only as long as your political party remains in power.

In education, while salaries may lag behind those in business and industry, tenure gives you greater job security. In addition, you have much longer vacations which permit you to travel, to work on personal or professional projects, or to experiment with other types of work while supplementing your income at the same time.

Under the hiring institutions that interest you, jot down those features of the job or the institution which for *you* are advantages or disadvantages. Don't use guesswork. Get facts before you make a judgment about your preferences. Keep in mind that if the work environment suits your personality, chances are you will find congenial colleagues and co-workers there.

It will be worth your while to do this analysis before you start any serious job-hunting. If you do, you will greatly improve your chances of landing a job in which you can thrive and prosper.

CURRENT OCCUPATIONS OF GRADUATES

Under each major, we list the actual occupations graduates entered over a period of 20 years.

Under the heading *1975-80*, three columns list the jobs alumni got and the number of men and women, separately and combined, who entered them during the six-year period immediately following graduation. For recent graduates of each major, these columns provide leads to jobs which have been most available at the entry level. They also show the beginning jobs that are more readily available either to men or to women in cases where hiring practices may differ. This information can help new graduates concentrate their job seeking efforts in those areas where their search is more likely to prove successful.

In the column titled *1960-74*, we list the jobs held by graduates who completed college during this 15-year period. Since the graduates in this group have been in the job market at least seven, and in some cases as many as 20, years, we can view their present jobs as indicating long-term career possibilities for that major.

Once you identify the things you do well, that give you satisfaction, and that have meaning for you — the process we described under Self-Assessment — you can begin to investigate those occupations of former graduates that appeal to you. In exploring career possibilities, you will need current and accurate occupational information. You can get this through recent publications, from summer jobs or internships in which you can test your skills, and by visiting and talking to people who are in the positions that interest you. In addition to your own resourcefulness and ingenuity, high school Guidance Offices, Career Counseling Centers in colleges, libraries, or community agencies can help you get the information you need.

JOB INDEX
MAJOR OF GRADUATES BY OCCUPATION

In the Index, we list alphabetically the positions which alumni currently hold, as well as the DOT numbers and the Holland letter identification for each job. Then we indicate the number of graduates from each major who occupy those positions. Here again we have two categories of graduates (1960-74; 1975-80), with the latter group showing separately the jobs men and women occupy.

The subdivisions under the 1975-80 category enable men and women to find entry positions listed by sex as well as those listed under their major. And the reader can find from the 1960-74 listings careers that graduates of related majors have entered. These tabulations show that graduates of 16 different majors are computer programers, those of 11 different majors are in public relations and hospital administration, and each of these occupations includes majors in English, economics, history, psychology, and sociology. Students in any one of these five majors, for example, according to their interests, could take electives in computer science, writing, or business management to compete more effectively for one of these positions.

The variety of jobs students in the humanities occupy can serve to reinforce the fact that training in history, English, or philosophy need not restrict job opportunities to the field in which the major concentrates. Our listings show that history majors hold jobs in research and development, philosophy majors in social welfare work, and English majors in hospital administration. And the large number of majors which appear under many occupations should impress the reader with the adaptability of almost every undergraduate course of study. You will find it heartening to see that administrative officers, business executives, lawyers, social workers, and systems analysts have all come from at least 16 different majors.

There is still another way you can use the Index to help you select either a major or a career. If you already have a major, you can see in which job categories it can lead to the greatest number of employment opportunities. You will note, for example, that business and economics majors abound in market research positions, and English majors in editing and reporting. A variety of majors, in almost equal numbers, are real-estate agents or hospital administrators. And there are also some positions that just a few graduates with a particular major seem to enter. For some reason, you do not find many buyers who majored in English, or copy writers who studied science. This information will help you prepare to present yourself more astutely and creatively in seeking jobs which fewer people with your major have entered. It will also show you that there are not many jobs for which your major disqualifies you.

Should you already have a career in mind — such as personnel manager, lawyer, business executive, or physician —

the Index can help you in choosing a major (or suitable electives). The information it contains can be especially helpful if you prefer studies that do not have a direct or logical connection with the career you wish to pursue. For example, if you want to be a business executive or an administrative officer but prefer to study the humanities, would you prejudice your chances for success by majoring in history or English? Here the Index shows that although most business executives have studied business administration, they came from *all* majors —and at least 20 percent of them from the humanities. Similarly, while 55 percent of lawyers majored in history, economics, or political science, at least 20 percent majored in English, modern languages, philosophy, or classics.

Once you are aware of the range of studies which qualify you for the career you think you prefer, you will feel more secure about choosing the major for which you have the greatest interest and aptitude. You will then avoid the common pitfall of choosing an inappropriate major — a misstep that can result in poor performance and eventual withdrawal from college.

PART FOUR

CAREERS BY DEPARTMENTAL MAJOR

Any fact is better established by two or three good testimonies than by a thousand arguments.

— Emmons

*The one thing that hurts more than paying an
income tax is not having to pay an income tax.*
— *Lord Dewar*

ACCOUNTANCY
GENERAL DESCRIPTION

Accountants analyze business records and prepare financial reports such as balance sheets, cost studies, and tax statements. They also audit accounts for business, financial, and industrial firms, and install and maintain a general accounting system. The major areas they specialize in are public, managerial, and governmental accounting.

Public accountants have their own business, or work for accounting firms. They may specialize in areas such as auditing, taxes, or estate-planning. Management accountants, employed by individual firms, deal with many aspects of corporate operations such as auditing, budgeting, taxes, costs and investments. Government accountants examine records of Federal agencies and audit private businesses whose operations must comply with government regulations. They may also function as agents of the Internal Revenue Service or the Federal Bureau of Investigation.

It is becoming increasingly important for accountants to be familiar with computer programing and to understand how electronic data processing can apply to accounting operations. It is also essential for them to be effective in oral and written communication, because much of an accountant's work involves conveying and interpreting data for clients. Competent public accountants can become managers or partners within their company, or, as is often the case, transfer to executive positions in private firms and corporations.

A bachelor's degree qualifies you for entry jobs in this field. Undergraduate accounting internships and some computer training can also help in securing beginning positions. A Certified Public Accountant certificate — the C.P.A. — can greatly broaden your opportunities to advance in the accounting field.

CAREER LEADS

DOT	JOB TITLE	HOC
160.167	Accountant (budget, cost, systems)	CES
020.167	Actuary	IAS
188.117	Administrative officer/government service	ESC
160.162	Auditor	CES
186.117	Bank officer	ESC
161.117	Budget officer	CES
160.207	Budget consultant	CES
160.167	Bursar/education	CES
189.167	Business/management trainee	ESC
162.157	Buyer	ECS
213.132	Computer-operations supervisor	CIS
020.187	Computer programer	IAS
186.117	Controller	ESC
191.267	Credit analyst	ESC
168.167	Credit-and-collection manager	SIE
169.167	Data processing manager	ESC
090.167	Department head, college	SIA
020.167	Financial analyst	IAS
187.117	Hospital administrator	SEC
109.067	Information scientist	IRC
250.257	Insurance agent/broker	ECS
168.267	Internal-revenue investigator	SIE
110.107	Lawyer	ESA
161.167	Management analyst	CES
189.117	Manager, industrial organization	ESC
050.067	Market-research analyst	IAS
169.167	Office manager	ESC
184.117	Operations manager	ESC
162.157	Purchasing agent	ECS
186.117	Real-estate agent	ESC
250.357	Real-estate broker	ECS
186.167	Securities trader/banking	ESC
375.167	Special agent/FBI	SRE
251.157	Stockbroker	ECS
012.167	Systems analyst	ERI
160.162	Tax accountant	CES
110.117	Tax attorney	ESA

DOT	JOB TITLE	HOC
160.167	Tax auditor	CES
090.227	Teacher/college	SIA
091.227	Teacher/high school	SAE
184.187	Traffic manager	ESC
161.117	Treasurer	CES
166.167	Wage-and-salary administrator	SEC

HIRING INSTITUTIONS

Accounting Firms
Advertising Companies
Banks, Savings/Commercial
Booking Agencies
Business Corporations
Chain Stores
Civic and Taxpayers' Associations
Colleges and Schools
Construction Companies
Credit Unions
Educational Institutions
Financial Institutions
Government Agencies
Hospitals
Industries, Manufacturing
Insurance Companies
Internal-Revenue Service
Investment Firms
Labor Unions
Law Firms
Management Consulting Firms
Marketing-Research Departments and Firms
Nursing Homes
Philanthropic Associations
Publishers
Radio/Television Stations
Real Estate Companies

Research-and-Development Firms
Retail Stores
Talent Booking Agencies
Tax-Consulting Firms
Trade Associations
Utility Companies

CURRENT OCCUPATIONS OF GRADUATES
WHO MAJORED IN ACCOUNTANCY

DOT	JOB TITLE	HOC	1960-1974	1975-1980 M	F	T
160.167	Accountant	CES	249	218	50	268
160.167	Accounting manager	CES	41	11	3	14
160.167	Accounting partner	CES	17	4		4
188.117	Administrative officer/ government service	ESC	9			
164.117	Advertising manager	AES	2			
— —	Armed services	—	16	2	1	3
160.162	Auditor	CES	69	40	7	47
186.117	Bank officer	ESC	24	9	6	15
183.117	Branch manager	ESC	1	3		3
186.117	Brokerage-house partner	ESC			1	1
161.117	Budget analyst	CES	7	2	1	3
189.117	Business executive	ESC	113	7		7
162.157	Buyer	ECS	1	1		1
186.117	Cashier, bank	ESC			1	1
120.007	Clergy	SAI	1	1		1
209.562	Clerk	CIE	5	8	4	12
213.362	Computer operator	CIS	1			
213.132	Computer-operations supervisor	CIS	6	1		1
020.187	Computer programer	IAS	2	4	1	5
869.664	Construction worker	REI	1			
160.167	Cost accountant	CES	13	7	1	8
160.267	Cost estimator	CES	1			
191.267	Credit analyst	ESC	2	2		2
168.167	Credit-and-collection manager	SIE	2	1	1	2

DOT	JOB TITLE	HOC	1960-1974	1975-1980		
				M	F	T
003.161	Development-and-planning engineer	IRE	2			
110.117	District attorney	ESA	1			
183.117	District manager	ESC	2	2		2
050.067	Economist/price	IAS	1			
828.261	Field engineer	RIC	1			
020.167	Financial/investment analyst	IAS	27		1	1
050.067	Financial planner	IAS	18	8	1	9
373.364	Firefighter	RSE		1		1
189.117	General manager	ESC	28	4	1	5
— —	Graduate student	—	3	2		2
045.107	Guidance counselor	SIA	2			
091.107	High-school official	SAE	2			
187.117	Hospital administrator	SEC	4			
250.257	Insurance agent/broker	ECS	7	1		1
241.217	Insurance-claim adjuster	CSE	1			
168.267	Insurance-claim examiner	SIE	1			
169.167	Insurance underwriter	ESC	2		1	1
376.367	Investigator	SRE	1			
166.167	Labor-relations consultant	SEC	1			
— —	Law student	—		2		2
110.107	Lawyer	ESA	18			
230.367	Mail carrier	CSR		2		2
012.167	Management/methods engineer	ERI	1			
189.167	Management trainee	ESC	2	2	1	3
163.117	Marketing manager	ESC	2			
050.067	Marketing-research analyst	IAS	3			
— —	Medical student	—		1		1
152.047	Music director	ASI	1			
152.041	Musician	ASI	1			
169.167	Office manager	ESC	21	1		1
184.167	Operations manager	ESC	8	2	1	3
166.117	Personnel manager	SEC	3	1		1
375.263	Police officer	SRE	1	1		1
189.117	Private-business owner	ESC	10	2		2
189.117	Product manager	ESC	5	1		1

DOT	JOB TITLE	HOC	1960-1974	1975-1980 M	F	T
183.117	Production manager	ESC		1		1
162.157	Purchasing agent	ECS	1		1	1
250.357	Real-estate agent/ broker	ECS	2	1		1
160.167	Revenue agent	CES	22	3		3
290.477	Sales clerk	ESC	1	2		2
290.477	Sales manager	ESC	2	2		2
279.357	Sales/service representative	ESC	2	2		2
186.167	Securities trader	ESC	1			
186.167	Security officer	ESC		1		1
600-800	Skilled trades	RIC		2	1	3
195.107	Social worker	SIC	1			
375.167	Special agent/FBI	SRE	6	1		1
251.157	Stockbroker	ECS	1	2		2
185.167	Store manager	ESI	1	1		1
070.101	Surgeon	ISA	1			
012.167	Systems analyst/electronic data processing	ERI	8			
160.162	Tax accountant	CES	18	10	1	11
160.167	Tax administrator	CES	6	2		2
110.117	Tax attorney	ESA	6			
090.227	Teacher/college	SIA	2			
091.227	Teacher/high school	SAE	7			
099.227	Teacher/other	SIR	1	1		1
159.147	Television/radio personnel	AES		1		1
184.117	Traffic analyst/manager	ESC	1	1		1
186.117	Trust officer/bank	ESC		1		1
073.101	Veterinarian	IRS	1			
			854	388	86	474

Every artist dips his brush in his own soul, and paints his own nature into the pictures.
— Henry Ward Beecher

ART HISTORY
GENERAL DESCRIPTION

T he art historian examines the significant achievements of artists, architects, and musicians to determine how their works have contributed to the development of culture. In this program students analyze and evaluate many forms of artistic expression, such as painting, sculpture, architecture, music, and cinematography.

Work-leads related to art history include teaching, lecturing, writing criticism or biographies of artists and performers. An art-history specialist can also serve as consultant to publishers, and to radio, TV, and movie producers, or function as a museum curator, copy writer, layout designer, or historic-preservationist.

Students with a bachelor's degree in art history can get beginning jobs in advertising and publishing firms, museums, educational institutions, and government agencies. They can also find employment in many types of business establishments where their training qualifies them to perform tasks related to interior and industrial design, buying, and advertising.

Art history can serve as background for additional studies —or in some cases apprenticeships — in medical illustration, photo-engraving, fashion design, or audiovisual technology. More responsible positions in museums or colleges and universities usually call for advanced degrees.

CAREER LEADS

DOT	JOB TITLE	HOC
763.381	Antiquer, furniture	RIC
191.287	Appraiser, art	ESC
001.061	Architect	AIR
101.167	Archivist	SAI
294.257	Art auctioneer	ESC
102.167	Art conservator/museum	AEI
131.067	Art critic	ASI
141.031	Art director	ASI
149.021	Art teacher	ASI
076.127	Art therapist	SIR
191.117	Artist's manager	ESC
188.117	Arts-and-Humanities-Council, director	ESC
191.117	Booking agent	ESC
018.261	Cartographic technician	RCI
141.061	Cartoonist	ASI
141.051	Color expert	ASI
970.381	Colorist/photography	AIR
141.081	Commercial designer (books, albums)	ASI
055.381	Conservator, artifacts	IAR
131.067	Critic (art, drama, film)	ASI
102.017	Curator (art galleries, museums)	AEI
142.061	Designer (banknote, textiles, furniture)	AIS
142.061	Designer (display, fashion, industrial, set, stage)	AIS
159.147	Disc jockey	AES
142.031	Display manager	AIS
142.081	Floral designer	AIS
141.061	Graphic designer	ASI
052.067	Historian/dramatic arts	SEI
141.061	Illustrator/medical and scientific	ASI
142.051	Interior designer	AIS
700.281	Jeweler	RIC
141.061	Layout artist	ASI
100.127	Librarian	SAI
191.117	Literary agent	ESC
131.067	Movie critic	ASI
102.381	Museum technician	AEI

DOT	JOB TITLE	HOC
131.067	Music critic	ASI
142.081	Package designer	AIS
144.061	Painter/sculptor	AIR
102.261	Paintings restorer	AEI
143.062	Photographer	AIR
144.061	Printmaker	AIR
109.267	Research assistant (documents and records)	IRC
277.457	Salesperson/art objects	ESC
142.061	Set decorator	AIS
142.061	Set designer (motion pictures, radio, TV)	AIS
017.281	Technical illustrator	RIA

HIRING INSTITUTIONS

Advertising Departments and Firms
Architectural Firms
Art Galleries
Business Corporations
Colleges and Schools
Community Organizations
     YM-YWCAs
     YM-YWHAs
     Scouts, etc.
Construction Firms
Department Stores
Educational Institutions
Engineering Firms
Film Companies
Furniture Manufacturers
Garment Industry
Government Agencies
Historical Societies
Insurance Companies
Interior-Design Companies
Libraries

Magazines
Motion-Picture Companies
Museums
National and State Parks
Pharmaceutical Companies
Photography Studios
Planetariums
Publishing Companies
Radio/Television Stations
Research Organizations
Restoration Firms
Textile Manufacturers

CURRENT OCCUPATIONS OF GRADUATES WHO MAJORED IN ART HISTORY

DOT	JOB TITLE	HOC	1960-1974	1975-1980 M	F	T
188.117	Administrative officer/ government service	ESC	1			
144.061	Artist	AIR	2			
099.167	Audiovisual specialist	SIE	1			
189.117	Business executive	ESC	1	1		1
162.157	Buyer	ECS	1			
120.007	Clergy member	SAI	1			
209.562	Clerk	CIE			1	1
090.117	College/university official	SIA			1	1
— —	Graduate student	—	1		1	1
045.107	Guidance counselor	SIA			1	1
110.107	Lawyer	ESA			1	1
189.117	Research/development director	ESC		1		1
290.477	Sales clerk	ESC	1			
195.107	Social worker	SIC	1			
003.167	Systems engineer	IRE	1			
090.227	Teacher/college	SIA	2			
092.227	Teacher/elementary	SAI			1	1
091.227	Teacher/high school	SAE	3			
184.117	Traffic analyst/manager	ESC			1	1
			16	2	7	9

*Whenever you examine an animal closely, you feel
as if a human being inside were making fun of you.*
— *Elias Canetti*

BIOLOGY
GENERAL DESCRIPTION

Biology is the science of living matter. It involves the study of the structure, evolutionary development, and functions of plants, animals, and micro-organisms — especially the ways in which they relate to our environment.

Biologists specialize in many fields such as agronomy, anatomy, botany, embryology, genetics, horticulture, oceanography, pathology, physiology, or zoology. Even within these subdivisions, numerous subspecialties exist. Under botany, for example, we find plant scientists, such as taxonomists, phytopathologists, bryologists, and mycologists. And the field of applied biology, such as the biomedical sciences, includes pharmacology, nutrition, immunology, and pathology. Agriculture has subdivisions such as agronomy, animal husbandry, and seed technology.

Employment opportunities for biologists occur in business and industry with firms that produce agricultural chemicals, pest controls, dietary supplements, foods and beverages. Manufacturers of textiles, petroleum and leather goods offer other opportunities. Pharmaceutical houses throughout the United States employ biologists in large numbers. Biological training, plus talent and interest in literary and graphic arts, can lead to jobs in scientific illustration and writing.

Students with a bachelor's degree can do testing and inspecting in laboratories, and can also function as sales and service representatives in business and industry, or find beginning jobs with zoos, arboretums, museums and many government agencies. Teaching in colleges and universities, and more responsible research and administrative positions, require advanced degrees. Most holders of doctorates work in higher education, with smaller numbers in government and industry.

CAREER LEADS

DOT	JOB TITLE	HOC
029.081	Air-pollution analyst	IRA
041.061	Anatomist	IRS
041.061	Animal ecologist	IRS
040.061	Animal scientist	RIS
041.061	Biochemist	IRS
143.362	Biological photographer	AIR
041.061	Biologist	IRS
019.061	Biomedical engineer	RIE
041.061	Biophysicist	IRS
041.061	Botanist	IRS
079.101	Chiropractor	SIR
029.281	Criminologist	IRA
102.017	Curator	AEI
102.017	Curator/medical museum	AEI
102.017	Curator/zoological museum	AEI
041.061	Cytologist	IRS
078.281	Cytotechnologist	ISR
072.101	Dentist	ISR
077.117	Dietitian	SIE
077.061	Dietitian/research	SIE
132.017	Editor (technical and scientific publications)	ASI
041.061	Entomologist	IRS
029.081	Environmental analyst	IRA
029.081	Environmental scientist	IRA
168.267	Food-and-drugs inspector	SIE
070.061	Forensic pathologist	ISA
040.061	Forester	RIS
041.061	Geneticist	IRS
041.061	Histopathologist	IRS
187.117	Hospital administrator	SEC
024.061	Hydrologist	IRA
079.161	Industrial hygienist	SIR
109.067	Information scientist	IRC
199.364	Laboratory assistant	ICR
110.107	Lawyer	ESA
041.061	Marine biologist	IRS

DOT	JOB TITLE	HOC
141.061	Medical illustrator	ASI
100.167	Medical librarian	SAI
078.361	Medical technologist	ISR
041.061	Microbiologist	IRS
102.381	Museum technician	AEI
041.061	Mycologist	IRS
041.061	Nematologist	IRS
078.361	Nuclear medical technologist	ISR
168.167	Occupational-safety-and-health inspector	SIE
024.061	Oceanographer	IRA
079.101	Optometrist	SIR
071.101	Osteopath	ISR
041.061	Parasitologist	IRS
070.061	Pathologist	ISA
262.157	Pharmaceutical detailer	ESR
074.161	Pharmacist	IES
041.061	Pharmacologist	IRS
076.121	Physical therapist	SIR
070.101	Physician	ISA
041.061	Plant pathologist	IRS
041.061	Plant physiologist	IRS
079.101	Podiatrist	SIR
045.107	Psychologist/industrial	SIA
079.117	Public-health educator	SIR
168.264	Safety inspector	SIE
012.167	Safety manager	ERI
262.357	Sales representative (chemicals and drugs)	ESR
079.117	Sanitarian	SIR
195.107	Social worker	SIC
040.061	Soil scientist	RIS
199.261	Taxidermist	ICR
090.227	Teacher/college	SIA
091.227	Teacher/high school	SAE
073.101	Veterinarian	IRS
073.061	Veterinarian/laboratory animal care	IRS
131.267	Writer/technical, scientific	ASI
041.061	Zoologist	IRS

HIRING INSTITUTIONS

Advertising Agencies
Aquariums
Arboretums
Beverage Companies
Botanical Gardens
Chemical Industries
Colleges and Schools
Consulting Firms
Cosmetic Companies
Doctors' Offices
Educational Institutions
Food Processors
Government Agencies
  Agriculture Department
  Energy Department
  Environmental Protection Agency
  Fish and Wildlife Service
  Health and Human Services Department
  National Institutes of Health
  National Science Foundation
  Patent Office
  Peace Corps
  Vista
Hatcheries
Hospitals
Libraries, Medical/Technical
Lumber Companies
Medical Clinics
Medical Laboratories
Medical-Supply Companies
Museums
National and State Parks
Nurseries
— Pharmaceutical Companies
Professional and Technical Journals
Publishers
Research-and-Development Firms
Textile Manufacturers
Zoological Parks

CURRENT OCCUPATIONS OF GRADUATES
WHO MAJORED IN BIOLOGY

DOT	JOB TITLE	HOC	1960-1974	1975-1980 M	F	T
160.167	Accountant	CES	1	1		1
150.047	Actor	ASE		1		1
070.101	Anesthesiologist	ISA	1			
— —	Armed services	—	13	2		2
041.061	Biochemist	IRS	1	1		1
041.061	Biologist	IRS	3	1		1
189.117	Business executive	ESC	1	2		2
189.167	Business/management trainee	ESC			1	1
022.161	Chemical-laboratory supervisor	IAR		1		1
022.061	Chemist	IAR	5	3	2	5
022.061	Chemist/analytical	IAR	2		2	
022.061	Chemist/quality control	IAR	1	1	1	2
022.061	Chemist/research	IAR	3	1	1	2
079.101	Chiropractor	SIR	1	1		1
120.007	Clergy member	SAI	1			
209.562	Clerk	CIE	2	2	2	4
090.117	College/university official	SIA	1			
020.187	Computer programer	IAS	2	1	2	3
869.664	Construction worker	REI		1		1
094.117	Coordinator of special services/education	SAI	1			
— —	Dental student	—	2	4	.	4
072.101	Dentist	ISR	35	3	1	4
092.137	Elementary-school official	SAI	1			
041.061	Endocrinologist	IRS	1			
189.117	General manager	ESC	2			
— —	Graduate student	—	20	22	10	32
091.107	High-school official	SAE	1			
040.061	Horticulturist	RIS	1			
187.117	Hospital administrator	SEC	3			
168.267	Insurance-claim examiner	SIE	1			
029.261	Laboratory technician	IRA	5	9	2	11
— —	Law student	—		2		2
110.107	Lawyer	ESA	2			

DOT	JOB TITLE	HOC	1960-1974	1975-1980 M	F	T
012.167	Management/methods engineer	ERI	1			
189.167	Management trainee	ESC			1	1
163.117	Marketing manager	ESC	1			
— —	Medical student	—	24	40	18	58
078.261	Medical technologist	ISR	2	1	2	3
041.061	Microbiologist	IRS	2	1	1	2
070.101	Obstetrician	ISA	8			
169.167	Office manager	ESC	1			
070.101	Ophthalmologist	ISA	7			
079.101	Optometrist	SIR	1			
070.101	Pediatrician	ISA	12	1		1
166.117	Personnel manager	SEC	1			
074.161	Pharmacist	IES	2			
— —	Pharmacy student	—	1			
070.101	Physician	ISA	98	7	2	9
079.101	Podiatrist	SIR	3			
— —	Podiatry student	—		2	1	3
189.117	Private-business owner	ESC	2			
163.267	Product-distribution manager		1		1	
183.117	Production manager	ESC	2			
070.107	Psychiatrist	ISA	7			
045.107	Psychologist	SIA	1			
070.101	Radiologist	ISA	8			
250.357	Real-estate agent/broker	ECS	1			
045.107	Rehabilitation counselor	SIA	1			
189.117	Research-and-development director	ESC	2	2	2	4
279.357	Sales/service representative	ESC	5	1	1	2
020.167	Securities analyst	IAS	1			
600-800	Skilled trades	RIC	1			
195.107	Social worker	SIC	1			
070.101	Surgeon	ISA	20			
012.167	Systems analyst/electronic data processing	ERI	1			
090.227	Teacher/college	SIA	9	1		1

DOT	JOB TITLE	HOC	1960-1974	1975-1980		
---	---	---	---	M	F	T
092.227	Teacher/elementary school	SAI	1	1	1	2
091.227	Teacher/high school	SAE	17	5	3	8
099.227	Teacher/other	SIR	3	1		1
184.117	Transportation manager	ESC			1	1
070.101	Urologist	ISA	3			
073.101	Veterinarian	IRS	1		1	1
			362	125	56	181

*Water is H$_2$O, hydrogen two parts, oxygen one, but
there is also a third thing that makes it water, and
nobody knows what that is.*
— *D.H. Lawrence*

CHEMISTRY
GENERAL DESCRIPTION

Chemists study the structure and make-up of substances,
and the way their interaction changes and transforms
them. In basic research, chemists
investigate properties of matter and the laws that come into
play when elements combine. Those in research and
development create new products, such as vaccines and
synthetics, and they find ways to apply new knowledge to such
fields as nutrition, genetics, electronics, drugs, and
environmental protection.

The more common specialties are: analytical chemistry
(the structure and composition of substances), organic
chemistry (living organisms and carbon compounds), inorganic
chemistry (compounds other than organic), physical chemistry
(transformation of energy). Often, by combining with other
sciences, these specialties produce new offshoots such as
biochemistry or chemical oceanography.

The largest number of chemists do research and
development in business and industry, most often with
chemical manufacturing companies. The next-highest sources
of employment are colleges and universities, followed by local,
State, and Federal government agencies.

Graduates with a bachelor's degree can get beginning
jobs in analysis and testing, or in technical sales and services.
With appropriate courses in education, they can qualify for
high-school teaching positions. You generally need the Ph.D. to
do research, to teach in colleges and universities, and to move
up in administrative positions.

CAREER LEADS

DOT	JOB TITLE	HOC
029.081	Air-pollution analyst	IRA
019.061	Biomedical engineer	RIE
041.061	Biochemist	IRS
008.061	Chemical engineer	IRE
022.161	Chemical-laboratory chief	IAR
559.130	Chemical-processing-plant supervisor	RIC
022.061	Chemist (analytical, quality control, research)	IAR
022.061	Chemist/food	IAR
022.061	Chemist/pollution control	IAR
078.261	Chemistry technologist/medical service	ISR
029.281	Criminalist	IRA
029.281	Crime-laboratory analyst	IRA
102.017	Curator/natural history (museum)	AEI
072.101	Dentist	ISR
077.117	Dietitian	SIE
077.061	Dietitian/research	SIE
132.017	Editor (technical and scientific publications)	ASI
029.081	Environmental analyst	IRA
029.081	Environmental scientist	IRA
168.267	Food-and-drug inspector	SIE
187.117	Hospital administrator	SEC
024.061	Hydrologist	IRA
012.167	Industrial-health engineer	ERI
109.067	Information scientist	IRC
199.364	Laboratory assistant	ICR
029.261	Laboratory technician	IRA
022.281	Laboratory tester	IAR
189.117	Manager/industrial organization	ESC
141.061	Medical illustrator	ASI
100.167	Medical librarian	SAI
078.361	Medical technologist	ISR
078.361	Nuclear medical technologist	ISR
168.167	Occupational-safety-and-health inspector	SIE
024.061	Oceanographer	IRA
079.101	Optometrist	SIR

DOT	JOB TITLE	HOC
071.101	Osteopath	ISR
110.117	Patent attorney	ESA
022.161	Perfumer	IAR
262.157	Pharmaceutical detailer	ESR
074.161	Pharmacist	IES
041.061	Pharmacologist	IRS
022.061	Physical chemist	IAR
070.101	Physician	ISA
029.281	Police chemist	IRA
183.117	Production manager	ESC
079.117	Public-health educator	SIR
012.167	Quality-control supervisor	ERI
012.167	Safety manager	ERI
262.357	Sales representative (chemicals and drugs)	ESR
079.117	Sanitarian	SIR
040.061	Soil scientist	RIS
090.227	Teacher/college	SIA
091.227	Teacher/high school	SAE
073.101	Veterinarian	IRS
029.081	Water-quality analyst	IRA
131.267	Writer, technical/scientific	ASI

HIRING INSTITUTIONS

Beverage Companies
Business Corporations
Chemical Industries
Colleges and Schools
Consulting Firms
Cosmetic Companies
Distributors of Scientific Equipment
Doctors' Offices
Educational Institutions
Engineering Firms
Food-Product Companies

Government Agencies
    Agriculture Department
    Consumer-Affairs Office
    Consumer Product Safety Commission
    Education Department
    Energy Department
    Environmental Protection Agency
    Fish and Wildlife Service
    Health and Human Services Department
    National Park Service
    National Science Foundation
    Patent Office
    Peace Corps
    Vista
Hospitals
Import/Export Companies
Industries, Manufacturing
Libraries, Medical/Technical
Lumber Companies
Manufacturing-and-Processing Firms
Medical Clinics
Medical Laboratories
Medical-Supply Companies
Mining Companies
Newspapers and Magazines
Paper Manufactuers
Petroleum Companies
Pharmaceutical Companies
Professional/Technical Journals
Publishers
Research-and-Development Firms
Textile Manufacturers
Utility Companies

CURRENT OCCUPATIONS OF GRADUATES
WHO MAJORED IN CHEMISTRY

DOT	JOB TITLE	HOC	1960-1974	1975-1980 M	F	T
188.117	Administrative officer/ government service	ESC	2			
— —	Armed services	—	7			
183.117	Branch manager	ESC	1			
189.117	Business executive	ESC	5		1	1
022.061	Chemist	IAR	33	4	3	7
022.061	Chemist/analytical	IAR	2			
022.061	Chemist/quality control	IAR	1			
022.061	Chemist/research	IAR	18			
120.007	Clergy member	SAI		1		1
090.117	College/university official	SIA	1			
213.132	Computer-operations supervisor	CIS	1			
020.187	Computer programer	IAS	1			
094.117	Coordinator of special services/education	SAI	1			
— —	Dental student	—		2		2
072.101	Dentist	ISR	5			
183.117	District manager	ESC	2			
092.137	Elementary-school official	SAI	1			
189.117	General manager	ESC	1			
— —	Graduate student	—	10	3	3	6
187.117	Hospital administrator	SEC		1		1
022.137	Laboratory supervisor	IAR	2			
029.261	Laboratory technician	IRA	1			
— —	Law student	—	1	1		1
110.107	Lawyer	ESA	1			
163.117	Marketing manager	ESC	5			
050.067	Market-research analyst	IAS	1			
— —	Medical student	—	3	7	1	8
041.061	Microbiologist	IRS	1			
169.167	Office manager	ESC	2			
070.101	Ophthalmologist	ISA	1			
110.117	Patent attorney	ESA	1			
041.061	Pharmacologist	IRS	1			
070.101	Physician	ISA	12	1		1

DOT	JOB TITLE	HOC	1960-1974	1975-1980		
				M	F	T
189.117	Private-business owner	ESC	2			
189.117	Product manager	ESC	4			
183.117	Production manager	ESC	3			
162.157	Purchasing agent	ECS	7			
012.167	Quality-control engineer	ERI	1			
070.101	Radiologist	ISA	1			
250.357	Real-estate agent/broker	ECS	1			
189.117	Research-and-development director	ESC	6			
160.167	Revenue agent	CES	1			
290.477	Sales clerk	ESC	1			
163.167	Sales manager	ESC	2			
279.357	Sales/service representative	ESC	6	1		1
012.167	Systems analyst/electronic data processing	ERI	1			
090.227	Teacher/college	SIA	8			
091.227	Teacher/high school	SAE	5			
099.227	Teacher/other	SIR	2	1		1
			175	22	8	30

Poetry heals the wounds inflicted by reason.
— *Novalis*

CLASSICS
GENERAL DESCRIPTION

In this major, people study the languages and civilization of the ancient Greek and Roman worlds. More specifically, students examine and evaluate the literary, intellectual, and artistic works of the authors, scholars, and artists of classical antiquity.

The study of the languages and the literary and art forms of antiquity lays bare the ideas and systems of communication that gave rise to our contemporary civilization, and in this way provides a background which you can apply in the arts, business, industry, the media, the professions, and education. Verbal and analytical skills deriving from classical studies qualify graduates for managerial and executive positions. You can also use the insights you acquire about human behavior in personnel work, or in educational and training activities for corporations, unions and social agencies. Your knowledge of the art and history of antiquity can lead to job opportunities in museums, art galleries, radio, television, and the theatre. And students who develop their writing and research skills will find that popular and learned magazines, newspapers, book publishers, and TV stations can use their services.

Persons with a bachelor's degree often find jobs in secondary school teaching or in business and finance. Additional training in the sciences, or in fields such as art, journalism, or library science can expand your job horizons. Those who continue their studies on the graduate level frequently become college teachers or lawyers.

CAREER LEADS

DOT	JOB TITLE	HOC
055.067	Anthropologist	IAR
055.067	Archeologist	IAR
101.167	Archivist	SAI
052.067	Biographer	SEI
131.067	Book critic	ASI
100.387	Cataloger	SAI
120.007	Clergy member	SAI
090.117	College/university official	SIA
139.087	Crossword-puzzle maker	ASI
102.017	Curator (art galleries, museums)	AEI
090.167	Department head, college/university	SIA
090.167	Director of institutional research	SIA
132.067	Editor/publications	ASI
132.067	Editor/dictionary	ASI
132.067	Editor/greeting card	ASI
132.267	Editorial assistant	ASI
131.067	Editorial writer	ASI
352.367	Flight attendant	ESA
131.267	Foreign correspondent	ASI
188.117	Foreign-service officer	ESC
055.067	Historical archeologist	IAR
184.117	Import/export agent	ESC
059.267	Intelligence specialist	SIA
051.067	International-relations specialist	SIA
110.107	Lawyer	ESA
100.127	Librarian	SAI
165.017	Lobbyist	AES
189.167	Management trainee	ESC
132.267	Manuscript reader (printing and publishing)	ASI
102.381	Museum technician	AEI
059.067	Philologist	SIA
209.387	Proofreader	CIE
109.267	Research assistant (documents and records)	IRC
277.357	Salesperson/books	ESC
059.067	Scientific linguist	SIA

DOT	JOB TITLE	HOC
131.087	Script reader	ASI
132.037	Story editor	ASI
090.227	Teacher/college	SIA
119.287	Title examiner	ESA
353.167	Tour guide	SRE
137.267	Translator	ASI
252.157	Travel agent	ECS
131.067	Writer (prose, fiction, and nonfiction)	ASI
131.267	Writer/technical publications	ASI

HIRING INSTITUTIONS

Air, Bus, and Rail Lines
Archives
Art Galleries
Business Corporations
Colleges and Schools
Educational Institutions
Film Companies
Government Agencies
      Civil Rights Commission
      Education Department
      Environmental Protection Agency
      Federal Trade Commission
      Government Printing Office
      Health and Human Services Department
      Labor Department
      Library of Congress
      National Labor Relations Board
Historical Societies
Import/Export Companies
Learned Periodicals
Libraries
Magazines
Museums
Newspapers
Publishing Companies
Radio/Television Stations
Travel Agencies

CURRENT OCCUPATIONS OF GRADUATES
WHO MAJORED IN CLASSICS

DOT	JOB TITLE	HOC	1960-1974	1975-1980 M	F	T
150.047	Actor	ASE	1			
188.117	Administrative officer/ government service	ESC	2			
— —	Armed services	—	1			
160.162	Auditor	CES	1			
189.117	Business executive	ESC	2		1	1
090.117	College/university official	SIA	2			
020.187	Computer programer	IAS	1			
183.117	District manager	ESC	1			
132.067	Editor	ASI		1		1
050.067	Financial planner	IAS		1		1
189.117	General manager	ESC	1			
— —	Graduate student	—	4	1		1
045.107	Guidance counselor	SIA	1			
119.267	Law clerk	ESA	1			
— —	Law student	—	1	1		1
110.107	Lawyer	ESA	14	1		1
189.167	Management trainee	ESC			1	1
070.101	Physician	ISA	1			
160.167	Revenue agent	CES	1			
290.477	Sales clerk	ESC		1		1
163.167	Sales manager	ESC	2			
600-800	Skilled trades	RIC	2			
185.167	Store manager	ESI	1			
070.101	Surgeon	ISA	1			
012.167	Systems analyst/ electronic data processing	ERI	1			
090.227	Teacher/college	SIA	5			
092.227	Teacher/elementary school	SAI	3		1	1
091.227	Teacher/high school	SAE	7			
099.227	Teacher/other	SIR	1			
			58	6	3	9

Economy is in itself a source of great revenue.
— *Seneca*

ECONOMICS
GENERAL DESCRIPTION

Economics is the study of how society uses its valuable resources to produce, distribute, and consume goods and services. Economists analyze the structure of institutions such as banks, the stock market, and labor unions. People trained in economics also deal with problems arising from inflation, unemployment, labor negotiations, taxes, and international trade.

Theoretical economists develop statistical and mathematical models to explain what causes such conditions as inflation, unemployment or recessions. Applied economists investigate the implications of theories in fields such as energy, finance, transportation, or industrial production. They also serve as advisers to business firms, financial institutions, or labor unions, and analyze data and prepare reports for these clients.

Economists specialize in many fields: advanced economic theory, econometrics, economic history, international economics, and public finance among them. Even as specialists, they can improve their job prospects by getting some training in mathematical methods of analysis and computer science. And since economists often have to present their findings verbally and in writing, they need effective communications skills.

Business, research and finance organizations employ the largest numbers of economists. Majors in this field also find jobs in local, State and Federal government agencies, as well as in secondary schools and colleges. They can qualify, in addition, as financial reporters, technical writers, and public relations practitioners.

Graduates with a bachelor's degree can get positions in business and industry as management and sales trainees. With some courses in statistics and computer science, they can get jobs in market research as well.

Those graduates who go on for advanced studies can achieve more responsible positions in business, research, and consulting firms, with the possibility of rising to top executive positions. A substantial number of economics majors go on to law school. In colleges and universities, they need the Ph.D. to get promotions and tenure.

CAREER LEADS

DOT	JOB TITLE	HOC
188.117	Administrative officer/government service	ESC
164.117	Advertising manager	AES
160.162	Auditor	CES
186.117	Bank officer	ESC
131.067	Book critic	ASI
162.157	Broker's floor representative	ECS
160.207	Budget consultant	CES
186.117	Business manager/education	ESC
162.157	Buyer	ECS
241.217	Claim adjuster	CSE
191.167	Claim agent	ESC
241.267	Claim examiner	CSE
131.067	Columnist/commentator	ASI
050.067	Commodity-industry analyst	IAS
213.132	Computer-operations supervisor	CIS
020.187	Computer programer	IAS
003.167	Computer-systems engineer	IRE
169.207	Conciliator	ESC
188.117	Consumer-affairs director	ESC
096.121	Consumer-services consultant	SRI
191.267	Credit analyst	ESC
168.167	Credit-and-collection manager	SIE
090.167	Department head/college	SIA
090.167	Director of institutional research	SIA
166.117	Director/industrial relations	SEC
050.117	Director/employment research planning	IAS
189.117	Director/research and development	ESC
188.167	Director of vital statistics	ESC

DOT	JOB TITLE	HOC
188.167	District customs director	ESC
050.067	Economist (financial, industrial, labor)	IAS
132.037	Editor, trade journal	ASI
012.167	Efficiency expert	ERI
166.267	Employment interviewer	SEC
001.061	Environmental planner	AIR
186.167	Estate planner	ESC
169.267	Financial-aid counselor	ESC
020.167	Financial analyst	IAS
184.167	Flight-reservations manager	ESC
293.157	Fund raiser/nonprofit organization	ESC
165.117	Fund-raising director	AES
166.267	Hospital-insurance representative	SEC
184.117	Import-export agent	ESC
109.067	Information scientist	IRC
250.257	Insurance agent/broker	ECS
059.267	Intelligence specialist	SIA
168.267	Internal-revenue investigator	SIE
050.067	International-trade economist	IAS
166.267	Job analyst	SEC
166.167	Labor-relations representative	SEC
110.107	Lawyer	ESA
050.067	Labor economist	IAS
165.017	Lobbyist	AES
161.167	Management analyst	CES
187.117	Manager/chamber of commerce	SEC
186.117	Manager/financial institution	ESC
050.067	Market-research analyst	IAS
166.067	Occupational analyst	SEC
166.117	Personnel manager	SEC
166.167	Placement director	SEC
165.067	Public-relations representative	AES
162.157	Purchasing agent	ECS
197.167	Purser	REI
250.357	Real-estate agent/broker	ECS
131.267	Reporter	ASI
161.267	Reports analyst	CES

DOT	JOB TITLE	HOC
012.167	Safety manager	ERI
251.257	Sales agent/financial services	ECS
163.167	Sales manager	ESC
186.167	Securities trader/banking	ESC
375.167	Special agent/ FBI	SRE
020.167	Statistician	IAS
251.157	Stockbroker	ECS
012.167	Systems analyst/electronic data processing	ERI
090.227	Teacher/college	SIA
166.227	Training instructor	SEC
161.117	Treasurer	CES
186.117	Trust officer/bank	ESC
166.167	Wage-and-salary administrator	SEC

HIRING INSTITUTIONS

Advertising Departments and Firms
Banks, Savings/Commercial
Brokerage Houses
Business Corporations
Chambers of Commerce
Civic and Taxpayer Associations
Colleges and Schools
Consulting Firms
Consumer Organizations
Department Stores
Educational Institutions
Employment Agencies
Financial Institutions
Fund-Raising Firms
Government Agencies
     Agriculture Department
     Airports
     Civil Rights Commission
     Consumer-Affairs Office
     Energy Department

Federal Communications Commission
Federal Trade Commission
Health and Human Services Department
Housing and Urban Development
International Trade Commission
Labor Department
Peace Corps
Social Security Administration
Treasury Department
Vista
Industries, Manufacturing
Insurance Companies
Investment Firms
Labor Unions
Magazines, Newspapers
Management Consulting Firms
Market-Research-Departments and Firms
Nursing Homes
Personnel Departments
Pharmaceutical Companies
Political-Action Groups
Professional/Technical Journals
Public-Relations Firms
Publishers
Real Estate Firms
Research-and-Development Firms
Trade Associations
Utility Companies

CURRENT OCCUPATIONS OF GRADUATES WHO MAJORED IN ECONOMICS

DOT	JOB TITLE	HOC	1960-1974	1975-1980		
				M	F	T
160.167	Accountant	CES	15	5		5
160.167	Accounting manager	CES	4			
188.117	Administrative officer/ government service	ESC	20			
164.117	Advertising manager	AES	1			
— —	Armed services	—	24	1		1
160.161	Auditor	CES	8	1		1
186.117	Bank officer	ESC	47	2	1	3
183.117	Branch manager	ESC	3			
186.117	Brokerage-house partner	ESC	1			
161.117	Budget analyst	CES	4		1	1
189.117	Business executive	ESC	43	4		4
162.157	Buyer	ECS	2			
186.117	Cashier/bank	ESC	3			
022.061	Chemist	IAR		1		1
022.061	Chemist/quality control	IAR		1		1
110.117	Claim attorney	ESA	1			
120.007	Clergy member	SAI	1			
209.562	Clerk	CIE	3	3		3
090.117	College/university official	SIA	2			
213.362	Computer operator	CIS	2	1		1
213.132	Computer-operations supervisor	CIS	8	1		1
020.187	Computer programer	IAS	6	3		3
119.267	Contract consultant	ESA	2			
094.117	Coordinator of special services/education	SAI	2			
110.117	Corporate counsel	ESA	1			
160.167	Cost accountant	CES	1		1	1
160.267	Cost estimator	CES	2			
191.267	Credit analyst	ESC	2	2	1	3
168.167	Credit-and-collection manager	SIE	2	1		1
188.167	Customs officer	ESC	1			
003.167	Data-processing engineer	IRE	1			
003.167	Development-and-planning engineer	IRE	2			

DOT	JOB TITLE	HOC	1960-1974	1975-1980		
				M	F	T
110.117	District attorney	ESA	1			
183.117	District manager	ESC	9		1	1
050.067	Economist	IAS	6		1	1
003.061	Electrical engineer	IRE	2	1		1
020.167	Financial/investment analyst	IAS	15	1		1
050.067	Financial planner	IAS	4			
373.364	Firefighter	RSE		1		1
189.117	General manager	ESC	24	3		3
— —	Graduate student	—	14	1	1	2
045.107	Guidance counselor	SIA	4			
091.107	High school official	SAE	3			
187.117	Hospital administrator	SEC	4			
250.257	Insurance agent/broker	ECS	7			
241.217	Insurance-claim adjuster	CSE	1			
168.267	Insurance-claim examiner	SIE	4			
186.117	Insurance-and-risk manager	ESC	1			
169.167	Insurance underwriter	ESC	3	2		2
376.367	Investigator	SRE	2			
111.107	Judge	ESA	1			
022.137	Laboratory supervisor	IAR	1			
119.267	Law clerk	ESA	1			
— —	Law student	—	3	2		2
110.107	Lawyer	ESA	38			
100.127	Librarian	SAI	1			
230.367	Mail carrier	CSR	1			
189.167	Management trainee	ESC	2	1	1	2
163.117	Marketing manager	ESC	2			
050.067	Market-research analyst	IAS	10	1		1
078.261	Medical technologist	ISR	1			
131.267	Newspaper reporter	ASI	1			
169.167	Office manager	ESC	8	1		1
184.167	Operations manager	ESC	2			
195.167	Parole/probation officer	SIC	2			
166.117	Personnel manager	SEC	9	1		1
074.161	Pharmacist	IES	2			

DOT	JOB TITLE	HOC	1960-1974	1975-1980 M	F	T
070.101	Physician	ISA	1			
375.263	Police officer	SRE	4			
189.117	Private-business owner	ESC	7			
189.117	Product manager	ESC	3			
183.117	Production manager	ESC	2	1		1
045.107	Psychologist	SIA	2			
165.067	Public-relations practitioner	AES	2			
162.157	Purchasing agent	ECS	3			
012.167	Quality-control-engineer	ERI	1			
250.357	Real-estate agent/ broker	ECS	1			
045.107	Rehabilitation counselor	SIA	1			
160.167	Revenue agent	CES	4			
290.477	Sales clerk	ESC	7			
163.167	Sales manager	ESC	8			
279.357	Sales/service representative	ESC	28	1		1
020.167	Securities analyst	IAS	5			
186.167	Securities trader	ESC	2	1		1
189.167	Security officer	ESC	1			
600-800	Skilled trades	RIC	2			
188.117	Social-welfare director	ESC	1			
195.107	Social worker	SIC	2	1		1
375.167	Special agent/FBI	SRE	4			
020.067	Statistician	IAS	1			
251.157	Stockbroker	ECS	2			
185.167	Store manager	ESI	1			
070.101	Surgeon	ISA	1			
012.167	Systems analyst/electronic data processing	ERI	8	2		2
003.167	Systems engineer	IRE	2			
160.162	Tax accountant	CES	1	1		1
160.167	Tax administrator	CES	1	1		1
110.117	Tax attorney	ESA	1			
090.227	Teacher/college	SIA	7			
092.227	Teacher/elementary school	SAI	8	2	1	3
091.227	Teacher/high school	SAE	14			

DOT	JOB TITLE	HOC	1960-1974	1975-1980		
				M	F	T
099.227	Teacher/other	SIR	2			
159.147	Television/radio personnel	AES	1			
184.117	Traffic analyst/manager	ESC	2	1		1
166.227	Training specialist	SEC	1			
184.117	Transportation manager	ESC	1			
186.117	Trust officer/bank	ESC	7			
199.167	Urban planner	ICR	2			
131.267	Writer/technical	ASI	1			
			558	52	9	61

What's done to children, they will do to society.
— *Karl Menninger*

EDUCATION
GENERAL DESCRIPTION

Education deals with methods of instruction which promote human development and learning. Although most graduates begin their careers in education as teachers, nearly half of the 5,000,000 persons working in this field do administrative and personnel work, or they supply technical and supportive services.

The employment situation continues to be rather competitive, although opportunities in special education, preschool education, and the teaching of science, industrial arts, and vocational subjects have continued to emerge. But now warnings are sounding from several sources that teacher shortages have begun to develop. The National Center for Educational Statistics, for one, predicts a growth of 13.7 percent in elementary enrollment by the end of this decade and projects that long before then — by 1986 — barely one teacher will be available for every teaching vacancy. In addition, the National Council for Accreditation of Teacher Education expects this anticipated shortage to become more critical in the late 1980's.

While waiting to get teaching jobs, graduates often find other positions which draw on the skills they have acquired by studying communications, administrative planning, training and motivating of young people, and learning-theory. Such positions involve personnel work, employment interviewing, job-training in unions and industry, employee educational-counseling in large corporations, as well as planning work with travel and recreational establishments.

A bachelor's degree is sufficient for achieving certification. Many states, however, require teachers to take courses in continuing education to maintain their skills. One usually needs additional degrees for salary-scale advances or for more responsible administrative posts.

CAREER LEADS

DOT	JOB TITLE	HOC
193.162	Air-traffic controller	RIE
090.117	Alumni secretary	SIA
153.227	Athletic coach	SRE
090.117	Athletic director/education	SIA
076.101	Audiologist	SIR
099.167	Audiovisual specialist	SIE
186.117	Business manager/education	ESC
099.167	Certification-and-selection specialist	SIE
188.117	Consumer-affairs director	ESC
096.121	Consumer-services consultant	SRE
188.117	Council-on-Aging director	ESC
045.107	Counselor (guidance, rehabilitation, vocational)	SIA
090.167	Department head, college/university	SIA
077.117	Dietitian	SIE
090.167	Director of admissions	SIA
090.167	Director of institutional research	SIA
090.167	Director of student affairs	SIA
099.117	Educational-program director	SIE
099.117	Education supervisor/correctional institution	SIE
094.227	Educational therapist	SAI
169.267	Financial-aid counselor	ESC
090.107	Foreign-student adviser	ESC
099.227	Instructor/correspondence school	SIE
153.227	Instructor/sports	SRE
100.127	Librarian	SAI
166.117	Personnel manager	SEC
166.167	Placement director	SEC
099.117	Principal/education	SIE
045.107	Psychologist/industrial	SIA
045.107	Psychologist/school	SIA
165.067	Public-relations representative	AES
162.157	Purchasing agent	ECS
195.167	Recreation director	SIC
090.167	Registrar, college/university	SIA

DOT	JOB TITLE	HOC
109.267	Research assistant	IRC
277.357	Salesperson/books	ESC
195.107	Social worker	SIC
076.107	Speech pathologist	SIR
099.227	Teacher/adult education	SIE
090.227	Teacher/college	SIA
092.227	Teacher/elementary school	SAI
094.227	Teacher/handicapped students	SAI
091.227	Teacher/high school	SAE
094.227	Teacher/mentally retarded	SAI
092.227	Teacher/preschool	SAI
166.227	Training instructor	SEC
099.227	Tutor	SIE

HIRING INSTITUTIONS

Adoption and Child Care Agencies
Boards of Education
Bookstores
Colleges and Schools
Community Organizations
    YM-YWCAs
    YM-YWHAs
    Scouts, etc.
Correctional Institutions
Day Care Centers
Educational Institutions
Educational Periodicals
Government Agencies
    Civil Rights Commission
    Consumer Affairs Office
    Education Department
    Environmental Protection Agency
    Federal Communications Commission
    Federal Labor Relations Authority
    Government Printing Office

Health and Human Services Department
Labor Department
Library of Congress
National Archives
Overseas Schools for Military Dependents
Peace Corps
Vista
Labor Unions
Libraries
Nursery Schools
Nursing Homes
Orphanages
Social-Service Agencies
Test-Development Corporations
Test-Preparation Institutes

CURRENT OCCUPATIONS OF GRADUATES
WHO MAJORED IN EDUCATION

DOT	JOB TITLE	HOC	1960-1974	1975-1980 M	F	T
188.117	Administrative officer/ government service	ESC	1			
164.117	Advertising manager	AES			1	1
— —	Armed services	—	1			
189.117	Business executive	ESC	1		3	3
209.562	Clerk	CIE	1		8	8
090.117	College/university official	SIA	1		2	2
213.132	Computer-operations supervisor	CIS	1		1	1
020.187	Computer programer	IAS	1	1		1
094.117	Coordinator of special services/education	SAI	2	1		1
168.167	Credit-and-collection manager	SIE	1			
092.137	Elementary-school official	SAI	1		1	1
189.117	General manager	ESC	1		2	2
— —	Graduate student	—	2	1	1	2

DOT	JOB TITLE	HOC	1960-1974	1975-1980		
				M	F	T
045.107	Guidance counselor	SIA	1			
250.257	Insurance agent/broker	ECS	1			
241.217	Insurance-claim investigator	ESC		1		1
029.261	Laboratory technician	IRA	1			
— —	Law student	—		3	1	4
163.117	Marketing manager	ESC			1	1
078.261	Medical technologist	ISR	1			
166.117	Personnel manager	SEC	1			
375.263	Police officer	SRE	1			
189.117	Private-business owner	ESC	1			
189.117	Research-and-development director	ESC	1			
290.477	Sales clerk	ESC		1		1
163.167	Sales manager	ESC	1			
279.357	Sales/service representative	ESC	1		1	1
600-800	Skilled trades	RIC	3	2		2
195.107	Social worker	SIC	2			
375.167	Special agent/FBI	SRE	2	1		1
090.227	Teacher/college	SIA	1		1	1
092.227	Teacher/elementary school	SAI	81	4	60	64
091.227	Teacher/high school	SAE	7	8	8	16
099.227	Teacher/other	SIR	15	1	21	22
094.227	Teacher/special education	SAI	1	2	4	6
252.157	Travel agent	ECS	1		2	2
			137	26	118	144

The artistic temperament is a disease that afflicts
amateurs.   *— G.K. Chesterton*

ENGLISH
GENERAL DESCRIPTION

Students of English investigate the ways in which the
written and spoken language takes form, and the
techniques for using it effectively. They also
evaluate the human response to experience as they find it
expressed through literary art forms such as poetry, drama, and
the novel. Such students develop theories of esthetics and
methods of literary criticism which they apply in analyzing the
major works of English and American literature.

Graduates who acquire the necessary skills can do
entry-level writing, editing, research or production in the
communications media. English majors with that kind of
training can also get into public relations, advertising, or
scientific-publishing jobs.

With this major, one can develop the ability to think
clearly, interpret data, and communicate results, especially in
writing. These skills can serve as a background for entry into
many fields of human endeavor: business management, social
work, library service, broadcasting, real estate, finance, and
travel.

To function effectively, most businesses need employees
who have good communications skills. English majors who
master these skills can further increase their job prospects by
taking business courses that attract them.

A bachelor's degree is usually sufficient for entry jobs in
advertising, publishing, journalism, radio, TV, and government
service, and trainee positions in business, industry, and
finance. Graduates who go on to advanced studies frequently
become lawyers, college professors, administrative officers and
business executives.

CAREER LEADS

DOT	JOB TITLE	HOC
188.117	Administrative officer/government service	ESC
164.117	Advertising manager	AES
159.147	Announcer (radio and TV)	AES
191.287	Appraiser/art	ESC
101.167	Archivist	SAI
131.067	Art critic	ASI
191.117	Artist's manager	ESC
188.117	Arts-and-Humanities-Council director	ESC
132.137	Assignment editor (radio and TV)	ASI
186.117	Bank officer	ESC
052.067	Biographer	SEI
131.067	Book critic	ASI
120.007	Clergy	SAI
131.067	Columnist/commentator	ASI
020.187	Computer programer	IAS
131.087	Continuity writer	ASI
131.067	Copy writer/advertising	ASI
131.267	Correspondent	ASI
131.267	Critic (book, drama, film)	ASI
139.087	Crossword-puzzle maker	ASI
159.147	Disc jockey	AES
132.067	Editor/dictionary	ASI
132.067	Editor/greeting card	ASI
132.037	Editor/house organ	ASI
132.067	Editor/news	ASI
132.067	Editor/publications	ASI
132.037	Editor/trade journal	ASI
132.267	Editorial assistant	ASI
131.267	Editorial writer	ASI
131.267	Foreign correspondent	ASI
293.157	Fund raiser	ESC
165.117	Fund-raising director	AES
250.257	Insurance agent/broker	ECS
110.107	Lawyer	ESA
100.127	Librarian	SAI
191.117	Literary agent	ESC

DOT	JOB TITLE	HOC
189.167	Management trainee	ESC
132.267	Manuscript reader	ASI
131.067	Movie critic	ASI
131.267	Newscaster	ASI
131.267	Newswriter	ASI
209.387	Proofreader	CIE
165.067	Public-relations practitioner	AES
131.267	Reporter	ASI
109.267	Research assistant	IRC
131.267	Rewriter	ASI
277.357	Salesperson/books	ESC
259.357	Sales representative (radio and TV)	ECS
131.087	Script reader	ASI
375.167	Special agent/FBI	SRE
251.157	Stockbroker	ECS
132.037	Story Editor	ASI
090.227	Teacher/college	SIA
252.157	Travel agent	ECS
131.267	Writer/technical, scientific	ASI

HIRING INSTITUTIONS

Advertising Departments and Firms

Air, Bus, and Rail Lines

Banks, Savings/Commercial

Bookstores

Business Corporations

Colleges and Schools

Consumer Organizations

Department Stores

Educational Institutions

Film Companies

Fund-Raising Firms

Government Agencies

     Consumer Affairs Office
     Education Department
     Environmental Protection Agency
     Federal Trade Commission
     Government Printing Office
     Health and Human Services Department
     Labor Department
     Library of Congress
     National Foundation on the Arts and the
        Humanities
     Social Security Administration
     Vista

Industries, Manufacturing

Insurance Companies

Investment Firms

Labor Unions

Libraries

Literary Periodicals

Magazines and Newspapers

Personnel Departments

Political-Action Groups

Public-Relations Firms

Publishing Companies

Radio/Television Stations

Real Estate Firms

Research-and-Development Firms

Travel Agencies

Utility Companies

CURRENT OCCUPATIONS OF GRADUATES WHO MAJORED IN ENGLISH

DOT	JOB TITLE	HOC	1960-1974	1975-1980 M	F	T
160.167	Accountant	CES	1	1		1
160.167	Accounting manager	CES	1			
150.047	Actor	ASE	1	1		1
188.117	Administrative officer/ government service	ESC	8	2		2
164.117	Advertising manager	AES	1		2	2
— —	Armed services	—	19	2		2
144.061	Artist	AIR	1		1	1
186.117	Bank officer	ESC	6			
189.117	Business executive	ESC	29		2	2
162.157	Buyer	ECS	3	1		1
022.061	Chemist/quality control	IAR	1			
120.007	Clergy member	SAI	1			
209.562	Clerk	CIE	9	7	5	12
090.117	College/university official	SIA	6		1	1
213.362	Computer operator	CIS		1		1
213.132	Computer-operations supervisor	CIS	1			
020.187	Computer programer	IAS	1	1		1
869.664	Construction worker	REI	1			
119.267	Contract consultant	ESA	1	1	1	2
110.117	Corporate counsel	ESA	1			
168.167	Credit/collection manager	SIE		1		1
003.167	Development-and-planning engineer	IRE	2			
110.117	District attorney	ESA	2			
183.117	District manager	ESC	3			
132.067	Editor	ASI	7		2	2
166.267	Employment interviewer	SEC	1		1	1
020.167	Financial/investment analyst	IAS	4		1	1
050.067	Financial planner	IAS	1		1	1
373.364	Firefighter	RSE	2			
189.117	General manager	ESC	8	4	1	5
— —	Graduate student	—	19	3	3	6
045.107	Guidance counselor	SIA	2			

DOT	JOB TITLE	HOC	1960-1974	1975-1980 M	F	T
091.107	High-school-department chairperson	SAE	3			
091.107	High-school official	SAE	3		1	1
187.117	Hospital administrator	SEC			1	1
187.117	Hotel/restaurant manager	SEC	1			
012.167	Industrial engineer	ERI	1		1	1
250.257	Insurance agent/broker	ECS	6			
241.217	Insurance-claim adjuster	CSE	3		1	1
168.267	Insurance-claim examiner	SIE	3		1	1
169.167	Insurance underwriter	ESC	3			
166.167	Labor-relations consultant	SEC	1			
119.267	Law clerk	ESA	1		1	1
110.107	Law-school professor	ESA	2			
— —	Law student	—	4		2	2
110.107	Lawyer	ESA	32	1		1
100.127	Librarian	SAI	6		4	4
189.167	Management trainee	ESC	2			
163.117	Marketing manager	ESC	3			
050.067	Market-research analyst	IAS			1	1
078.261	Medical technologist	ISR	1			
152.041	Musician	ASI	1			
131.267	Newspaper reporter	ASI	4	1	1	2
169.167	Office manager	ESC	11		1	1
184.167	Operations manager	ESC	1			
195.167	Parole/probation officer	SIC	1			
166.117	Personnel manager	SEC	3			
143.062	Photographer	AIR	2			
196.263	Pilot/airplane	IRC	1			
375.263	Police officer	SRE		1		1
189.117	Private-business owner	ESC	8		1	1
163.267	Product-distribution manager	ESC	1			
189.117	Product manager	ESC.	2			
183.117	Production manager	ESC	1			
165.067	Public-relations practitioner	AES	8	1	1	2
045.107	Rehabilitation counselor	SIA	1			
290.477	Sales clerk	ESC	3			

DOT	JOB TITLE	HOC	1960-1974	1975-1980 M	F	T
163.167	Sales manager	ESC	8	1	1	2
279,357	Sales/service representative	ESC	9	2	1	3
600-800	Skilled trades	RIC	1	1		1
188.117	Social-welfare director	ESC	1		1	1
195.107	Social worker	SIC	7		1	1
070.101	Surgeon	ISA	1			
012.167	Systems analyst/electronic data processing	ERI	4			
160.167	Tax administrator	CES	1			
090.227	Teacher/college	SIA	24			
092.227	Teacher/elementary school	SAI	21	2	2	4
091.227	Teacher/high school	SAE	86	2	3	5
099.227	Teacher/other	SIR	16	1	4	5
094.227	Teacher/special education	SAI	1			
159.147	Television/radio personnel	AES	1			
184.117	Traffic analyst/manager	ESC	1		1	1
166.227	Training specialist	SEC	2			
252.157	Travel agent	ECS	1			
045.107	Vocational counselor	SIA	1			
131.067	Writer (fiction and nonfiction)	ASI	2			
131.267	Writer/technical	ASI	3	2		2
			457	40	52	92

*Not to know what happened before one was born is
to remain a child.*   — *Cicero*

HISTORY
GENERAL DESCRIPTION

History gives us a narrative account of the political, social, and cultural events and achievements that mankind has placed on record. Historians evaluate and analyze documents and record data relating to aspirations and deeds that past generations have left us, and use this knowledge to understand and interpret the present.

Historians frequently focus on an area that has special interest for them. Their specialties might embrace a period of time, an individual country, or the history of a field of human endeavor such as medicine, art, philosophy, feminism, military affairs.

In addition to being archivists and museum curators, historians can serve as consultants to publishers, TV, and movie producers, and they can do research for business and industrial firms, social and governmental agencies.

Students who major in history for their own educational development can use this training to enter a wide variety of occupations that suit their personalities and interests. The knowledge and training students gain in this major — together with additional skills they acquire through electives — have enabled many to find congenial employment in sales, brokerage and publishing houses, the media, insurance, and government. As they build up experience, graduates have frequently progressed to executive positions.

With a bachelor's degree, you can get entry jobs in government service, communications, banking, finance, and sales. You need an advanced degree to consider yourself a professional historian and to find jobs in research or archival work. Those who go on for additional training often become lawyers or college teachers.

CAREER LEADS

DOT	JOB TITLE	HOC
188.117	Administrative officer/government service	ESC
191.287	Appraiser/art	ESC
101.167	Archivist	SAI
188.117	Arts-and-Humanities-Council director	ESC
186.117	Bank officer	ESC
052.067	Biographer	SEI
100.387	Cataloger	SAI
090.117	College/university official	SIA
131.067	Columnist/commentator	ASI
131.087	Continuity writer	ASI
131.267	Correspondent	ASI
131.067	Critic (book, drama, film)	ASI
188.117	Cultural-affairs officer	ESC
168.267	Customs inspector	SIE
102.017	Curator (art galleries, museums)	AEI
090.161	Department head/college	SIA
090.167	Director of institutional research	SIA
052.167	Director/research (motion picture, radio, TV)	SEI
052.067	Director/state-historical society	SEI
132.067	Editor/news	ASI
132.067	Editor/publications	ASI
188.167	Election supervisor	ESC
055.067	Ethnologist	IAR
131.267	Foreign correspondent	ASI
188.117	Foreign-service officer	ESC
293.157	Fund raiser	ESC
052.067	Genealogist	SEI
052.067	Historian	SEI
052.067	Historian/dramatic arts	SEI
055.067	Historical archaeologist	IAR
250.257	Insurance agent/broker	ECS
059.267	Intelligence specialist	SIA
110.107	Lawyer	ESA
100.127	Librarian	SAI
189.167	Management trainee	ESC
187.117	Manager/chamber of commerce	SEC

DOT	JOB TITLE	HOC
132.267	Manuscript reader	ASI
131.067	Movie critic	ASI
102.381	Museum technician	AEI
131.267	Newscaster	ASI
131.267	News editor	ASI
119.267	Paralegal assistant	ESA
051.067	Political scientist	SIA
165.067	Public-relations practitioner	AEC
090.167	Registrar, college/university	SIA
259.357	Sales representative, radio/television time	ECS
131.087	Script reader	ASI
195.107	Social worker	SIC
102.117	Supervisor/historic sites	AEI
119.287	Title examiner	ESA
090.227	Teacher/college	SIA
091.227	Teacher/high school	SAE
353.167	Tour guide	SRE
252.157	Travel agent	ECS
131.067	Writer (prose, fiction, nonfiction)	ASI

HIRING INSTITUTIONS

Air, Bus, and Rail Lines
Archives
Banks, Savings/Commercial
Business Corporations
Chambers of Commerce
Colleges and Schools
Educational Institutions
Film Companies
Foundations, Non-Profit
Government Agencies
 Civil Rights Commission
 Consumer Affairs Office
 Education Department
 Environmental Protection Agency
 Federal Communications Agency
 Foreign Service Department
 Government Printing Office
 Health and Human Services Department
 International Trade Commission
 Justice Department
 Labor Department
 Library of Congress
 National Archives
 Social Security Administration
 Vista
Historical Societies
Industries, Manufacturing
Insurance Companies
Investment Firms
Libraries
Magazines and Newspapers
Museums
National and State Parks
Professional Periodicals
Public-Relations Firms
Publishing Companies
Radio/Television Stations
Social-Service Agencies
Travel Agencies

CURRENT OCCUPATIONS OF GRADUATES WHO MAJORED IN HISTORY

DOT	JOB TITLE	HOC	1960-1974	1975-1980 M	F	T
160.167	Accountant	CES	5	2		2
160.167	Accounting manager	CES	2	1		1
188.117	Administrative officer/ government service	ESC	8			
164.117	Advertising manager	AES	2			
001.061	Architect	AIR		1		1
— —	Armed services	—	37	7		7
160.162	Auditor	CES	2	1		1
186.117	Bank officer	ESC	16	1		1
183.117	Branch manager	ESC	2			
161.117	Budget analyst	CES		1		1
189.117	Business executive	ESC	20	3		3
162.157	Buyer	ECS	2			
186.117	Cashier/bank	ESC	2			
120.007	Clergy member	SAI	4			
209.562	Clerk	CIE	4			
090.117	College/university official	SIA	11	1		1
213.362	Computer operator	CIS	1	1		1
213.132	Computer-operations supervisor	CIS	1			
020.187	Computer programer	IAS	7		1	1
169.664	Construction worker	REI		1	1	2
182.167	Contractor	ERI	1			
094.117	Coordinator of special services/education	SAI	6			
110.117	Corporate counsel	ESA	4			
160.167	Cost accountant	CES	1			
160.267	Cost estimator	CES	1			
191.267	Credit analyst	ESC	1	1		1
186.167	Credit-and-collection manager	SIE	2			
188.167	Customs officer	ESC	2			
— —	Dental student		1			
003.167	Development-and-planning engineer	IRE	1			
110.117	District attorney	ESA	2			
183.117	District manager	ESC	2			

DOT	JOB TITLE	HOC	1960-1974	1975-1980 M	F	T
050.067	Economist	IAS	1			
132.067	Editor	ASI	1			
092.137	Elementary-school official	SAI				
166.267	Employment interviewer	SEC	2			
186.167	Estate planner	ESC	5			
020.167	Financial/investment analyst	IAS	4			
050.067	Financial planner	IAS			1	1
373.364	Firefighter	RSE	2	1		1
189.117	General manager	ESC	15	1		1
— —	Graduate student	—	21	9	1	10
045.107	Guidance counselor	SIA	5		1	1
091.107	High-school-department chairperson	SAE	6			
091.107	High-school official	SAE	7			
187.117	Hospital administrator	SEC	5			
187.117	Hotel/restaurant manager	SEC	1			
012.167	Industrial engineer	ERI	2			
250.257	Insurance agent/broker	ECS	7	1		1
241.217	Insurance-claim adjuster	CSE	1	1		1
168.267	Insurance-claim examiner	SIE	7	1	2	3
169.167	Insurance underwriter	ESC	8	1		1
376.367	Investigator	SRE	2	1		1
111.107	Judge	ESA	1			
029.261	Laboratory technician	IRA	2			
119.267	Law clerk	ESA	4	3		3
— —	Law student	—	15	2	2	4
110.107	Lawyer	ESA	72	4	3	7
100.127	Librarian	SAI	5		2	2
189.167	Management trainee	ESC	3	3		3
163.117	Marketing manager	ESC	3	1		1
050.067	Market-research analyst	IAS	3			
078.261	Medical technologist	ISR	1			
131.267	Newspaper reporter	ASI	3			
169.167	Office manager	ESC	13			
184.167	Operations manager	ESC	1			
195.167	Parole/probation officer	SIC	4			

DOT	JOB TITLE	HOC	1960-1974	1975-1980 M	F	T
166.117	Personnel manager	SEC	5	1	1	2
143.062	Photographer	AIR	1			
070.101	Physician	ISA	1			
196.263	Pilot/airplane	IRC	1			
375.263	Police officer	SRE	5	5		5
189.117	Private-business owner	ESC	12	1		1
163.267	Product-distribution manager	ESC	2			
189.117	Product manager	ESC	3			
183.117	Production manager	ESC	3			
045.107	Psychologist	SIA	4			
165.067	Public-relations practitioner	AES		1		1
070.101	Radiologist	ISA	1			
250.357	Real-estate agent/broker	ECS		1		1
045.107	Rehabilitation counselor	SIA	1			
189.117	Research-and-development director	ESC	1		1	1
160.167	Revenue agent	CES	7	1		1
290.477	Sales clerk	ESC	1		1	1
163.167	Sales manager	ESC	5			
279.357	Sales/service representative	ESC	23	5		5
186.167	Securities trader	ESC	3			
189.167	Security officer	ESC	1	1		1
— —	Seminarian	—	2	1		1
600-800	Skilled trades	RIC	6	2		2
188.117	Social-welfare director	ESC	2			
195.107	Social worker	SIC	7	1		1
375.167	Special agent/FBI	SRE	1			
251.157	Stock broker	ECS	2			
185.167	Store manager	ESI	4	1		1
012.167	Systems analyst/electronic data processing	ERI	2			
003.167	Systems engineer	IRE	1			
090.227	Teacher/college	SIA	13			
092.227	Teacher/elementary school	SAI	30	5	3	8
091.227	Teacher/high school	SAE	72	7	2	9

DOT	JOB TITLE	HOC	1960-1974	1975-1980 M	F	T
099.227	Teacher/other	SIR	21	1		1
094.227	Teacher/special education	SAI	1			
184.117	Traffic analyst/manager	ESC	2	1		1
166.227	Training specialist	SEC	5			
184.117	Transportation manager	ESC	1	1		1
199.167	Urban planner	ICR	1			
			637	86	22	108

Let your advance worrying become advance thinking and planning. — *Sir Winston Churchill*

MANAGEMENT
GENERAL DESCRIPTION

Business managers plan, organize, staff, and direct a business or institution. They may run an entire organization or one of its units.

They become involved in such areas as managing human resources, labor relations, resolving conflicts, motivating and evaluating subordinates, negotiating and decision-making. A variety of fast-paced, action-oriented activities make effective writing and speaking skills a must for business managers — on the phone, in staff meetings, or at large conferences.

Managers need flexibility to play different roles at different times: institutional symbol, spokesperson, negotiator. As employees advance in any kind of organizational structure —manufacturer, hospital, financial institution, college, or consulting firm — they can expect to take on managerial responsibilities that call for increasingly-specialized knowledge and skills.

Places of employment usually include firms which manufacture products such as machinery, food and clothing, or those that provide services, such as airlines and telephone companies. You can improve your chances of advancing in your job if you develop proficiency in data-processing and statistics. And if you train yourself to write clearly and to speak effectively, you will have the tools that most executives say you need to succeed in business.

The bachelor's degree in management, with electives in communications and the new technologies, opens up a wide variety of beginning jobs in business, industry, and government. Additional education such as an MBA, in the same or a related field, is helpful and often essential as you take on greater managerial responsibilities.

CAREER LEADS

DOT	JOB TITLE	HOC
160.167	Accountant (budget, cost, systems)	CES
164.167	Account executive	AES
020.167	Actuary	IAS
188.117	Administrative officer/government service	ESC
164.117	Advertising manager	AES
193.162	Air-traffic controller	RIE
160.162	Auditor	CES
186.117	Bank officer	ESC
162.157	Broker's floor representative	ECS
160.207	Budget consultant	CES
161.117	Budget officer	CES
160.167	Bursar	CES
186.117	Business manager/education	ESC
241.217	Claim adjustor	CSE
191.167	Claim agent	ESC
241.267	Claim examiner	CSE
161.267	Clerical-methods analyst	CES
213.132	Computer-operations supervisor	CIS
020.187	Computer programer	IAS
169.207	Conciliator	ESC
096.121	Consumer-service consultant	SRI
119.267	Contract consultant	ESA
186.117	Controller	ESC
191.267	Credit analyst	ESC
168.167	Credit-and-collection manager	SIE
166.117	Director/industrial relations	SEC
189.117	Director/research and development	ESC
166.267	Employment interviewer	SEC
132.037	Editor/trade journal	ASI
012.167	Efficiency expert	ERI
169.267	Financial-aid counselor	ESC
020.167	Financial analyst	IAS
161.267	Forms analyst	CES
187.117	Hospital administrator	SEC
184.117	Import-export agent	ESC
012.167	Industrial engineer	ERI
109.067	Information scientist	IRC

DOT	JOB TITLE	HOC
250.257	Insurance agent/broker	ECS
168.267	Internal-revenue investigator	SIE
166.267	Job analyst	SEC
166.167	Labor-relations representative	SEC
110.107	Lawyer	ESA
186.267	Loan officer	ESC
161.117	Management analyst	CES
189.167	Management trainee	ESC
187.167	Manager/casino	SEC
187.117	Manager/chamber of commerce	SEC
163.117	Manager/contracts	ESC
186.117	Manager/financial institution	ESC
163.117	Manager/promotion	ESC
185.167	Manager/retail store	ESI
050.067	Market-research analyst	IAS
169.167	Office manager	ESC
184.117	Operations manager	ESC
166.117	Personnel manager	SEC
166.167	Placement director	SEC
189.117	Product manager	ESC
183.117	Production manager	ESC
163.167	Property-disposal officer	ESC
162.157	Purchasing agent	ECS
197.167	Purser	REI
250.357	Real-estate agent/broker	ECS
160.167	Revenue agent	CES
161.267	Reports analyst	CES
168.264	Safety inspector	SIE
251.257	Sales agent/financial services	ECS
186.167	Securities trader	ESC
357.167	Special agent/FBI	SRE
251.157	Stock broker	ECS
012.167	Systems analyst	ERI
090.227	Teacher/college	SIA
119.287	Title examiner	ESA
184.167	Traffic manager	ESC
166.227	Training instructor	SEC
186.117	Trust officer/bank	ESC

DOT	JOB TITLE	HOC
166.167	Wage-and-salary administrator	SEC
131.267	Writer/technical publications	ASI

HIRING INSTITUTIONS

Accounting Firms
Advertising Departments and Agencies
Air, Bus, and Rail Lines
Banks, Savings/Commercial
Brokerage Houses
Business Corporations
Civic and Taxpayers' Associations
Colleges and Schools
Department Stores
Educational Institutions
Engineering Firms
Foundations, Non-Profit
Government Agencies
     Civil Service Commission
     Consumer Affairs Office
     Energy Department
     General Accounting Office
     International Trade Commission
     Labor Department
     Management and Budget Office
     Securities and Exchange Commission
     Social Security Administration
     Vista
Hospitals
Industries, Manufacturing
Insurance Companies
Investment Firms
Magazines, Newspapers
Management-Consulting Firms
Manufacturing and Processing Firms
Market Research Departments and Firms

Nursing Homes
Personnel Departments
Professional Journals
Publishing Companies
Radio/Television Stations
Regional-Planning Councils and Associations
Research-and-Development Firms
Trade Associations
Utility Companies

CURRENT OCCUPATIONS OF GRADUATES WHO MAJORED IN MANAGEMENT

DOT	JOB TITLE	HOC	1960-1974	1975-1980		
				M	F	T
160.167	Accountant	CES	16	18	2	20
160.167	Accounting manager	CES	6	2	3	5
160.167	Accounting partner	CES	1			
020.167	Actuary	IAS	1			
188.117	Administrative officer/ government service	ESC	19	3	2	5
164.117	Advertising manager	AES	4	1		1
— —	Armed services	—	17	8		8
099.167	Audiovisual specialist	SIE	1			
160.162	Auditor	CES	11	4		4
186.117	Bank officer	ESC	46	19	5	24
183.117	Branch manager	ESC	10	3		3
161.117	Budget analyst	CES	5	4	2	6
189.117	Business executive	ESC	52	12	5	17
162.157	Buyer	ECS	6	3	2	5
186.117	Cashier/bank	ESC	2	3	2	5
022.061	Chemist/research	IAR	1			
079.101	Chiropractor	SIR	1			
110.117	Claim attorney	ESA			1	1
120.007	Clergy member	SAI	3			
209.562	Clerk	CIE	12	12	7	19
090.117	College/university official	SIA	2	1		1
213.362	Computer operator	CIS	2		2	2
213.132	Computer-operations supervisor	CIS	4	8		8

DOT	JOB TITLE	HOC	1960-1974	1975-1980 M	F	T
020.187	Computer programer	IAS	21	24	2	26
869.664	Construction worker	REI	1	2		2
119.267	Contract consultant	ESA	1			
094.117	Coordinator of special services/education	SAI	1			
160.167	Cost accountant	CES	8	1		1
160.267	Cost estimator	CES	1	2		2
191.267	Credit analyst	ESC	2	3	1	4
168.167	Credit-and-collection manager	SIE	5	3	2	5
188.167	Customs officer	ESC	1	1		1
003.167	Development-and-planning engineer	IRE	4	2		2
183.117	District manager	ESC	7	3		3
050.067	Economist	IAS	1			
050.067	Economist/price	IAS		1		1
132.067	Editor	ASI	1			
003.061	Electrical engineer	IRE	4	2		2
092.137	Elementary-school official	SAI	1			
166.267	Employment interviewer	SEC	2			
020.167	Financial/investment analyst	IAS	3	1		1
050.067	Financial planner	IAS	5	2	3	5
373.364	Firefighter	RSE	2	2		2
187.167	Funeral director	SEC		1	1	2
189.117	General manager	ESC	45	37	5	42
— —	Graduate student	—	5	1	1	2
045.107	Guidance counselor	SIA	2			
091.107	High-school-department chairperson	SAE	1			
091.107	High-school official	SAE	2			
187.117	Hospital administrator	SEC	1	1	2	3
012.167	Industrial engineer	ERI	9	2	2	4
250.257	Insurance agent/broker	ECS	16	6		6
241.217	Insurance-claim adjuster	CSE	4	5		5
168.267	Insurance-claim examiner	SIE	6	2	2	4
241.217	Insurance-claim investigator	CSE	2	1		1

DOT	JOB TITLE	HOC	1960-1974	1975-1980 M	F	T
186.117	Insurance-and-risk manager	ESC	1	1		1
169.167	Insurance underwriter	ESC	14	1		1
142.051	Interior designer/decorator	AIS	1			
376.367	Investigator	SRE	3	1		1
111.107	Judge	ESA	1			
029.261	Laboratory technician	IRA		1		1
166.167	Labor-relations consultant	SEC	1		1	1
119.267	Law clerk	ESA	2	1		1
— —	Law student	—		3		3
110.107	Lawyer	ESA	6		1	1
100.127	Librarian	SAI			1	1
230.367	Mail carrier	CSR	2		1	1
012.167	Management/methods engineer	ERI	6			
189.167	Management trainee	ESC	4	11	5	16
163.117	Marketing manager	ESC	9	2		2
050.067	Market-research analyst	IAS	11		1	1
— —	Medical student	—		1		1
152.041	Musician	ASI	1			
169.167	Office manager	ESC	42	7	2	9
184.167	Operations manager	ESC	7	15		15
079.101	Optometrist	SIR		1		1
195.167	Parole/probation officer	SIC	2			
166.117	Personnel manager	SEC	16	9	4	13
196.263	Pilot/airplane	IRC	2			
375.263	Police officer	SRE	4	7		7
189.117	Private-business owner	ESC	13	1		1
163.267	Product-distribution manager	ESC	1			
189.117	Product manager	ESC	14	8	1	9
183.117	Production manager	ESC	14	7	1	8
165.067	Public-relations practitioner	AES	5	3		3
162.157	Purchasing agent	ECS	12	1	1	2
012.167	Quality-control engineer	ERI	1	1		1
070.101	Radiologist	ISA	1			
250.357	Real-estate agent/broker	ECS	4	1	2	3

DOT	JOB TITLE	HOC	1960-1974	1975-1980		
				M	F	T
045.107	Rehabilitation counselor	SIA	1			
189.117	Research-and-development director	ESC	5		1	1
160.167	Revenue agent	CES	3			
290.477	Sales clerk	ESC	14	5	1	6
163.167	Sales manager	ESC	24	5		5
279.357	Sales/service representative	ESC	36	19	3	22
020.167	Securities analyst	IAS		2		2
186.167	Securities trader	ESC	2	1		1
186.167	Security officer	ESC		1		1
600-800	Skilled trades	RIC	10	10		10
195.107	Social worker	SIC	3	2		2
054.067	Sociologist	SIA		1		1
375.167	Special agent/FBI	SRE	2			
020.067	Statistician	IAS	1			
251.157	Stock broker	ECS	2	5		5
185.167	Store manager	ESI		5		5
070.101	Surgeon	ISA	1			
012.167	Systems analyst/electronic data processing	ERI	23	2		2
003.167	Systems engineer	IRE	3			
160.167	Tax administrator	CES			1	1
090.227	Teacher/college	SIA	3	1		1
092.227	Teacher/elementary school	SAI	3			
091.227	Teacher/high school	SAE	17	2	3	5
099.227	Teacher/other	SIR	4	1	2	3
184.117	Traffic analyst/manager	ESC	5	3		3
137.267	Translator	ASI	1			
184.117	Transportation manager	ESC	4	2		2
186.117	Trust officer/bank	ESC	4			
			757	356	86	442

Invention is the mother of necessity.
— *Thorstein Veblen*

MARKETING
GENERAL DESCRIPTION

Marketing seeks to satisfy the needs and wants of consumers by exchanging goods for money or credit. Marketing also aims to use efficiently an economy's assets and productive capacity.

Managers in charge of marketing develop practices to control the flow of goods from production-stage to point-of-purchase. They find ways to anticipate and stimulate demand for a product or service. Their activities include advertising, marketing research, brand management, international distribution, and transportation. In marketing, they analyze the opinions and tastes of the buying public, the means of disseminating information — radio, TV, magazines, direct mail — and the most efficient, economical ways to get products to the marketplace and to the consumer.

Since the marketing manager's activities touch on so many aspects of a business enterprise, you can improve your prospects in this field with courses in economics, sociology, psychology, political science, statistics — and especially in speech and writing.

Employers include large business and industrial firms but also smaller companies, private research organizations, and advertising agencies. Retail and wholesale trade, insurance, travel, and real estate are other areas where your training can open up job opportunities.

While the bachelor's degree qualifies you for a broad range of beginning jobs, you will probably need a master's degree for more responsible positions.

CAREER LEADS

DOT	JOB TITLE	HOC
160.167	Accountant (budget, cost, systems)	CES
164.167	Account executive	AES
020.167	Actuary	IAS
188.117	Administrative officer/government service	ESC
164.117	Advertising manager	AES
188.167	Appraiser	ESC
191.117	Artist's manager	ESC
186.117	Bank officer	ESC
191.117	Booking agent	ESC
160.207	Budget consultant	CES
186.117	Business manager/education	ESC
241.217	Claim adjustor	CSE
191.167	Claim agent	ESC
241.267	Claim examiner	CSE
213.132	Computer-operations supervisor	CIS
020.186	Computer programer	IAS
169.207	Conciliator	ESC
188.117	Consumer affairs/director	ESC
096.121	Consumer-service consultant	SRI
094.117	Coordinator of special services/education	SAI
191.267	Credit analyst	ESC
168.167	Credit-and-collection manager	SIE
166.117	Director/industrial relations	SEC
189.117	Director/research and development	ESC
166.267	Employment interviewer	SEC
132.037	Editor/trade journal	ASI
169.267	Financial-aid counselor	ESC
020.167	Financial analyst	IAS
166.267	Hospital-insurance representative	SEC
184.117	Import-export agent	ESC
187.117	Hotel/restaurant manager	SEC
012.167	Industrial engineer	ERI
109.067	Information scientist	IRC
250.257	Insurance agent/broker	ECS
168.267	Internal-revenue investigator	SIE
166.167	Labor-relations representative	SEC
110.107	Lawyer	ESA

DOT	JOB TITLE	HOC
191.117	Literary agent	ESC
189.167	Management trainee	ESC
187.117	Manager/chamber of commerce	SEC
186.117	Manager/financial institution	ESC
184.167	Manager/flight reservations	ESC
163.117	Manager/promotion	ESC
185.167	Manager/retail store	ESI
050.067	Market-research analyst	IAS
169.167	Office manager	ESC
184.117	Operations manager	ESC
166.117	Personnel manager	SEC
262.157	Pharmaceutical detailer	ESR
166.167	Placement director	SEC
189.117	Product manager	ESC
183.117	Production manager	ESC
163.167	Property-disposal officer	ESC
165.067	Public-relations representative	AES
162.157	Purchasing agent	ECS
197.167	Purser	REI
250.357	Real-estate agent/broker	ECS
161.267	Reports analyst	CES
160.167	Revenue agent	CES
251.257	Sales agent/financial services	ECS
251.257	Sales agent/psychological tests	ECS
163.167	Sales manager	ESC
275.257	Sales representative (computers and electronic data processing systems)	ESI
186.167	Securities trader	ESC
020.167	Statistician	IAS
251.157	Stock broker	ECS
012.167	Systems analyst	ERI
090.227	Teacher/college	SIA
184.167	Traffic manager	ESC
166.227	Training instructor	SEC
186.117	Trust officer/bank	ESC
199.167	Urban planner	ICR
131.267	Writer/technical publications	ASI

HIRING INSTITUTIONS

Accounting Firms
Advertising Departments and Agencies
Air, Bus, and Rail Lines
Banks, Savings/Commercial
Brokerage Houses
Business Corporations
Chambers of Commerce
Civic and Taxpayers' Associations
Colleges and Schools
Consumer Organizations
Department Stores
Educational Institutions
Employment Agencies
Film Companies
Foundations, Non-Profit
Fund-Raising Firms
Government Agencies
      Consumer Affairs Office
      International Trade Commission
      Securities and Exchange Commission
      Social Security Administration
Import/Export Companies
Industries, Manufacturing
Insurance Companies
Investment Firms
Labor Unions
Magazines, Newspapers
Manufacturing and Processing Firms
Market Research Departments and Firms
Personnel Departments
Pharmaceutical Companies
Professional Journals
Public-Relations Firms
Publishing Companies
Radio/Television Stations
Research-and-Development Firms
Trade Associations
Travel Agencies
Utility Companies

CURRENT OCCUPATIONS OF GRADUATES
WHO MAJORED IN MARKETING

DOT	JOB TITLE	HOC	1960-1974	1975-1980 M	F	T
160.167	Accountant	CES	11	3	2	5
160.167	Accounting manager	CES	2	1	1	2
150.047	Actor	ASE	1			
020.167	Actuary	IAS			1	1
188.117	Administrative officer/ government service	ESC	21	1	1	2
164.117	Advertising manager	AES	2	1		1
070.101	Anesthesiologist	ISA			1	1
— —	Armed services	—	18			
144.061	Artist	AIR		1		1
160.162	Auditor	CES	5	1		1
186.117	Bank officer	ESC	24	3	1	4
183.117	Branch manager	ESC	4			
161.117	Budget analyst	CES	6			
189.117	Business executive	ESC	45	7	2	9
162.157	Buyer	ECS	10	1	2	3
186.117	Cashier, bank	ESC	4	1		1
209.562	Clerk	CIE	6	11	3	14
090.117	College/university official	SIA	2			
213.363	Computer operator	CIS	4	5	1	6
213.132	Computer-operations supervisor	CIS	1			
020.187	Computer programer	IAS	7	10	1	11
869.664	Construction worker	REI	2			
094.117	Coordinator of special services/education	SAI	3			
160.167	Cost accountant	CES	2			
191.267	Credit analyst	ESC	2	1		1
168.167	Credit-and-collection manager	SIE	4	2		2
003.167	Development-and-planning engineer	IRE	3			
183.117	District manager	ESC	9	1		1
050.067	Economist	IAS	2		1	1
050.067	Economist/price	IAS	1			
132.067	Editor	ASI	1		1	1
166.267	Employment interviewer	SEC			1	1

DOT	JOB TITLE	HOC	1960-1974	1975-1980 M	F	T
020.167	Financial/investment analyst	IAS	8	1		1
050.067	Financial planner	IAS	1		1	1
373.364	Firefighter	RSE	1			
187.167	Funeral director	SEC	1			
189.117	General manager	ESC	24	2	2	4
— —	Graduate student	—	3	1		1
045.107	Guidance counselor	SIA	2			
091.107	High-school-department chairperson	SAE	1			
091.107	High school official	SAE	1			
187.117	Hotel/restaurant manager	SEC		1		1
012.167	Industrial engineer	ERI	2	2		2
250.257	Insurance agent/broker	ECS	8	1	2	3
241.217	Insurance-claim adjuster	CSE	1	2		2
168.267	Insurance-claim examiner	SIE	6			
241.217	Insurance-claim investigator	CSE	1			
169.167	Insurance underwriter	ESC	4	1		1
119.267	Law clerk	ESA		1		1
— —	Law student	—	2	1		1
110.107	Lawyer	ESA	15			
100.127	Librarian	SAI		2		2
230.367	Mail carrier	CSR	1	1		1
012.167	Management/methods engineer	ERI	2			
189.167	Management trainee	ESC	6	2		2
163.117	Marketing manager	ESC	7	3	1	4
050.067	Market-research analyst	IAS	9	4	2	6
169.167	Office manager	ESC	12	3	1	4
184.167	Operations manager	ESC	5	3		3
166.117	Personnel manager	SEC	11	2	2	4
070.101	Physician	ISA	1			
196.263	Pilot/airplane	IRC	1			
375.263	Police officer	SRE	2	1		1
189.117	Private-business owner	ESC	10	2		2
163.267	Product-distribution manager	ESC	4			

DOT	JOB TITLE	HOC	1960-1974	1975-1980 M	F	T
189.117	Product manager	ESC	9	1	3	4
183.117	Production manager	ESC	4	2		2
045.107	Psychologist	SIA		1		1
165.067	Public-relations practitioner	AES	4		1	1
162.157	Purchasing agent	ECS	3	3		3
012.167	Quality-control engineer	ERI		1		1
250.357	Real-estate agent/broker	ECS	2	1		1
189.117	Research-and-development director	ESC	5			
160.167	Revenue agent	CES	1			
290.477	Sales clerk	ESC	20	6		6
163.167	Sales manager	ESC	27	11	1	12
279.357	Sales/service representative	ESC	41	10	3	13
020.167	Securities analyst	IAS	2			
186.167	Securities trader	ESC	1			
— —	Seminarian	—	1			
600-800	Skilled trades	RIC	7	1		1
195.107	Social worker	SIC	3		1	1
020.167	Statistician	IAS		1		1
251.157	Stock broker	ECS	5			
185.167	Store manager	ESI	3	1	1	2
012.167	Systems analyst/electronic data processing	ERI	9	1		1
160.162	Tax accountant	CES	1			
090.227	Teacher/college	SIA	1			
092.227	Teacher/elementary school	SAI	2	1	1	2
091.227	Teacher/high school	SAE	17	1		1
099.227	Teacher/other	SIR	4		1	1
094.227	Teacher/special education	SAI		1		1
184.117	Traffic analyst/manager	ESC	1	2	1	3
166.227	Training specialist	SEC	1			
184.117	Transportation manager	ESC	1	1		1
186.117	Trust officer/bank	ESC	1		1	1
199.167	Urban planner	ICR	1			
131.267	Writer/technical	ASI	1			
			532	**132**	**44**	**176**

Difficulties strengthen the mind, as labor does the body.   *—Seneca*

MATHEMATICS AND COMPUTER SCIENCE
GENERAL DESCRIPTION

Mathematicians study concepts and theories to help them solve problems that involve quantitative relationships. Those who do research to discover new theories or to increase basic knowledge call themselves *theoretical* mathematicians. Those who develop techniques and approaches to solve problems in the physical and social sciences, or in business and industry, refer to themselves as *applied* mathematicians.

Computer scientists learn how to structure and operate computer systems and they study the principles that underlie their design and programing. Students work with circuitry, logic, programing languages, file structures, and systems architectures. As computer scientists, they also explore new areas of intellectual activity where computers can come creatively into play.

Although for a while opportunities in colleges and universities had dwindled for mathematicians as a result of shrinking enrollments, math graduates still found employment as statisticians, economists, systems analysts, and life scientists by taking a minor in one of these subjects while in college.

Computer-science graduates generally find jobs as programers and systems analysts, with many specialties in each area. A background in accounting, management, or economics may qualify you for work in the business sector; for jobs in scientifically-oriented establishments you can improve your prospects by getting some training in the physical sciences, mathematics, or engineering.

In many colleges, computer science has developed as part of the Mathematics Department, but there is a growing tendency for these two disciplines to become independent departments.

CAREER LEADS

DOT	JOB TITLE	HOC
160.167	Accountant (budget, cost, systems)	CES
020.167	Actuary	IAS
196.167	Airplane navigator	IRC
196.263	Airplane pilot	IRC
193.162	Air-traffic controller	RIE
001.061	Architect	AIR
161.117	Budget officer	CES
160.167	Bursar/education	CES
018.261	Cartographer	RCI
020.062	Computer-applications engineer	IAS
020.187	Computer programer	IAS
003.167	Computer-systems engineer	IRE
020.067	Computing analyst	IAS
199.267	Cryptanalyst	ICR
102.017	Curator (art galleries, museums)	AEI
169.167	Data-processing manager	ESC
020.162	Data-reduction analyst	IAS
020.167	Demographer	IAS
090.167	Department head/college	SIA
090.167	Director of institutional research	SIA
188.167	Director of vital statistics	ESC
017.261	Draftsman	RIA
012.167	Efficiency expert	ERI
020.067	Engineering analyst	IAS
001.061	Environmental planner	AIR
186.167	Estate planner	ESC
020.167	Financial analyst	IAS
293.157	Fund raiser	ESC
018.167	Geodetic computer	RCI
109.067	Information scientist	IRC
250.257	Insurance agent/broker	ECS
168.267	Internal-revenue investigator	SIE
110.107	Lawyer	ESA
189.167	Management trainee	ESC
050.067	Market-research analyst	IAS
020.162	Mathematical technician	IAS
020.067	Mathematician (applied, research)	IAS

DOT	JOB TITLE	HOC
025.062	Meteorologist	IRA
020.067	Operations-research analyst	IAS
099.117	Principal/education	SIE
162.157	Purchasing agent	ECS
012.167	Quality-control supervisor	ERI
275.257	Sales representative (computer and electronic data processing systems)	ESI
186.167	Securities trader/banking	ESC
020.167	Statistician/applied	IAS
020.067	Statistician/mathematical	IAS
251.157	Stockbroker	ECS
002.061	Stress analyst	IRE
012.167	Systems analyst	ERI
020.067	Systems analyst/engineering-scientific	IAS
090.227	Teacher/college	SIA
017.281	Technical illustrator	RIA

HIRING INSTITUTIONS

Banks, Savings/Commercial
Business Corporations
Colleges and Schools
Educational Institutions
Engineering Firms
Government Agencies
       Agriculture Department
       Airports
       Civil Service Commission
       Consumer Affairs Commission
       Defense Department
       Energy Department
       Federal Communications Commission
       General Accounting Office
       Internal Revenue Service
       Management and Budget Office
       National Science Foundation
       Nuclear Regulation Commission

Securities and Exchange Commission
Social Security Administration
Treasury Department
Industries, Manufacturing
Insurance Companies
Investment Firms
Market-Research Departments and Firms
Professional/Technical Journals
Publishing Companies
Research-and-Development Firms
Test-Development Corporations
Utility Companies
Weather Bureaus and Companies

CURRENT OCCUPATIONS OF GRADUATES WHO MAJORED IN MATHEMATICS/COMPUTER SCIENCE

DOT	JOB TITLE	HOC	1960-1974	1975-1980 M	F	T
160.167	Accountant	CES	2			
160.167	Accounting manager	CES	3			
020.167	Actuary	IAS	8	1	1	2
188.117	Administrative officer/ government service	ESC	3			
— —	Armed services	—	12			
160.162	Auditor	CES	1	1		1
186.117	Bank officer	ESC	8			
183.117	Branch manager	ESC	1			
161.117	Budget analyst	CES	1	1		1
189.117	Business executive	ESC	15	1	1	2
022.161	Chemist	IAR		1		1
022.061	Chemist research	IAR	1			
120.007	Clergy member	SAI	1			
209.562	Clerk	CIE	2	2	1	3
090.117	College/university official	SIA	1		1	1
213.362	Computer operator	CIS	1	3		3
213.132	Computer-operations supervisor	CIS	10	1	3	4
020.187	Computer programer	IAS	45	17	9	26
119.267	Contract consultant	ESA	1			

DOT	JOB TITLE	HOC	1960-1974	1975-1980		
				M	F	T
160.167	Cost accountant	CES	1			
160.267	Cost estimator	CES			1	1
168.167	Credit-and-collection manager	SIE	3			
188.167	Customs officer	ESC	1			
003.167	Data-processing engineer	IRE	1	1		1
003.167	Development-and-planning engineer	IRE	6	1	1	2
183.117	District manager	ESC	3			
050.067	Economist	IAS	1			
003.061	Electrical engineer	IRE	2		1	1
092.137	Elementary-school official	SAI	1			
020.167	Financial/investment analyst	IAS	3			
050.067	Financial planner	IAS			1	1
189.117	General manager	ESC	13	1		1
— —	Graduate student	—	11	1	2	3
045.107	Guidance counselor	SIA	2			
091.107	High-school-department chairperson	SAE	2			
091.107	High-school official	SAE	3			
250.257	Insurance agent/broker	ECS	5			
168.267	Insurance-claim examiner	SIE	1			
186.117	Insurance-and-risk manager	ESC	1	1		1
169.167	Insurance underwriter	ESC	3			
029.261	Laboratory technician	IRA		1		1
— —	Law student	—	1		2	2
110.107	Lawyer	ESA	5			
100.127	Librarian	SAI	1			
012.167	Management/methods engineer	ERI	2	1		1
189.167	Management trainee	ESC	2			
163.117	Marketing manager	ESC	3			
050.067	Market-research analyst	IAS	5			
020.067	Mathematician	IAS	3	1	1	2
— —	Medical student	—	1			
169.167	Office manager	ESC	8	1		1

DOT	JOB TITLE	HOC	1960-1974	1975-1980		
				M	F	T
184.167	Operations manager	ESC	4	1		1
166.117	Personnel manager	SEC	5			
196.263	Pilot/airplane	IRC		1		1
375.263	Police officer	SRE	1			
189.117	Private-business owner	ESC	3			
189.117	Product manager	ESC	2			
165.067	Public-relations practitioner	AES	1			
189.117	Research-and-development director	ESC	2			
290.477	Sales clerk	ESC	2			
163.167	Sales manager	ESC	1			
279.357	Sales/service representative	ESC	4			
600-800	Skilled trades	RIC	8			
195.107	Social worker	SIC	4			
020.067	Statistician	IAS	1			
251.157	Stockbroker	ECS	1			
185.167	Store manager	ESI	2	1		1
012.167	Systems analyst/ electronic data processing	ERI	32	1		1
003.167	Systems engineer	IRE	1			
090.227	Teacher/college	SIA	20			
092.227	Teacher/elementary school	SAI	5	1		1
091.227	Teacher/high school	SAE	61	4	6	10
099.227	Teacher/other	SIR	13		2	2
094.227	Teacher/special education	SAI	1			
166.227	Training specialist	SEC	1			
186.117	Trust officer/bank	ESC	1			
			386	46	33	79

*When you travel, remember that a foreign country is
not designed to make you comfortable. It is
designed to make its own people comfortable.*
— *Clifton Fadiman*

MODERN LANGUAGES
GENERAL DESCRIPTION

L anguage is the system people use to express the ideas
and feelings they share as human beings. Through that
process, studying a language gives us a way to
understand the range of experience a particular culture has
enjoyed.

Jobs that require a foreign language as a primary skill
can be somewhat limited in number. Such jobs include teaching in schools and colleges, interpreting at the United Nations
or in foreign service, or broadcasting for radio and cable TV stations that transmit programs in Spanish, Italian, Japanese, and
other languages.

Language-study helps you to think quickly and logically,
to use words effectively, and to sharpen your memory. You can
apply this kind of training to electives in business, finance, or
other subjects you like, to round out further your preparation
for a career. You can improve your job prospects by finding
firms that will consider your language training an asset: multi-
national corporations with offices all over the world that deal in
oil, electronics, automobiles, and heavy machinery, and companies that export such products as tires, food, tools, hardware,
and other basic commodities.

Fields where you can apply your language training
include also travel and tourism, hotel service (there are 150
multilingual hotels in the United States), English newspapers
and magazines with foreign departments or editions
(*Reader's Digest* has 26 foreign-language editions), motion pictures, libraries, museums, and publishing companies.

Those who wish to become college instructors or professional linguists will need advanced training beyond the bachelor's degree.

CAREER LEADS

DOT	JOB TITLE	HOC
159.147	Announcer (radio and TV)	AES
055.067	Anthropological linguist	IAR
191.287	Appraiser/art	ESC
188.117	Arts-and-Humanities-Council director	ESC
099.167	Audiovisual specialist	SIE
052.067	Biographer	SEI
131.067	Book critic	ASI
100.387	Cataloger	SAI
090.117	College/university official	SIA
195.167	Community-organization worker	SIC
020.187	Computer programer	IAS
131.067	Copy writer/advertising	ASI
139.087	Crossword-puzzle maker	ASI
168.267	Customs inspector	SIE
090.167	Department head/college	SIA
132.067	Editor/greeting cards	ASI
166.267	Employment interviewer	SEC
059.067	Etymologist	SIA
352.367	Flight attendant	ESA
184.167	Flight-reservations manager	ESC
188.117	Foreign-service officer	ESC
090.107	Foreign-student advisor	SIA
165.117	Fund-raising director	AES
168.167	Immigration inspector	SIE
184.117	Import-export agent	ESC
059.267	Intelligence specialist	SIA
051.067	International-relations specialist	SIA
137.267	Interpreter	ASI
110.107	Lawyer	ESA
100.127	Librarian	SAI
189.167	Management trainee	ESC
132.267	Manuscript reader (print and publications)	ASI
102.381	Museum technician	AEI
131.267	Newswriter/foreign languages	ASI
059.067	Philologist	SIA
070.101	Physician	ISA

DOT	JOB TITLE	HOC
165.067	Public-relations representative	AES
109.267	Research assistant	IRC
059.067	Scientific linguist	SIA
195.107	Social worker	SIC
375.167	Special agent/FBI	SRE
090.227	Teacher/college	SIA
091.227	Teacher/high school	SAE
353.167	Tour guide	SRE
166.227	Training instructor	SEC
137.267	Translator	ASI
252.157	Travel agent	ECS
131.067	Writer (prose, fiction and nonfiction)	ASI
131.267	Writer/technical publications	ASI

HIRING INSTITUTIONS

Advertising Departments and Agencies
Air, Bus, and Rail Lines
Banks, Savings/Commercial
Bookstores
Business Corporations
Colleges and Schools
Department Stores
Film Companies
Fund-Raising Firms
Government Agencies
      Agency for International Development
      Airports
      Civil Rights Commission
      Civil Service Commission
      Commerce Department
      Consumer Affairs Office
      Educational Department
      Federal Communications Commission
      Federal Trade Commission
      Foreign Service Department
      Government Printing Office

Immigration and Naturalization Service
International Trade Commission
Library of Congress
National Archives
National Foundation on the Arts and
the Humanities
Peace Corps
Vista
Hotel Chains
Import/Export Companies
Industries, Manufacturing
Investment Firms
Labor Unions
Libraries
Literary Periodicals
Magazines, Newspapers
Museums
Professional Periodicals
Public-Relations Firms
Publishing Companies
Radio/Television Stations
Social-Service Agencies
Technical-Writing Services
Travel Agencies
United Nations

CURRENT OCCUPATIONS OF GRADUATES WHO MAJORED IN MODERN LANGUAGES

DOT	JOB TITLE	HOC	1960-1974	1975-1980 M	F	T
160.167	Accounting manager	CES	1			
150.047	Actor	ASE	1			
188.117	Administrative officer/ government service	ESC	3			
— —	Armed services	—	5	1		1
186.117	Bank officer	ESC	4	1	1	2
161.117	Budget analyst	CES	1			
189.117	Business executive	ESC	4		1	1
162.157	Buyer	ECS	1			
079.101	Chiropractor	SIR	1			
120.007	Clergy member	SAI	2	1		1
209.562	Clerk	CIE			5	5
090.167	College-department head	SIA	1	1		1
090.117	College/university official	SIA	3			
119.267	Contract consultant	ESA			1	1
131.067	Copy writer	ASI	1			
188.167	Customs officer	ESC	1			
132.067	Editor	ASI	2			
189.117	General manager	ESC	1		1	1
— —	Graduate student	—	4		1	1
045.107	Guidance counselor	SIA			1	1
091.107	High-school official	SAE	1			
187.117	Hospital administrator	SEC	1			
250.257	Insurance agent/broker	ECS	2			
119.267	Law clerk	ESA	1			
110.107	Lawyer	ESA	5	1		1
230.367	Mail carrier	CSR	1			
189.167	Management trainee	ESC			1	1
050.067	Market-research analyst	IAS	1			
— —	Medical student	—	1		1	1
152.041	Musician	ASI	1			
169.167	Office manager	ESC	2			
166.117	Personnel manager	SEC	2	1	1	2
045.107	Psychologist	SIA	1			
165.067	Public-relations practitioner	AES			1	1

DOT	JOB TITLE	HOC	1960-1974	1975-1980 M	F	T
290.477	Sales clerk	ESC	1			
163.167	Sales manager	ESC	1			
279.357	Sales/service representative	ESC	5		3	3
— —	Seminarian	—	1			
188.117	Social-welfare director	ESC	3		1	1
195.107	Social worker	SIC	2		2	2
375.167	Special agent/FBI	SRE	1			
185.167	Store manager	ESI	1			
012.167	Systems analyst/electronic data processing	ERI	1			
090.227	Teacher/college	SIA	14	1		1
092.227	Teacher/elementary	SAI	5	1		1
091.227	Teacher/high school	SAE	34		1	1
099.227	Teacher/other	SIR	10	1	1	2
094.227	Teacher/special education	SAI	1			
159.147	Television/radio personnel	AES	1			
137.267	Translator	ASI	1		1	1
			137	9	24	33

Through space the universe grasps me and swallows me up like a speck; through thought I grasp it.
— *Pascal*

NATURAL SCIENCE
GENERAL DESCRIPTION

This is a composite major which includes courses in biology, chemistry, mathematics, and physics. Students who want a broad background in several sciences usually choose this major. That way, they can keep their options open before making a commitment to professional studies or to a single science upon entering graduate school. This program also prepares students for certification to teach in elementary or secondary schools, to attend medical school, or to become involved with other health-oriented programs such as physical therapy.

A bachelor's degree equips students to enter a variety of graduate programs which include the natural sciences, medicine, law, business and finance. With appropriate electives in business, accounting, or computer science, they can also qualify for a large range of positions in business and industry as trainees, managers, or technical sales and service representatives.

Natural science majors can also find entry jobs as assistants to life scientists, medical researchers, and environmentalists. By developing effective writing skills, they can become science reporters, editors, and technical-report writers.

With advanced degrees, graduates can get into independent research, administrative positions, or teaching posts in colleges and universities.

CAREER LEADS

DOT	JOB TITLE	HOC
029.081	Air-pollution analyst	IRA
041.061	Anatomist	IRS
041.061	Animal ecologist	IRS
040.061	Animal scientist	RIS
021.067	Astronomer	IAR
041.061	Biochemist	RIS
041.061	Biophysicist	IRS
041.061	Botanist	IRS
262.357	Chemical-sales representative	ESR
079.101	Chiropractor	SIR
020.187	Computer programer	IAS
131.067	Copy writer	ASI
029.281	Crime-laboratory analyst	IRA
029.281	Criminalist	IRA
102.017	Curator/medical museum	AEI
102.017	Curator/natural history museum	AEI
041.061	Cytologist	IRS
072.101	Dentist	ISR
077.117	Dietitian	SIE
132.017	Editor/scientific publications	ASI
041.061	Entomologist	IRS
029.081	Environmental analyst	IRA
168.267	Food-and-drugs inspector	SIE
022.061	Food chemist	IAR
070.061	Forensic pathologist	ISA
040.061	Forester	RIS
045.107	Guidance counselor	SIA
187.117	Hospital administrator	SEC
024.061	Hydrologist	IRA
079.161	Industrial hygienist	SIR
045.107	Industrial psychologist	SIA
109.067	Information scientist	IRC
199.364	Laboratory assistant	ICR
029.261	Laboratory technician	IRA
110.107	Lawyer	ESA
189.167	Management trainee	ESC
141.061	Medical illustrator	ASI

DOT	JOB TITLE	HOC
100.167	Medical librarian	SAI
078.361	Medical technologist	ISR
102.381	Museum technician	AEI
078.361	Nuclear medical technologist	ISR
168.167	Occupational-safety-and-health inspector	SIE
024.061	Oceanographer	IRA
119.167	Patent examiner	ESA
022.161	Perfumer	IAR
074.161	Pharmacist	IES
076.121	Physical therapist	SIR
041.061	Plant pathologist	IRS
029.281	Police chemist	IRA
022.061	Pollution-control chemist	IAR
163.267	Product-distribution manager	ESC
189.117	Product manager	ESC
183.117	Production manager	ESC
012.167	Quality-control engineer	ERI
045.107	Rehabilitation counselor	SIA
168.264	Safety inspector	SIE
079.117	Sanitarian	SIR
040.061	Soil scientist	RIS
199.261	Taxidermist	ICR
090.227	Teacher/college	SIA
091.227	Teacher/high school	SAE
131.267	Technical writer	ASI
029.081	Water-quality analyst	IRA
025.267	Weather observer	IRA

HIRING INSTITUTIONS

Arboretums
Botanical Gardens
Business Corporations
Educational Institutions
Engineering Firms
Government Agencies
      Agriculture Department
      Airports
      Civil Service Commission
      Consumer Affairs Office
      Education Department
      Energy Department
      Environmental Protection Agency
      Federal Communications Commission
      Fish and Wildlife Services
      Government Printing Office
      Health and Human Services Department
      Library of Congress
      National Park Service
      National Science Foundation
      Nuclear Regulation Commission
      Peace Corps
      Vista
Hospitals
Libraries, Medical/Technical
Magazines, Newspapers
Manufacturing/Processing Firms
Medical Laboratories
Mining Companies
Petroleum Companies
Pharmaceutical Companies
Professional/Technical Journals
Publishing Companies
Radio/Television Stations
Research-and-Development Firms
Utility Companies

CURRENT OCCUPATIONS OF GRADUATES
WHO MAJORED IN NATURAL SCIENCE

DOT	JOB TITLE	HOC	1960-1974	1975-1980 M	F	T
160.167	Accountant	CES			1	1
188.117	Administrative officer/ government service	ESC	1			
— —	Armed services	—	5	1	1	2
041.061	Biologist	IRS	1			
189.117	Business executive	ESC	2			
186.117	Cashier/bank	ESC			1	1
022.061	Chemist	IAR	3	1		1
022.061	Chemist/research	IAR	2	2		2
079.101	Chiropractor	SIR		2		2
120.007	Clergy member	SAI	1			
209.562	Clerk	CIE	1		1	1
213.132	Computer-operations supervisor	CIS	1			
020.187	Computer programer	IAS	1	1		1
131.067	Copy writer	ASI	1			
091.267	Credit analyst	ESC		1		1
— —	Dental student	—	1	2		2
072.101	Dentist	ISR	8	1		1
189.117	General Manager	ESC	2	2	1	3
— —	Graduate student	—	8	10	6	16
045.107	Guidance counselor	SIA	2			
091.107	High-school department chairperson	SAE	1			
012.167	Industrial engineer	ERI	1	1		1
250.257	Insurance agent/broker	ECS		1		1
029.261	Laboratory technician	IRA	6	3		3
— —	Law student	—	1	1	1	2
110.107	Lawyer	ESA	3	1	1	2
230.367	Mail carrier	CSR		1		1
163.117	Marketing manager	ESC	1			
— —	Medical student	—	5	13	5	18
078.261	Medical technologist	ISR	3	1	1	2
169.167	Office manager	ESC	3			
184.167	Operations manager	ESC	1			
074.161	Pharmacist	IES	1	1		1

DOT	JOB TITLE	HOC	1960-1974	1975-1980		
				M	F	T
070.101	Physician	ISA	7	2		2
023.061	Physicist	IAR		1		1
079.101	Podiatrist	SIR	1			
163.267	Product-distribution manager	ESC	1			
189.117	Product manager	ESC	2			
045.107	Psychologist	SIA	1		1	1
012.167	Quality-control engineer	ERI	1	1		1
045.107	Rehabilitation counselor	SIA			1	1
290.447	Sales clerk	ESC		1		1
279.357	Sales/service representative	ESC	3	2		2
186.167	Security officer	ESC		1	1	2
600-800	Skilled trades	RIC	2			
070.101	Surgeon	ISA	1			
012.167	Systems analyst/electronic data processing	ERI	1			
092.227	Teacher/elementary school	SAI	2		1	1
091.227	Teacher/high school	SAE	10	3	2	5
099.227	Teacher/other	SIR	2		1	1
184.117	Transportation manager	ESC		1		1
199.167	Urban planner	ICR			1	1
073.101	Veterinarian	IRS	1			
			101	58	27	85

The natural flights of the human mind are not from pleasure to pleasure but from hope to hope.
— *Dr. Johnson*

PHILOSOPHY
GENERAL DESCRIPTION

As a branch of learning, philosophy probes the nature of the human species and the ways people seek to understand their world. Topics that philosophers investigate include reality, perception, morality, ethics, knowledge, aesthetics, and existence.

Students of philosophy learn to analyze and evaluate, by logical processes, the premises on which we base our ideas about life.

This helps students develop flexibility in their thinking, along with the ability to apply their training to a variety of other subjects. Such reasoning skills are essential in almost every area of human endeavor: business, industry, the arts, publishing, social services, politics, or diplomacy.

Business leaders most frequently cite the ability to learn in new situations and the capacity to analyze, evaluate, and interpret data as two of the most important qualities that successful executives must possess. Still another necessary skill for success in any field is the ability to communicate clearly and effectively in speech and writing. As our technology continues its rapid expansion, these communications skills take on added importance not only to exploit our technology, but to use it judiciously.

A bachelor's degree can qualify you for trainee jobs that lead to managerial or personnel positions in business, jobs with non-profit organizations such as the Red Cross or Catholic Relief Services, and entry-level administrative posts with most government agencies.

Graduates who have refined their communications skills can become editors, reporters, or technical writers. Or they can find their way into writing and announcing jobs with radio, network, and cable TV stations.

Students frequently go on for graduate studies in law, the ministry, finance, psychological counseling, and diplomacy. Those who wish to teach in colleges will need a doctorate.

CAREER LEADS

DOT	JOB TITLE	HOC
188.117	Administrative officer/government service	ESC
055.067	Anthropological linguist	IAR
055.067	Anthropologist	IAR
101.167	Archivist	SAI
052.067	Biographer	SEI
131.067	Book critic	ASI
100.387	Cataloger	SAI
120.007	Clergy member	SAI
090.117	College/university official	SIA
131.067	Columnist/commentator	ASI
131.067	Critic (book, drama, film)	ASI
188.117	Cultural-affairs officer	ESC
102.017	Curator (art galleries, museums)	AEI
090.167	Department head/college	SIA
090.167	Director of institutional research	SIA
132.067	Editor/dictionary	ASI
132.067	Editor/publications	ASI
132.267	Editorial assistant	ASI
131.067	Editorial writer	ASI
059.067	Etymologist	SIA
131.267	Foreign correspondent	ASI
188.117	Foreign-service officer	ESC
052.067	Genealogist	SEI
168.167	Immigration inspector	SIE
250.257	Insurance agent/broker	ECS
059.267	Intelligence specialist	SIA
051.067	International-relations specialist	SIA
110.107	Lawyer	ESA
100.127	Librarian	SAI
189.167	Management trainee	ESC
132.167	Manuscript reader	ASI
102.381	Museum technician	AEI
132.067	News editor (radio, TV)	ASI
119.267	Paralegal assistant	ESA
166.117	Personnel manager	SEC
059.067	Philologist	SIA
070.101	Physician	ISA

DOT	JOB TITLE	HOC
209.387	Proofreader	CIE
070.107	Psychiatrist	ISA
045.107	Psychologist	SIA
165.067	Public-relations representative	AES
131.267	Reporter (print and publications)	ASI
109.267	Research assistant	IRC
277.357	Salesperson/books	ESC
195.107	Social worker	SIC
375.167	Special agent/FBI	SRE
090.227	Teacher/college	SIA
119.287	Title examiner	ESA
353.167	Tour guide	SRE
166.227	Training instructor	SEC
252.157	Travel agent	ECS
131.067	Writer (prose, fiction, nonfiction)	ASI

HIRING INSTITUTIONS

Archives, Federal/Municipal
Bookstores
Business Corporations
Churches and Religious Organizations
Colleges and Schools
Educational Institutions
Foundations, Non-Profit
Government Agencies
    Civil Rights Commission
    Civil Service Commission
    Consumer Affairs Office
    Education Department
    Energy Department
    Environmental Protection Agency
    Federal Communications Commission
    Foreign Service
    Government Printing Office
    Health and Human Services Department
    Labor Department
    Library of Congress
    National Archives
    National Foundations on the Arts
      and the Humanities
    Peace Corps
    Vista
Industries/Manufacturing
Insurance Companies
Learned Periodicals
Libraries
Magazines and Newspapers
Museums
Professional Periodicals
Public-Relations Firms
Publishing Companies
Radio/Television Stations
Research Institutes
Social-Service Agencies
Travel Agencies

CURRENT OCCUPATIONS OF GRADUATES WHO MAJORED IN PHILOSOPHY

DOT	JOB TITLE	HOC	1960-1974	1975-1980 M	F	T
— —	Armed services	—	1			
189.117	Business executive	ESC	2			
209.562	Clerk	CIE			1	1
020.187	Computer programer	IAS	1			
110.117	District attorney	ESA	1			
189.117	General manager	ESC	1	1		1
— —	Graduate student	—	4	1		1
186.117	Insurance-and-risk manager	ESC	1			
— —	Law student	—		1	1	2
110.107	Lawyer	ESA	5	1		1
100.117	Librarian	SAI	1			
230.367	Mail carrier	CSR	1			
189.167	Management trainee	ESC			1	1
169.167	Office manager	ESC	1			
163.167	Sales manager	ESC	1			
— —	Seminarian	—	1			
600-800	Skilled trades	RIC	1			
195.107	Social worker	SIC	4			
185.167	Store manager	ESI		1		1
003.167	Systems engineer	IRE	1			
091.227	Teacher/high school	SAE	3			
			30	5	3	8

Nature, to be commanded, must be obeyed.
                                    — *Sir Francis Bacon*

PHYSICS
GENERAL DESCRIPTION

Physicists analyze the structure of matter and the way it interacts with various forms of energy such as heat, light, sound, electricity, and magnetism. From their research, physicists construct theories and formulate laws to explain how the universe works.

Most physicists engage in research and development, and specialize in one or more branches of the science — such as optics, acoustics, electronics, and nuclear or plasma physics. And others combine physics with a related science such as geophysics, astrophysics, or biophysics. The basic research that physicists do often finds applications in areas they could not have foreseen: solid-state physics led to the development of transistors, and the laser beam became an instrument for surgery.

With a bachelor's degree, you can carry on applied research or develop new products for companies that manufacture defense matériel, or electrical or scientific equipment. In hospitals and other health facilities, you can also get jobs that involve working with radiation and advanced types of life-support equipment, and with firms that develop and operate computers and electronic data-processing equipment. Or you can locate with government agencies such as the Air Force, Defense, and Energy Departments, the Nuclear Regulatory Commission, the Environmental Protection Agency, the National Science Foundation, or the Goddard Space Flight Center.

Physicists who wish to conduct research projects or teach in colleges must plan to earn advanced degrees.

CAREER LEADS

DOT	JOB TITLE	HOC
002.061	Aerodynamist	IRE
196.167	Airplane navigator	IRC
196.263	Airplane pilot	IRC
001.061	Architect	AIR
021.067	Astronomer	IAR
199.267	Ballistics expert	ICR
041.061	Biophysicist	IRS
020.187	Computer programer	IAS
003.167	Computer-systems engineer	IRE
029.281	Crime laboratory analyst	IRA
029.281	Criminalist	IRA
102.017	Curator/natural history	AEI
132.067	Editor/science	ASI
132.017	Editor (technical and scientific publications)	ASI
131.067	Editorial writer	ASI
029.081	Environmental analyst	IRA
029.081	Environmental scientist	IRA
018.167	Geodetic computer	RCI
024.061	Geologist	IRA
079.021	Health physicist	SIR
024.061	Hydrologist	IRA
012.167	Industrial-health engineer	ERI
079.161	Industrial hygienist	SIR
109.067	Information scientist	IRC
022.281	Laboratory tester	IAR
110.107	Lawyer	ESA
100.127	Librarian	SAI
189.167	Management trainee	ESC
078.361	Medical technologist	ISR
011.061	Metallurgist	IRE
025.062	Meteorologist	IRA
024.061	Oceanographer	IRA
079.101	Optometrist	SIR
110.117	Patent attorney	ESA
018.261	Photogrammetrist	RCI
029.280	Photo-optics technician	IRA

DOT	JOB TITLE	HOC
029.067	Physical geographer	IRA
070.101	Physician	ISA
023.061	Physicist (acoustic, atomic, electronic heat, light, mechanic, nuclear, solid state)	IAR
023.061	Physicist/cryogenics	IAR
023.061	Physicist/plasma	IAR
023.067	Physicist/theoretical	IAR
029.281	Police chemist	IRA
078.362	Radiologic (X-ray) technologist	ISR
012.167	Safety manager	ERI
024.061	Seismologist	IRA
002.061	Stress analyst	IRE
090.227	Teacher/college	SIA
017.281	Technical illustrator	RIA
025.267	Weather observer	IRA
131.267	Writer/technical publications	ASI

HIRING INSTITUTIONS

Air, Bus, and Rail Lines
Airports
Atomic and Nuclear Laboratories
Colleges and Schools
Educational Institutions
Engineering Firms
Government Agencies
    Agriculture Department
    Commerce Department
    Consumer Affairs Office
    Energy Department
    Federal Communications Commission
    Health and Human Services Department
    National Science Foundation
    Nuclear Regulation Commission
    Peace Corps
    Vista

Hospitals
Magazines, Newspapers
Manufacturing and Processing Firms
Mining Companies
Nuclear Plants
Petroleum Companies
Professional/Technical Journals
Publishing Companies
Radio/Television Stations
Research-and-Development Firms
Utility Companies
Weather Bureaus and Companies

CURRENT OCCUPATIONS OF GRADUATES WHO MAJORED IN PHYSICS

DOT	JOB TITLE	HOC	1960-1974	1975-1980 M	F	T
160.167	Accounting manager	CES	1			
188.117	Administrative officer/ government service	ESC	1			
002.061	Aeronautical engineer	IRE	2			
— —	Armed services	—	3			
186.117	Bank officer	ESC	1			
189.117	Business executive	ESC	4	1		1
022.061	Chemist	IAR	2			
209.562	Clerk	CIE	1			
213.132	Computer-operations supervisor	CIS	3			
020.187	Computer programer	IAS	2			
003.167	Data-processing engineer	IRE	1			
— —	Dental student	—	1			
183.117	District manager	ESC	1			
003.061	Electrical engineer	IRE	7			
020.167	Financial/investment analyst	IAS	1			
189.117	General manager	ESC	1			
— —	Graduate student	—	3			
091.107	High-school department chairperson	SAE	2			

DOT	JOB TITLE	HOC	1960-1974	1975-1980		
				M	F	T
012.167	Industrial engineer	ERI	1			
376.367	Investigator	SRE	1			
110.107	Lawyer	ESA	1			
012.167	Management/methods engineer	ERI	1			
163.117	Marketing manager	ESC	2			
— —	Medical student	—	2			
169.167	Office manager	ESC	3			
184.167	Operations manager	ESC	1			
023.061	Physicist	IAR	12	1		1
189.117	Private-business owner	ESC	2			
183.117	Production manager	ESC	1			
189.117	Research-and-development director	ESC	2			
160.167	Revenue agent	CES	1			
290.477	Sales clerk	ESC	1			
012.167	Systems analyst/electronic data processing	ERI	2			
003.167	Systems engineer	IRE	3			
090.227	Teacher/college	SIA	3			
091.227	Teacher/high school	SAE	7	1		1
099.227	Teacher/other	SIR	1			
			84	3		3

*The times are not so bad as they seem; they couldn't
be.*   *— Jay Franklin*

POLITICAL SCIENCE
GENERAL DESCRIPTION

Political scientists explore the way people organize,
administer, and operate the institutions that govern
their society. Such specialists investigate phenomena in
the areas of public opinion, political parties, elections, the uses
of power, and international relations, as well as of the
presidency, Congress, and the judicial system. They also trace
how ideas about the rights and privileges of citizens evolved,
and they develop theories about political processes.

Graduate specialties include comparative politics,
international relations, political theory and behavior, public
policy, and foreign-area studies.

With a bachelor's degree, you can get jobs in Federal
agencies that deal with civil rights, consumer affairs, labor, and
foreign relations, or you can serve as legislative assistant to
Senators and Representatives. Corporations can use your skills
to analyze political conditions abroad, evaluate tax proposals,
and lobby for their interests in Congress. You can conduct
public opinion surveys, and analyze election results for political
parties, labor unions, and public interest groups.

For jobs in public relations, finance, and advertising
that require oral and written presentations, you will gain a
distinct advantage by developing your communications skills.
Such skills will also put jobs in journalism, radio/TV reporting,
and foreign correspondence within your reach.

Graduate studies can prepare you for positions in
research, foreign service, college teaching, or high-level
administrative posts.

CAREER LEADS

DOT	JOB TITLE	HOC
188.117	Administrative officer/government service	ESC
055.067	Anthropologist	IAR
101.167	Archivist	SAI
052.067	Biographer	SEI
131.067	Book critic	ASI
090.117	College/university official	SIA
131.067	Columnist/commentator	ASI
209.362	Congressional-district aide	CIE
188.117	Consular officer	ESC
131.267	Correspondent	ASI
131.067	Critic (book, drama, film)	ASI
188.117	Cultural-affairs officer	ESC
168.267	Customs inspector	SIE
054.067	Demographer	SIA
090.167	Department head/college	SIA
188.117	Diplomatic officer	ESC
090.167	Director of institutional research	SIA
132.067	Editor/publications	ASI
188.167	Election supervisor	ESC
131.267	Foreign correspondent	ASI
188.117	Foreign-service officer	ESC
184.117	Import-export agent	ESC
059.267	Intelligence specialist	SIA
051.067	International-relations specialist	SIA
166.167	Labor-relations representative	SEC
110.107	Lawyer	ESA
165.017	Legislative advocate	AES
165.017	Lobbyist	AES
187.117	Manager/chamber of commerce	SEC
050.067	Market-research analyst	IAS
131.267	Newscaster	ASI
119.267	Paralegal assistant	ESA
195.167	Parole officer	SIC
051.067	Political scientist	SIA
195.167	Probation/parole officer	SIC
165.067	Public-relations representative	AES
250.357	Real-estate agent/broker	ECS

DOT	JOB TITLE	HOC
131.267	Reporter (print and publications)	ASI
109.267	Research assistant	IRC
195.107	Social worker	SIC
375.167	Special agent/FBI	SRE
090.227	Teacher/college	SIA
119.287	Title examiner	ESA
353.167	Tour guide	SRE
199.167	Urban planner	ICR
131.067	Writer (prose, fiction, nonfiction)	ASI

HIRING INSTITUTIONS

Archives, Federal/Municipal
Business Corporations
Chambers of Commerce
Civic and Taxpayers' Associations
Colleges and Schools
Correctional Institutions
Court System
Educational Institutions
Government Agencies
    Civil Rights Commission
    Civil Service Commission
    Commerce Department
    Consumers Affairs Office
    Defense Department
    Education Department
    Energy Department
    Environmental Protection Agency
    Federal Bureau of Investigation
    Federal Trade Commission
    Foreign Service
    Government Printing Office
    Housing and Urban Development
    Labor Department
    Treasury Department
    Veteran's Administration
Historical Societies

Import/Export Companies
Labor Unions
Libraries
Magazines, Newspapers
Market-Research-Departments and Firms
Political-Action Committees
Political-Party Headquarters
Professional Periodicals
Public-Opinion-Research Companies
Public-Relations Firms
Radio/Television Stations
Regional-Planning Councils and Associations
Senators/Representatives/Local Officials
Social-Service Agencies

CURRENT OCCUPATIONS OF GRADUATES WHO MAJORED IN POLITICAL SCIENCE

DOT	JOB TITLE	HOC	1960-1974	1975-1980 M	F	T
160.167	Accountant	CES	1	1		1
160.167	Accounting manager	CES		1		1
188.117	Administrative officer/ government service	ESC	2			
164.117	Advertising manager	AES	1			
— —	Armed services	—	5	3		3
186.117	Bank officer	ESC	4		1	1
183.117	Branch manager	ESC	1			
189.117	Business executive	ESC	7		3	3
162.157	Buyer	ECS	2			
209.562	Clerk	CIE	1	2		2
090.167	College-department head	SIA			1	1
090.117	College/university official	SIA	1		1	1
119.267	Contract consultant	ESA	1			
094.117	Coordinator of special services/education	SAI		1		1
003.167	Development-and-planning engineer	IRE	2			
373.364	Firefighter	RSE	1			
189.117	General manager	ESC	4			

DOT	JOB TITLE	HOC	1960-1974	1975-1980 M	F	T
— —	Graduate student	—	2	4	1	5
045.107	Guidance counselor	SIA	1			
250.257	Insurance agent/broker	ECS	1			
169.167	Insurance underwriter	ESC	4	1		1
376.367	Investigator	SRE	1			
119.267	Law clerk	ESA	2			
— —	Law student	—	7	6	6	12
110.107	Lawyer	ESA	40	5		5
012.167	Management/methods engineer	ERI	1			
189.167	Management trainee	ESC	1	1		1
163.117	Marketing manager	ESC			1	1
050.067	Market-research analyst	IAS	1			
025.062	Meteorologist	IRA	1			
131.267	Newspaper reporter	ASI	1	1		1
169.167	Office manager	ESC	2			
184.167	Operations manager	ESC	2	1		1
195.167	Parole/probation officer	SIC	2	1		1
116.117	Personnel manager	SEC	3	1		1
375.263	Police officer	SRE		1		1
163.267	Product-distribution manager	ESC	1			
189.117	Product manager	ESC	1			
183.117	Production manager	ESC	1			
165.067	Public-relations practitioner	AES	1	1		1
162.157	Purchasing agent	ECS		1		1
250.357	Real-estate agent/broker	ECS	1	1		1
160.167	Revenue agent	CES	1			
290.477	Sales clerk	ESC	2			
163.167	Sales manager	ESC	1			
279.357	Sales/service representative	ESC	3	2		2
020.167	Securities analyst	IAS	1			
189.167	Security officer	ESC	1	1		1
— —	Seminarian	—	1			
600-800	Skilled trades	RIC	1	1		1
188.117	Social-welfare director	SIC		1		1

DOT	JOB TITLE	HOC	1960-1974	1975-1980 M	F	T
195.107	Social worker	SIC	6			
185.167	Store manager	ESI	1			
092.227	Teacher/elementary school	SAI	2	1		1
091.227	Teacher/high school	SAE	10			
099.227	Teacher/other	SIR	2			
166.227	Training specialist	SEC	1			
186.117	Trust officer/bank	ESC	1			
199.167	Urban planner	ICR	2			
045.107	Vocational counselor	SIA		1		1
131.067	Writer (fiction and nonfiction)	ASI	1			
			147	**40**	**14**	**54**

*Life is like an onion: You peel off one layer at a time,
and sometimes you weep.*
— *Carl Sandburg*

PSYCHOLOGY
GENERAL DESCRIPTION

Psychologists examine the behavior of individuals in order to understand and explain how and why they act as they do. By learning about people's traits and tendencies through interviews, tests, and experiments, practitioners in this field can help their clients improve their personal adjustments. These behavioral scientists also analyze conditions that affect human behavior outside the individual — such as social, political, demographic, environmental conditions — to discover ways of improving the quality of life. Some fields in which psychologists specialize are clinical, social, counseling, experimental, physiological, personality, space, and industrial psychology.

Holders of a bachelor's degree can assist psychologists and other professionals in hospitals, rehabilitation centers, and correctional institutions. They also find jobs in business and industry doing market research, testing job applicants, or training new employees.

You need at least a master's degree for professional work in which you might administer and interpret psychological tests, counsel college students with educational or emotional problems, or help the handicapped find suitable training and employment.

With a doctorate, you can get certified to conduct private practice, and you can qualify for more responsible research and counseling positions in hospitals, clinics, and other health facilities. The largest number of Ph.D.'s work as teachers, counselors or administrators in colleges and universities, where you must have a doctorate to advance or receive tenure.

CAREER LEADS

DOT	JOB TITLE	HOC
164.117	Advertising manager	AES
052.067	Biographer	SEI
019.061	Biomedical engineer	RIE
131.067	Book critic	ASI
045.061	Child psychologist	SIA
120.007	Clergy member	SAI
090.117	College/university official	SIA
131.067	Columnist/commentator	ASI
195.167	Community-organization worker	SIC
020.187	Computer programer	IAS
188.117	Consumer-affairs director	ESC
096.121	Consumer-services consultant	SRI
131.067	Copy writer	ASI
188.117	Council-on-Aging/director	ESC
045.107	Counselor (guidance, rehabilitation, residence, vocational)	SIA
054.067	Criminologist	SIA
090.167	Department-head/college	SIA
090.167	Director of institutional research	SIA
132.067	Editor/publications	ASI
012.167	Efficiency expert	ERI
187.117	Hospital administrator	SEC
045.061	Human-factors specialist	SIA
012.167	Industrial engineer	ERI
076.167	Industrial therapist	SIR
109.067	Information scientist	IRC
166.267	Job analyst	SEC
110.107	Lawyer	ESA
189.167	Management trainee	ESC
166.117	Manager/employee welfare	SEC
050.067	Market-research analyst	IAS
076.121	Occupational therapist	SIR
054.067	Penologist	SIA
166.117	Personnel manager	SEC
070.101	Physician	ISA
166.167	Placement director	SEC
166.267	Prisoner-classification interviewer	SEC

DOT	JOB TITLE	HOC
195.167	Probation officer	SIC
070.107	Psychiatrist	ISA
055.067	Psychological anthropologist	IRA
045.107	Psychologist/clinical	SIA
045.061	Psychologist/developmental	SIA
045.061	Psychologist/engineering	SIA
045.061	Psychologist/experimental	SIA
045.107	Psychologist/industrial-organizational	SIA
045.107	Psychologist/school	SIA
045.067	Psychometrist	SIA
165.067	Public-relations representative	AES
195.167	Recreation director	SIC
076.124	Recreational therapist	SIR
109.267	Research assistant	IRC
251.257	Sales agent (psychological tests and industrial relations)	ECS
195.107	Social worker	SIC
375.167	Special agent/FBI	SRE
076.107	Speech pathologist	SIR
020.167	Statistician/applied	IAS
090.227	Teacher/college	SIA
094.227	Teacher/handicapped	SAI
094.227	Teacher/mentally retarded	SAI
131.067	Writer (prose, fiction, nonfiction)	ASI
131.267	Writer/technical publications	ASI

HIRING INSTITUTIONS

Adoption and Child Care Agencies
Advertising Departments and Agencies
Air, Bus, and Rail Lines
Business Corporations
Churches and Religious Organizations
Colleges and Schools
Community Organizations
    Recreation Departments
    YM - YWCAs
    YM - YWHAs
    Scouts, etc.
Correctional Institutions
Court System
Department Stores
Educational Institutions
Educational Periodicals
Government Agencies
    Civil Rights Commission
    Consumer Affairs Office
    Environmental Protection Agency
    Federal Communications Commission
    Foreign Service
    Health and Human Services Department
    Labor Department
    National Science Foundation
    Peace Corps
    Veteran's Administration
    Vista
Hospitals
Industries/Manufacturing
Magazines, Newspapers
Management-Consulting Firms
Market-Research Departments and Firms
Mental-Health Associations
Nursing Homes
Orphanages
Personnel Departments
Professional/Technical Journals

Public-Opinion-Research Companies
Public-Relations Firms
Publishing Companies
Research Institutes
Social-Service Agencies
Test-Development Corporations

CURRENT OCCUPATIONS OF GRADUATES WHO MAJORED IN PSYCHOLOGY

DOT	JOB TITLE	HOC	1960-1974	1975-1980 M	F	T
160.167	Accountant	CES		2	1	3
188.117	Administrative officer/ government service	ESC	1			
— —	Armed services	—	2	2		2
189.117	Business executive	ESC	2			
079.101	Chiropractor	SIR		1		1
209.562	Clerk	CIE		1	1	2
090.117	College/university official	SIA	1			
020.187	Computer programer	IAS	1			
— —	Dental student	—	1			
072.101	Dentist	ISR	1			
003.061	Electrical engineer	IRE	1			
187.167	Funeral director	SEC	1			
189.117	General manager	ESC	2	1	1	2
— —	Graduate student	—	15	13	6	19
045.107	Guidance counselor	SIA			1	1
187.117	Hospital administrator	SEC	1	1	2	3
250.257	Insurance agent/broker	ECS			1	1
241.217	Insurance-claim adjuster	CSE		1		1
241.217	Insurance-claim investigator	ESC			1	1
186.117	Insurance-and-risk manager	ESC		1		1
110.107	Lawyer	ESA		1		1
230.367	Mail carrier	CSR		1		1
189.167	Management trainee	ESC			1	1
— —	Medical student	—	3		1	1
078.261	Medical technologist	ISR			1	1
166.117	Personnel manager	SEC	1	1		1

DOT	JOB TITLE	HOC	1960-1974	1975-1980		
				M	F	T
070.101	Physician	ISA	1			
187.167	Private-business owner	ESC		1		1
189.117	Product manager	ESC		1	1	2
070.107	Psychoanalyst	ISA	1			
045.107	Psychologist	SIA	11	1	3	4
165.067	Public-relations practitioner	AES	1			
045.107	Rehabilitation counselor	SIA	4			
189.117	Research-and-development director	ESC	2			
163.167	Sales manager	ESC	1			
279.357	Sales/service representative	ESC	1			
600-800	Skilled trades	RIC	1			
188.117	Social-welfare director	ESC	1			
195.107	Social worker	SIC	1		5	5
076.107	Speech therapist	SIR	1			
185.167	Store manager	ESI		1		1
012.167	Systems analyst/electronic data processing	ERI	1			
003.167	Systems engineer	IRE	1			
090.227	Teacher/college	SIA	9			
092.227	Teacher/elementary school	SAI	2		2	2
091.227	Teacher/high school	SAE	2	1	2	3
099.227	Teacher/other	SIR	2	2		2
094.227	Teacher/special education	SAI		1		1
159.147	Television/radio personnel	AES		1		1
045.107	Vocational counselor	SIA	2	1	1	2
			78	36	31	67

It is easier to know man in general than to
understand one man in particular.
                                    — La Rouchefoucauld

SOCIOLOGY
GENERAL DESCRIPTION

Sociologists investigate how people behave in social groups — families, tribes, communities, and governments. They analyze the behavior patterns of social, political, religious, and business organizations, and how such groups influence the total society. Sociologists also do research to help identify the causes of social problems such as crime, divorce, poverty, and racism.

Students can specialize in areas such as social psychology, rural and urban sociology, criminology, demography, gerontology, and social ecology. Besides doing theoretical research, sociologists use their techniques to see how well government programs such as income-assistance or Medicare are helping people, to ascertain whether job training is reducing unemployment, or to find out if communities harboring toxic-waste sites have a high incidence of cancer.

With a bachelor's degree, students can get jobs doing case work for child-welfare agencies or family courts, or they can counsel ex-offenders, or mental patients at halfway houses. Graduates can also get jobs in business and industry where they can use their ability to analyze group-behavior as one means of improving sales and services, or to predict the public's response to radio and TV programs or printed publications. With some training in statistics, you can get into the computer and data-processing fields.

You will need advanced degrees to teach in college, to hold senior positions in research and administration, or to do consulting work.

CAREER LEADS

DOT	JOB TITLE	HOC
188.117	Administrative officer/government service	ESC
164.117	Advertising manager	AES
055.067	Anthropologist	IAR
052.067	Biographer	SEI
131.067	Book critic	ASI
120.007	Clergy member	SAI
090.117	College/university official	SIA
131.067	Columnist/commentator	ASI
195.167	Community-organization worker	SIC
188.117	Consumer-affairs director	ESC
096.121	Consumer-services consultant	SRI
131.067	Copy writer	ASI
188.117	Council-on-Aging/director	ESC
045.107	Counselor (guidance, rehabilitation, vocational)	SIA
054.067	Criminologist	SIA
054.067	Demographer	SIA
090.167	Department head/college	SIA
090.167	Director of institutional research	SIA
132.067	Editor/publications	ASI
055.067	Ethnologist	IAR
187.117	Hospital administrator	SEC
059.267	Intelligence specialist	SIA
166.167	Labor-relations representative	SEC
110.107	Lawyer	ESA
189.167	Management trainee	ESC
166.117	Manager/employee welfare	SEC
050.067	Market-research analyst	IAS
054.067	Medical sociologist	SIA
054.067	Penologist	SIA
166.117	Personnel manager	SEC
166.167	Placement director	SEC
166.267	Prisoner-classification interviewer	SEC
195.167	Probation officer	SIC
045.107	Psychologist/industrial	SIA
079.117	Public-health educator	SIR
165.067	Public-relations representative	AES

DOT	JOB TITLE	HOC
195.167	Recreation director	SIC
109.267	Research assistant	IRC
054.067	Research worker/social welfare	SIA
054.067	Rural sociologist	SIA
012.167	Safety manager	ERI
054.067	Social-problems specialist	SIA
054.067	Social ecologist	SIA
195.107	Social worker	SIC
054.067	Sociologist	SIA
020.167	Statistician/applied	IAS
090.227	Teacher/college	SIA
199.167	Urban planner	ICR
054.067	Urban sociologist	SIA
131.267	Writer/technical publications	ASI

HIRING INSTITUTIONS

Adoption and Child Care Agencies
Advertising Departments and Agencies
Business Corporations
Churches and Religious Organizations
Colleges and Schools
Community Organizations
>Recreation Department
>YM - YWCAs
>YM - YWHAs
>Scouts, etc.
Correctional Institutions
Court Systems
Educational Institutions
Educational Periodicals
Government Agencies
>Civil Rights Commission
>Civil Service Commission
>Consumer Affairs Office
>Defense Department
>Education Department
>Federal Communications Commission
>Federal Housing Administration

Federal Trade Commission
Foreign Service
Housing and Urban Development
Labor Department
National Labor Relations Board
Peace Corps
Veteran's Administration
Vista
Hospitals
Industries, Manufacturing
Labor Unions
Magazines, Newspapers
Market Research Departments and Firms
Personnel Departments
Professional Periodicals
Public-Opinion-Research Companies
Public-Relations Firms
Publishing Companies
Research Institutes
Social-Service Agencies

CURRENT OCCUPATIONS OF GRADUATES WHO MAJORED IN SOCIOLOGY

DOT	JOB TITLE	HOC	1960-1974	1975-1980 M	F	T
188.117	Administrative officer/ government service	ESC	3		1	1
— —	Armed services	—	6	1		1
153.341	Athlete	SRE	1			
160.162	Auditor	CES	2			
186.117	Bank officer	ESC	2			
183.117	Branch manager	ESC	1			
189.117	Business executive	ESC	4		1	1
162.157	Buyer	ECS	2			
022.061	Chemist/quality control	IAR	1			
079.101	Chiropractor	SIR		1		1
209.562	Clerk	CIE	4	2	1	3
090.117	College/university official	SIA	1			
213.132	Computer-operations supervisor	CIS	1			
020.187	Computer programer	IAS	5			

DOT	JOB TITLE	HOC	1960-1974	1975-1980		
				M	F	T
094.117	Coordinator of special services/education	SAI	1			
160.167	Cost accountant	CES	1			
168.167	Credit-and-collection manager	SIE			1	1
132.067	Editor	ASI	1			
003.061	Electrical engineer	IRE	1			
166.267	Employment interviewer	SEC	2		1	1
189.117	General manager	ESC	4	2	1	3
— —	Graduate student	—	8	1	1	2
045.107	Guidance counselor	SIA	4	1		1
091.107	High-school official	SAE	2			
052.067	Historian	SEI	1			
187.117	Hospital administrator	SEC	3		1	1
250.257	Insurance agent/broker	ECS		1		1
241.217	Insurance-claim investigator	CSE	1			
186.117	Insurance-and-risk manager	ESC		1		1
169.167	Insurance underwriter	ESC	1			
376.367	Investigator	SRE		1		1
166.167	Labor-relations consultant	SEC	1			
119.267	Law clerk	ESA	1			
110.107	Lawyer	ESA	8	1		1
100.127	Librarian	SAI	1			
230.367	Mail carrier	CSR		1		1
189.167	Management trainee	ESC	1			
163.117	Marketing manager	ESC	2	1		1
— —	Medical student	—	1			
169.167	Office manager	ESC	3	1		1
184.167	Operations manager	ESC	1			
195.167	Parole/probation officer	SIC	6			
166.117	Personnel manager	SEC	5		2	2
070.101	Physician	ISA	3			
196.263	Pilot/airplane	IRC	1			
183.117	Production manager	ESC	2		1	1
070.107	Psychiatrist	ISA	1			
045.107	Psychologist	SIA	4			
165.067	Public-relations practitioner	AES	2			

DOT	JOB TITLE	HOC	1960-1974	1975-1980 M	F	T
162.157	Purchasing agent	ECS	1	1		1
250.357	Real-estate agent/broker	ECS	1			
045.107	Rehabilitation counselor	SIA	1			
189.117	Research-and-development director	ESC	1			
290.477	Sales clerk	ESC	1	1	1	2
163.167	Sales manager	ESC	1			
279.357	Sales/service representative	ESC	8	1		1
186.167	Securities trader	ESC	1			
189.167	Security officer	ESC	1			
188.117	Social-welfare director	ESC	1			
195.107	Social worker	SIC	23	2	4	6
054.067	Sociologist	SIA	1			
020.167	Statistician	IAS			1	1
251.157	Stockbroker	ECS	1			
185.167	Store manager	ESI	1			
012.167	Systems analyst/electronic data processing	ERI	4			
090.227	Teacher/college	SIA	10	1		1
092.227	Teacher/elementary school	SAI	6		3	3
091.227	Teacher/high school	SAE	10	3	1	4
099.227	Teacher/other	SIR	9		1	1
159.147	Television/radio personnel	AES	1			
166.227	Training specialist	SEC	1			
184.117	Transportation manager	ESC		1		1
199.167	Urban planner	ICR	4		1	1
045.107	Vocational counselor	SIA	1			
131.067	Writer (fiction and nonfiction)	ASI	1			
			196	**25**	**23**	**48**

He conquers who endures. — *Persius*

URBAN STUDIES
GENERAL DESCRIPTION

U rban Studies concerns itself with the history, expression, and evaluation of the way people live in cities. Students in this field study the cultural resources of the city, together with such problems as poverty, violence, and crime which affect the quality of urban living. They also explore the way ethnic groups, social classes, and politics influence community planning and social reform.

Depending on their personalities and individual preferences, graduates can enter a variety of fields that relate to urban concerns. If you enjoy direct contact with people, you can either teach or perform social services — within a court system, for example, or at a correctional facility.

Perhaps you prefer managerial work. For that, you can look into hospital administration, or activities dealing with city life — such as community relations programs — that business and financial organizations sponsor.

And graduates striving to improve our physical environment can work for engineering firms that design subways and parking facilities, or for urban renewal agencies that rehabilitate schools, housing, shopping centers, and playgrounds.

With a bachelor's degree, students can find entry-level jobs in urban administration and planning, private social agencies, community-organization projects, and social welfare. They can also go on to graduate studies in urban and regional planning, architecture or law. A master's degree will qualify individuals to get a start as urban and regional planners at local, State, and Federal levels. With an additional range of experience, you can do consulting work for land-developers, engineering firms, research organizations, or government agencies.

CAREER LEADS

DOT	JOB TITLE	HOC
188.117	Administrative officer/government service	ESC
001.061	Architect	AIR
131.067	Book critic	ASI
188.117	City manager	ESC
090.117	College/university official	SIA
195.167	Community-organization worker	SIC
096.121	Consumer-services consultant	SRI
169.167	Contact representative	ESC
119.267	Contract consultant	ESA
188.117	Council-on-Aging/director	ESC
054.067	Demographer	SIA
188.167	Election supervisor	ESC
165.117	Fund-raising director	AES
188.167	Director of vital statistics	ESC
099.117	Educational-program director	SIE
166.267	Employment interviewer	SEC
001.061	Environmental planner	AIR
187.117	Hospital administrator	SEC
188.117	Housing-management officer	ESC
166.267	Job analyst	SEC
166.167	Labor-relations representative	SEC
110.107	Lawyer	ESA
165.017	Lobbyist	AES
161.167	Management analyst	CES
189.167	Management trainee	ESC
187.117	Manager/chamber of commerce	SEC
166.117	Manager/employee welfare	SEC
166.067	Occupational analyst	SEC
169.167	Office manager	ESC
119.267	Paralegal assistant	ESA
166.267	Prisoner-classification interviewer	SEC
195.167	Probation officer	SIC
165.067	Public-relations representative	SIR
162.157	Purchasing agent	ECS
250.357	Real-estate agent/broker	ECS
195.167	Recreation director	SIC
131.267	Reporter (print and publications)	ASI

DOT	JOB TITLE	HOC
012.167	Safety manager	ERI
195.117	Social-welfare director	SIC
195.107	Social worker	SIC
090.227	Teacher/college	SIA
119.287	Title examiner	ESA
184.167	Transportation manager	ESC
199.167	Urban planner	ICR
054.067	Urban sociologist	SIA

HIRING INSTITUTIONS

Adoption and Child Care Agencies
Business Corporations
Chambers of Commerce
Civic and Taxpayers' Associations
Colleges and Schools
Community Organizations

> Recreation Departments
> YM - YWCAs
> YM - YWHAs
> Scouts, etc.

Correctional Institutions
Court Systems
Educational Institutions
Government Agencies

> Civil Rights Commission
> Civil Service Commission
> Consumer Affairs Office
> Education Department
> Environmental Protection Agency
> Federal Housing Administration
> Federal Labor Relations Board
> Federal Trade Commission
> Foreign Service
> Health and Human Services Department
> Housing and Urban Development

Labor Department
Peace Corps
Veteran's Administration
Vista
Hospitals
Housing Authorities
Industries, Manufacturing
Labor Unions
Libraries
Magazines, Newspapers
Municipalities
Professional Periodicals
Public-Relations Firms
Regional Planning Councils and
  Associations
Social-Service Agencies
Urban-Renewal Agencies

CURRENT OCCUPATIONS OF GRADUATES
WHO MAJORED IN URBAN STUDIES

DOT	JOB TITLE	HOC	1960-1974	1975-1980 M	F	T
160.167	Accounting manager	CES	1			
188.117	Administrative officer/ government service	ESC	2	2	1	3
— —	Armed services	—	2	1		1
160.162	Auditor	CES		1		1
186.117	Bank officer	ESC			2	2
161.117	Budget analyst	CES	3			
189.117	Business executive	ESC	1		1	1
120.007	Clergy member	SAI	2			
209.562	Clerk	CIE	1	1	2	3
119.267	Contract consultant	ESA		1		1
191.267	Credit analyst	ESC			1	1
187.167	Funeral director	SEC		1		1
189.117	General manager	ESC	3			
— —	Graduate student			1	5	6

DOT	JOB TITLE	HOC	1960-1974	1975-1980 M	F	T
045.107	Guidance counselor	SIA			1	1
187.117	Hospital administrator	SEC	2			
187.117	Hotel/restaurant manager	SEC	1			
250.257	Insurance agent/broker	ECS	1	1		1
376.367	Investigator	SRE			1	1
166.167	Labor-relations consultant	SEC			1	1
119.267	Law clerk	ESA	2			
— —	Law student	—			1	1
110.107	Lawyer	ESA	2			
230.367	Mail carrier	CSR	1			
131.267	Newspaper reporter	ASI		1		1
169.167	Officer manager	ESC	3		2	2
166.267	Personnel manager	SEC			1	1
375.263	Police officer	SRE	1	1		1
183.117	Production manager	ESC	1			
045.107	Psychologist	SIA			1	1
165.067	Public-relations practitioner	AES			1	1
162.157	Purchasing agent	ECS	1	1		1
250.357	Real-estate agent/broker	ECS	1			
189.117	Research-and-development director	ESC	1		1	1
290.477	Sales clerk	ESC	1			
163.167	Sales manager	ESC		1		1
279.357	Sales/service representative	ESC			1	1
189.167	Security officer	ESC	1			
600-800	Skilled trades	RIC	1	1		1
188.117	Social-welfare director	ESC	1		3	3
195.107	Social worker	SIC	5		6	6
251.157	Stockbroker	ECS		1		1
012.167	Systems analyst/electronic data processing	ERI	1			
090.227	Teacher/college	SIA	3			
092.227	Teacher/elementary school	SAI	1			
091.227	Teacher/high school	SAE	1			
099.227	Teacher/other	SIR	1	1	1	2
184.117	Transportation manager	ECS		1		1
199.167	Urban planner	ICR	1	1		1
045.107	Vocational counselor	SIA	3		1	1
			52	18	34	52

PART FIVE

JOB INDEX: MAJOR OF GRADUATES BY OCCUPATION

A book without an index is much like a compass-box without the needle, perplexing instead of directive to the point we would reach. — Anon.

PART FIVE
THE MAJORS OF GRADUATES —
BY OCCUPATION

DOT	JOB TITLE	HOC	1960-1974	1975-1980 M	F	T
160.167	**Accountant** .... CES					
	Accountancy		249	218	50	268
	Biology		1	1		1
	Economics		15	5		5
	English		1	1		1
	History		5	2		2
	Management		16	18	2	20
	Marketing		11	3	2	5
	Math/Computer Science		2			
	Natural Science				1	1
	Political Science		1	1		1
	Psychology			2	1	3
			301	251	56	307
160.167	**Accounting Manager** ...... CES					
	Accountancy		41	11	3	14
	Economics		4			
	English		1			
	History		2	1		1
	Management		6	2	3	5
	Marketing		2	1	1	2
	Math/Computer Science		3			
	Modern Languages		1			
	Physics		1			
	Political Science			1		1
	Urban Studies		1			
			62	16	7	23
160.167	**Accounting Partner** .... CES					
	Accountancy		17	4		4
	Management		1			
			18	4		4

DOT	JOB TITLE	HOC	1960-1974	1975-1980 M	F	T
150.047	**Actor** .... ASE					
	Biology			1		1
	Classics		1			
	English		1	1		1
	Marketing		1			
	Modern Languages		1			
			4	2		2
020.167	**Actuary** .... IAS					
	Management		1			
	Marketing				1	1
	Math/Computer Science		8	1	1	2
			9	1	2	3
169.167	**Administrative Officer Government Service/** ..... ESC					
	Accountancy		9			
	Art History		1			
	Chemistry		2			
	Classics		2			
	Economics		20			
	Education		1			
	English		8	2		2
	History		8			
	Management		19	3	2	5
	Marketing		21	1	1	2
	Math/Computer Science		3			
	Modern Languages		3			
	Natural Science		1			
	Physics		1			
	Political Science		2			
	Psychology		1			
	Sociology		3		1	1
	Urban Studies		2	2	1	3
			107	8	5	13

DOT	JOB TITLE	HOC	1960-1974	1975-1980		
				M	F	T
164.117	**Advertising Manager**	AES				
	Accountancy		2			
	Economics		1			
	Education				1	1
	English		1		2	2
	History		2			
	Management		4	1		1
	Marketing		2	1		1
	Political Science		1			
			13	2	3	5
002.061	**Aeronautical Engineer**	IRE				
	Physics		2			
			2			
070.101	**Anesthesiologist** .... (see Medical Doctor)	ISA				
001.061	**Architect**	AIR				
	History			1		1
				1		1
— —	**Armed Services**	—				
	Accountancy		16	2	1	3
	Biology		13	2		2
	Chemistry		7			
	Classics		1			
	Economics		24	1		1
	Education		1			
	English		19	2		2
	History		37	7		7
	Management		17	8		8

DOT	JOB TITLE	HOC	1960-1974	1975-1980 M	F	T
	Marketing		18			
	Math/Computer Science		12			
	Modern Languages		5	1		1
	Natural Science		5	1	1	2
	Philosophy		1			
	Physics		3			
	Political Science		5	3		3
	Psychology		2	2		2
	Sociology		6	1		1
	Urban Studies		2	1		1
			194	31	2	33
144.061	**Artist**	AIR				
	Art History		2			
	English		1		1	1
	Marketing			1		1
			3	1	1	2
153.341	**Athlete**	SRE				
	Sociology		1			
			1			
099.167	**Audiovisual Specialist**	SIE				
	Art History		1			
	Management		1			
			1			
160.162	**Auditor**	CES				
	Accountancy		69	40	7	47
	Classics		1			
	Economics		8	1		1

DOT	JOB TITLE	HOC	1960-1974	1975-1980		
				M	F	T
	History		2	1		1
	Management		11	4		4
	Marketing		5	1		1
	Math/Computer Science		1	1		1
	Sociology		2			
	Urban Studies			1		1
			99	49	7	56
186.117	**Bank Officer**	ESC				
	Accountancy		24	9	6	15
	Economics		47	2	1	3
	English		6			
	History		16	1		1
	Management		46	19	5	24
	Math/Computer Science		8			
	Marketing		24	3	1	4
	Modern Languages		4	1	1	2
	Physics		1			
	Political Science		4		1	1
	Sociology		2			
	Urban Studies				2	2
			182	35	17	52
041.061	**Biochemist**	IRS				
	Biology		1	1		1
			1	1		1
041.061	**Biologist**	IRS				
	Biology		3	1		1
	Natural Science		1			
			4	1		1

DOT	JOB TITLE	HOC	1960-1974	1975-1980 M	F	T
183.117	**Branch Manager**	ESC				
	Accountancy		1	3		3
	Chemistry		1			
	Economics		3			
	History		2			
	Management		10	3		3
	Marketing		4			
	Math/Computer Science		1			
	Political Science		1			
	Sociology		1			
			24	6		6
186.117	**Brokerage-House Partner**	ESC				
	Accountancy				1	1
	Economics		1			
			1		1	1
161.117	**Budget Analyst**	CES				
	Accountancy		7	2	1	3
	Economics		4		1	1
	History			1		1
	Management		5	4	2	6
	Marketing		6			
	Math/Computer Science		1	1		1
	Modern Languages		1			
	Urban Studies		3			
			27	8	4	12
189.117	**Business Executive**	ESC				
	Accountancy		113	7		7
	Art History		1	1		1
	Biology		1	2		2

DOT	JOB TITLE	HOC	1960-1974	1975-1980 M	F	T
	Chemistry		5		1	1
	Classics		2		1	1
	Economics		43	4		4
	Education		1		3	3
	English		29		2	2
	History		20	3		3
	Managment		52	12	5	17
	Marketing		45	7	2	9
	Math/Computer Science		15	1	1	2
	Modern Languages		4		1	1
	Natural Science		2			
	Philosophy		2			
	Physics		4	1		1
	Political Science		7		3	3
	Psychology		2			
	Sociology		4		1	1
	Urban Studies		1		1	1
			353	38	21	59
162.157	**Buyer** .... ECS					
	Accountancy		1	1		1
	Art History		1			
	Economics		2			
	English		3	1		1
	History		2			
	Management		6	3	2	5
	Marketing		10	1	2	3
	Modern Languages		1			
	Political Science		2			
	Sociology		2			
			30	6	4	10

DOT	JOB TITLE	HOC	1960-1974	1975-1980 M	F	T
186.117	**Cashier, Bank**	ESC				
	Accountancy				1	1
	Economics		3			
	History		2			
	Management		2	3	2	5
	Marketing		4	1		1
	Natural Science				1	1
			11	4	4	8
022.061	**Chemist**	IAR				
	Biology		5	3	2	5
	Chemistry		33	4	3	7
	Economics			1		1
	Math/Computer Science			1		1
	Natural Science		3	1		1
	Physics		2			
			43	10	5	15
022.061	**Chemist, Analytical**	IAR				
	Biology			2		2
	Chemistry		2			
			2	2		2
022.061	**Chemist/ Quality Control**	IAR				
	Biology		1	1	1	2
	Chemistry		1			
	Economics			1		1
	English		1			
	Sociology		1			
			4	2	1	3

DOT	JOB TITLE	HOC	1960-1974	1975-1980 M	F	T
022.061	**Chemist/Research**	IAR				
	Biology		3	1	1	2
	Chemistry		18			
	Management		1			
	Math/Computer Science		1			
	Natural Science		2	2		2
			25	3	1	4
079.101	**Chiropractor**	SIR				
	Biology		1	1		1
	Management		1			
	Modern Languages		1			
	Natural Science			2		2
	Psychology			1		1
	Sociology			1		1
			3	5		5
110.117	**Claim Attorney**	ESA				
	Economics		1			
	Business Management				1	1
			1		1	1
120.007	**Clergy Member**	SAI				
	Accountancy		1	1		1
	Art History		1			
	Biology		1			
	Chemistry			1		1
	Economics		1			
	English		1			
	History		4			
	Management		3			
	Math/Computer Science		1			

DOT	JOB TITLE	HOC	1960-1974	1975-1980 M	F	T
	Modern Languages		2	1		1
	Natural Science		1			
	Urban Studies		2			
			18	3		3
209.562	**Clerk** .... CIE					
	Accountancy		5	8	4	12
	Art History			1		1
	Biology		2	2	2	4
	Economics		3	3		3
	Education		1		8	8
	English		9	7	5	12
	History		4			
	Management		12	12	7	19
	Marketing		6	11	3	14
	Math/Computer Science		2	2	1	3
	Modern Languages				5	5
	Natural Science		1		1	1
	Philosophy				1	1
	Physics		1			
	Political Science		1	2		2
	Psychology			1	1	2
	Sociology		4	2	1	3
	Urban Studies		1	1	2	3
			52	51	42	93
090.167	**College Department Head** .... SIA					
	Modern Languages		1	1		1
	Political Science				1	1
			1	1	1	2

DOT	JOB TITLE	HOC	1960-1974	1975-1980 M	F	T
090.117	**College/University Official**	SIA				
	Art History				1	1
	Biology		1			
	Chemistry		1			
	Classics		2			
	Economics		2			
	Education		1		2	2
	English		6		1	1
	History		11	1		1
	Management		2	1		1
	Marketing		2			
	Math/Computer Science		1		1	1
	Modern Languages		3			
	Political Science		1		1	1
	Psychology		1			
	Sociology		1			
			35	2	6	8
213.362	**Computer Operator**	CIS				
	Accountancy		1			
	Economics		2	1		1
	English			1		1
	History		1	1		1
	Management		2		2	2
	Marketing		4	5	1	6
	Math/Computer Science		1	3		3
			11	11	3	14
213.132	**Computer-Operations Supervisor**	CIS				
	Accountancy		6	1		1
	Chemistry		1			
	Economics		8	1		1
	Education		1		1	1

DOT	JOB TITLE	HOC	1960-1974	1975-1980 M	F	T
	English		1			
	History		1			
	Management		4	8		8
	Marketing		1			
	Math/Computer Science		10	1	3	4
	Natural Science		1			
	Physics		3			
	Sociology		1			
			38	**11**	**4**	**15**
020.187	**Computer Programer** ..... IAS					
	Accountancy		2	4	1	5
	Biology		2	1	2	3
	Chemistry		1			
	Classics		1			
	Economics		6	3		3
	Education		1	1		1
	English		1	1		1
	History		7		1	1
	Management		21	24	2	26
	Marketing		7	10	1	11
	Math/Computer Science		45	17	9	26
	Natural Science		1	1		1
	Philosophy		1			
	Physics		2			
	Psychology		1			
	Sociology		5			
			104	**62**	**16**	**78**
869.664	**Construction Worker** ..... REI					
	Accountancy		1			
	Biology				1	1
	English		1			

DOT	JOB TITLE	HOC	1960-1974	1975-1980 M	F	T
	History			1	1	2
	Management		1	2		2
	Marketing		2			
			5	4	1	5
119.267	**Contract Consultant**	ESA				
	Economics		2			
	English		1	1	1	2
	Management		1			
	Math/Computer Science		1			
	Modern Languages				1	1
	Political Science		1			
	Urban Studies			1		1
			6	2	2	4
182.167	**Contractor**	ERI				
	History		1			
			1			
094.117	**Coordinator of Special Studies/ Education**	SAI				
	Biology		1			
	Chemistry		1			
	Economics		2			
	Education		2	1		1
	History		6			
	Management		1			
	Marketing		3			
	Political Science			1		1
	Sociology		1			
			17	2		2

DOT	JOB TITLE	HOC	1960-1974	1975-1980 M	F	T
131.067	**Copy Writer**	ASI				
	Modern Languages		1			
	Natural Science		1			
			2			
110.117	**Corporate Counsel**	ESA				
	Economics		1			
	English		1			
	History		4			
			6			
160.167	**Cost Accountant**	CES				
	Accountancy		13	7	1	8
	Economics		1		1	1
	History		1			
	Management		8	1		1
	Marketing		2			
	Math/Computer Science		1			
	Sociology		1			
			27	8	2	10
160.267	**Cost Estimator**	CES				
	Accountancy		1			
	Economics		2			
	History		1			
	Management		1	2		2
	Math/Computer Science				1	1
			5	2	1	3
191.267	**Credit Analyst**	ESC				
	Accountancy		2	2		2
	Economics		2	2	1	3
	History		1	1		1

DOT	JOB TITLE	HOC	1960-1974	1975-1980 M	F	T
	Management		2	3	1	4
	Marketing		2	1		1
	Natural Science			1		1
	Urban Studies				1	1
			9	10	3	13
168.167	**Credit-and-Collection Manager** .... SIE					
	Accountancy		2	1	1	2
	Economics		2	1		1
	Education		1			
	English			1		1
	History		2			
	Management		5	3	2	5
	Marketing		4	2		2
	Math/Computer Science		3			
	Sociology				1	1
			19	8	4	12
188.167	**Customs Officer** .... ESC					
	Economics		1			
	History		2			
	Management		1	1		1
	Math/Computer Science		1			
	Modern Languages		1			
			6	1		1
003.167	**Data-Processing Engineer** .... IRE					
	Economics		1			
	Math/Computer Science		1	1		1
	Physics		1			
			3	1		1

DOT	JOB TITLE	HOC	1960-1974	1975-1980 M	F	T
— —	**Dental Student**	—				
	Biology		2	4		4
	Chemistry			2		2
	History		1			
	Natural Science		1	2		2
	Physics		1			
	Psychology		1			
			6	8		8
072.101	**Dentist**	ISR				
	Biology		35	3	1	4
	Chemistry		5			
	Natural Science		8	1		1
	Psychology		1			
			49	4	1	5
003.167	**Development-and-Planning Engineer**	IRE				
	Accountancy		2			
	Economics		2			
	English		2			
	History		1			
	Management		4	2		2
	Marketing		3			
	Math/Computer Science		6	1	1	2
	Natural Science			1		1
	Political Science		2			
			22	4	1	5
110.117	**District Attorney**	ESA				
	Accountancy		1			
	Economics		1			
	English		2			

DOT	JOB TITLE	HOC	1960-1974	1975-1980 M	F	T
	History		2			
	Philosophy		1			
			7			
183.117	**District Manager** .... ESC					
	Accountancy		2	2		2
	Chemistry		2			
	Classics		1			
	Economics		9		1	1
	English		3			
	History		2			
	Management		7	3		3
	Marketing		9	1		1
	Math/Computer Science		3			
	Physics		1			
			39	6	1	7
050.067	**Economist** .... IAS					
	Economics		6		1	1
	History		1			
	Management		1			
	Marketing		2		1	1
	Math/Computer Science		1			
			11		2	2
050.067	**Economist/Price** .... IAS					
	Accountancy		1			
	Management				1	1
	Marketing		1			
			2	1		1

DOT	JOB TITLE	HOC	1960-1974	1975-1980 M	F	T
132.067	**Editor**	ASI				
	Classics			1		1
	English		7		2	2
	History		1			
	Management		1			
	Marketing		1		1	1
	Modern Languages		2			
	Sociology		1			
			13	1	3	4
003.061	**Electrical Engineer**	IRE				
	Economics		2	1		1
	Managment		4	2		2
	Math/Computer Science		2		1	1
	Physics		7			
	Psychology		1			
	Sociology		1			
			17	3	1	4
092.137	**Elementary-School Official**	SAI				
	Biology		1			
	Chemistry		1			
	Education		1			
	History		2			
	Management		1			
	Math/Computer Science		1			
			7			
166.267	**Employment Interviewer** ...	SEC				
	English		1		1	1
	History		2			
	Management		2			

DOT	JOB TITLE	HOC	1960-1974	1975-1980 M	F	T
	Marketing				1	1
	Sociology		2		1	1
			7		3	3
041.061	**Endocrinologist**	IRS				
	Biology		1			
			1			
186.167	**Estate Planner**	ESC				
	History		5			
			5			
828.261	**Field Engineer**	RIC				
	Accountancy		1			
			1			
020.167	**Financial/Investment Analyst**	IAS				
	Accountancy		27		1	1
	Economics		15	1		1
	English		4		1	1
	History		4			
	Management		3	1		1
	Marketing		8	1		1
	Math/Computer Science		3			
	Physics		1			
			65	3	2	5
050.067	**Financial Planner**	IAS				
	Accountancy		18	8	1	9
	Classics				1	1
	Economics		4			

DOT	JOB TITLE	HOC	1960-1974	1975-1980		
				M	F	T
	English		1		1	1
	History				1	1
	Management		5	2	3	5
	Marketing		1		1	1
	Math/Computer Science				1	1
			29	11	8	19
373.364	**Firefighter**	RSE				
	Accountancy				1	1
	Economics				1	1
	English		2			
	History		2	1		1
	Management		2	2		2
	Marketing		1			
	Political Science		1			
			8	5		5
187.167	**Funeral Director**	SEC				
	Management			1	1	2
	Marketing		1			
	Psychology		1			
	Urban Studies			1		1
			2	2	1	3
189.117	**General Manager**	ESC				
	Accountancy		28	4	1	5
	Biology		2			
	Chemistry		1			
	Classics		1			
	Economics		24	3		3
	Education		1		2	2
	English		8	4	1	5
	History		15	1		1

DOT	JOB TITLE	HOC	1960-1974	1975-1980 M	F	T
	Management		45	37	5	42
	Marketing		24	2	2	4
	Math/Computer Science		13	1		1
	Modern Languages		1		1	1
	Natural Science		2	2	1	3
	Philosophy		1	1		1
	Physics		1			
	Political Science		4			
	Psychology		2	1	1	2
	Sociology		4	2	1	3
	Urban Studies		3			
			180	58	15	73
— —	**Graduate Student** .... —					
	Accountancy		3	2		2
	Art History		1		1	1
	Biology		20	22	10	32
	Chemistry		10	3	3	6
	Classics		4	1		1
	Economics		14	1	1	2
	Education		2	1	1	2
	English		19	3	3	6
	History		21	9	1	10
	Management		5	1	1	2
	Marketing		3	1		1
	Math/Computer Science		11	1	2	3
	Modern Languages		4		1	1
	Natural Science		8	10	6	16
	Philosophy		4	1		1
	Physics		3			
	Political Science		2	4	1	5
	Psychology		15	13	6	19
	Sociology		8	1	1	2
	Urban Studies			1	5	6
			157	75	43	118

DOT	JOB TITLE	HOC	1960-1974	1975-1980 M	F	T
045.107	**Guidance Counselor**	SIA				
	Accountancy		2			
	Art History				1	1
	Classics		1			
	Economics		4			
	Education		1			
	English		2			
	History		5		1	1
	Management		2			
	Marketing		2			
	Math/Computer Science		2			
	Modern Languages				1	1
	Natural Science		2			
	Political Science		1			
	Psychology				1	1
	Sociology		4	1		1
	Urban Studies				1	1
			28	1	5	6
091.107	**High-School Department Chairperson**	SAE				
	English		3			
	History		6			
	Management		1			
	Marketing		1			
	Math/Computer Science		2			
	Natural Science		1			
	Physics		2			
			16			
091.107	**High-School Official**	SAE				
	Accountancy		2			
	Biology		1			
	Economics		3			

DOT	JOB TITLE	HOC	1960-1974	1975-1980		
				M	F	T
	English		3		1	1
	History		7			
	Management		2			
	Marketing		1			
	Math/Computer Science		3			
	Modern Languages		1			
	Sociology		2			
			25		1	1
052.067	**Historian**	SEI				
	Sociology		1			
			1			
040.061	**Horticulturist**	RIS				
	Biology		1			
			1			
187.117	**Hospital Administrator** ...	SEC				
	Accountancy		4			
	Biology		3			
	Chemistry			1		1
	Economics		4			
	English				1	1
	History		5			
	Management		1	1	2	3
	Modern Languages		1			
	Psychology		1	1	2	3
	Sociology		3		1	1
	Urban Studies		2			
			24	3	6	9

DOT	JOB TITLE	HOC	1960-1974	1975-1980 M	F	T
187.117	**Hotel/Restaurant Manager**	SEC				
	English		1			
	History		1			
	Marketing			1		1
	Urban Studies		1			
			3	1		1
012.167	**Industrial Engineer**	ERI				
	English		1		1	1
	History		2			
	Management		9	2	2	4
	Marketing		2	2		2
	Natural Science		1	1		1
	Physics		1			
			16	5	3	8
250.257	**Insurance-Agent/Broker** ..	ECS				
	Accountancy		7	1		1
	Economics		7			
	Education		1			
	English		6			
	History		7	1		1
	Management		16	6		6
	Marketing		8	1	2	3
	Math/Computer Science		5			
	Modern Languages		2			
	Natural Science			1		1
	Political Science		1			
	Psychology				1	1
	Sociology			1		1
	Urban Studies		1	1		1
			61	12	3	15

DOT	JOB TITLE	HOC	1960-1974	1975-1980 M	F	T
241.217	**Insurance-Claim Adjuster**	CSE				
	Accountancy		1			
	Economics		1			
	English		3		1	1
	History		1	1		1
	Management		4	5		5
	Marketing		1	2		2
	Psychology			1		1
			11	9	1	10
168.267	**Insurance-Claim Examiner**	SIE				
	Accountancy		1			
	Biology		1			
	Economics		4			
	English		3		1	1
	History		7	1	2	3
	Management		6	2	2	4
	Marketing		6			
	Math/Computer Science		1			
			29	3	5	8
241.217	**Insurance-Claim Investigator**	CSE				
	Education			1		1
	Management		2	1		1
	Marketing		1			
	Psychology				1	1
	Sociology		1			
			4	2	1	3

DOT	JOB TITLE	HOC	1960-1974	1975-1980		
				M	F	T
186.117	**Insurance-and-Risk Manager**	ESC				
	Economics		1			
	Management		1	1		1
	Math/Computer Science		1	1		1
	Philosophy		1			
	Psychology			1		1
	Sociology			1		1
			4	4		4
169.167	**Insurance Underwriter**	ESC				
	Accountancy		2		1	1
	Economics		3	2		2
	English		3			
	History		8	1		1
	Management		14	1		1
	Math/Computer Science		3			
	Marketing		4	1		1
	Political Science		4	1		1
	Sociology		1			
			42	6	1	7
142.051	**Interior Designer/ Decorator**	AIS				
	Management		1			
			1			
376.367	**Investigator**	SRE				
	Accountancy		1			
	Economics		2			
	History		2	1		1

DOT	JOB TITLE	HOC	1960-1974	1975-1980		
				M	F	T
	Management		3	1		1
	Physics		1			
	Political Science		1			
	Sociology			1		1
	Urban Studies				1	1
			10	3	1	4
111.107	**Judge** .... ESA					
	Management		1			
	Economics		1			
	History		1			
			3			
022.137	**Laboratory Supervisor** .... IAR					
	Chemistry		2			
	Economics		1			
			3			
029.261	**Laboratory Technician** .... IRA					
	Biology		5	9	2	11
	Chemistry		1			
	Education		1			
	English				1	1
	History		2			
	Management			1		1
	Math/Computer Science			1		1
	Natural Science		6	3		3
			15	14	3	17
166.167	**Labor-Relations Consultant** .... SEC					
	Accountancy		1			
	English		1			
	Management		1		1	1

DOT	JOB TITLE	HOC	1960-1974	1975-1980 M	F	T
	Sociology		1			
	Urban Studies				1	1
			4		2	2
119.267	**Law Clerk**	ESA				
	Classics		1			
	Economics		1			
	English		1		1	1
	History		4	3		3
	Management		2	1		1
	Marketing			1		1
	Modern Languages		1			
	Political Science		2			
	Sociology		1			
	Urban Studies		2			
			15	5	1	6
110.107	**Law-School Professor**	SIA				
	English		2			
			2			
— —	**Law Student**	—				
	Accountancy			2		2
	Biology			2		2
	Chemistry		1	1		1
	Classics		1	1		1
	Economics		3	2		2
	Education			3	1	4
	English		4		2	2
	History		15	2	2	4
	Management			3		3
	Marketing		2	1		1

DOT	JOB TITLE	HOC	1960-1974	1975-1980 M	F	T
	Math/Computer Science		1		2	2
	Natural Science		1	1	1	2
	Philosophy			1	1	2
	Political Science		7	6	6	12
	Urban Studies				1	1
			35	25	16	41
110.107	**Lawyer** .... ESA					
	Accountancy		18			
	Art History				1	1
	Biology		2			
	Chemistry		1			
	Classics		14	1		1
	Economics		38			
	English		32	1		1
	History		72	4	3	7
	Management		6		1	1
	Marketing		15			
	Math/Computer Science		5			
	Modern Languages		5	1		1
	Natural Science		3	1	1	2
	Philosophy		5	1		1
	Physics		1			
	Political Science		40	5		5
	Psychology			1		1
	Sociology		8	1		1
	Urban Studies		2			
			267	16	6	22
100.127	**Librarian** .... SAI					
	Economics		1			
	English		6		4	4
	History		5		2	2

DOT	JOB TITLE	HOC	1960-1974	1975-1980 M	F	T
	Management				1	1
	Marketing			2		2
	Math/Computer Science		1			
	Philosophy		1			
	Sociology		1			
			15	2	7	9
230.367	**Mail Carrier** .... CSR					
	Accountancy			2		2
	Economics		1			
	Management		2		1	1
	Marketing		1	1		1
	Modern Languages		1			
	Natural Science			1		1
	Philosophy		1			
	Psychology			1		1
	Sociology			1		1
	Urban Studies		1			
			7	6	1	7
012.167	**Management/Methods Engineer** .... ERI					
	Accountancy		1			
	Biology		1			
	Management		6			
	Marketing		2			
	Math/Computer Science		2	1		1
	Physics		1			
	Political Science		1			
			14	1		1
189.167	**Management Trainee** ...... ESC					
	Accountancy		2	2	1	3
	Biology				1	1
	Classics				1	1

DOT	JOB TITLE	HOC	1960-1974	1975-1980 M	F	T
	Economics		2	1	1	2
	English		2			
	History		3	3		3
	Management		4	11	5	16
	Marketing		6	2		2
	Math/Computer Science		2			
	Modern Languages				1	1
	Philosophy				1	1
	Political Science		1	1		1
	Psychology				1	1
	Sociology		1			
			23	20	12	32
163.117	**Marketing Manager**	ESC				
	Accountancy		2			
	Biology		1			
	Chemistry		5			
	Economics		2			
	Education				1	1
	English		3			
	History		3	1		1
	Management		9	2		2
	Marketing		7	3	1	4
	Math/Computer Science		3			
	Natural Science		1			
	Physics		2			
	Political Science				1	1
	Sociology		2	1		1
			40	7	3	10
050.067	**Market-Research Analyst**	IAS				
	Accountancy		3			
	Chemistry		1			
	Economics		10	1		1

DOT	JOB TITLE	HOC	1960-1974	1975-1980		
				M	F	T
	English				1	1
	History		3			
	Management		11		1	1
	Marketing		9	4	2	6
	Math/Computer Science		5			
	Modern Languages		1			
	Political Science		1			
			44	5	4	9
020.067	**Mathematician**	IAS				
	Math/Computer Science		3	1	1	2
			3	1	1	2
070.	**Medical Doctor**	ISA				
	Accountancy		1			
	Biology		164	8	2	10
	Chemistry		14	1		1
	Classics		2			
	Economics		2			
	English		1			
	History		2			
	Management		2			
	Marketing		1			
	Natural Science		8		2	2
	Psychology		2			
	Sociology		4			
			203	9	4	13
— —	**Medical Student**	—				
	Accountancy			1		1
	Biology		24	40	18	58
	Chemistry		3	7	1	8
	Management			1		1

DOT	JOB TITLE	HOC	1960-1974	1975-1980 M	F	T
	Math/Computer Science		1			
	Modern Languages		1		1	1
	Natural Science		5	13	5	18
	Physics		2			
	Psychology		3		1	1
	Sociology		1			
			40	62	26	88
078.261	**Medical Technologist** ..... ISR					
	Biology		2	1	2	3
	Economics		1			
	Education		1			
	English		1			
	History		1			
	Natural Science		3	1	1	2
	Psychology				1	1
			9	2	4	6
025.062	**Meteorologist** .... IRA					
	Political Science		1			
			1			
041.061	**Microbiologist** .... IRS					
	Biology		2	1	1	2
	Chemistry		1			
			3	1	1	2
152.047	**Music Director** .... ASI					
	Accountancy		1			
			1			

DOT	JOB TITLE	HOC	1960-1974	1975-1980 M	F	T
152.041	**Musician**	ASI				
	Accountancy		1			
	English		1			
	Management		1			
	Modern Languages		1			
			4			
131.267	**Newspaper Reporter**	ASI				
	Economics		1			
	English		4	1	1	2
	History		3			
	Political Science		1	1		1
	Urban Studies			1		1
			9	**3**	**1**	**4**
070.101	**Obstetrician** .... (see Medical Doctor)	ISA				
169.167	**Office Manager**	ESC				
	Accountancy		21	1		1
	Biology		1			
	Chemistry		2			
	Economics		8	1		1
	English		11		1	1
	History		13			
	Management		42	7	2	9
	Marketing		12	3	1	4
	Math/Computer Science		8	1		1
	Modern Languages		2			
	Natural Science		3			
	Philosophy		1			
	Physics		3			
	Political Science		2			
	Sociology		3	1		1
	Urban Studies		3		2	2
			135	**14**	**6**	**20**

DOT	JOB TITLE	HOC	1960-1974	1975-1980 M	F	T
184.167	**Operations Manager**	ESC				
	Accountancy		8	2	1	3
	Economics		2			
	English		1			
	History		1			
	Management		7	15		15
	Marketing		5	3		3
	Math/Computer Science		4	1		1
	Natural Science		1			
	Physics		1			
	Political Science		2	1		1
	Sociology		1			
			33	22	1	23
070.101	**Ophthalmologist** .... (see Medical Doctor)	ISA				
079.101	**Optometrist**	SIR				
	Biology		1			
	Management			1		1
			1	1		1
195.167	**Parole/Probation Officer**	SIC				
	Economics		2			
	English		1			
	History		4			
	Management		2			
	Political Science		2	1		1
	Sociology		6			
			17	1		1
110.117	**Patent Attorney**	ESA				
	Chemistry		1			
			1			

DOT	JOB TITLE	HOC	1960-1974	1975-1980 M	F	T
070.101	**Pediatrician** .... (see Medical Doctor)	ISA				
166.117	**Personnel Manager**	SEC				
	Accountancy		3	1		1
	Biology		1			
	Economics		9	1		1
	Education		1			
	English		3			
	History		5	1	1	2
	Management		16	9	4	13
	Marketing		11	2	2	4
	Math/Computer Science		5			
	Modern Languages		2	1	1	2
	Political Science		3	1		1
	Psychology		1	1		1
	Sociology		5		2	2
	Urban Studies				1	1
			65	17	11	28
074.161	**Pharmacist**	IES				
	Biology		2			
	Economics		2			
	Natural Science		1	1		1
			5	1		1
041.061	**Pharmacologist**	IRS				
	Chemistry		1			
			1			
— —	**Pharmacy Student**	—				
	Biology		1			
			1			

DOT	JOB TITLE	HOC	1960-1974	1975-1980 M	F	T
143.062	**Photographer**	AIR				
	English		2			
	History		1			
			3			
070.101	**Physician**	ISA				
	(see Medical Doctor)					
023.061	**Physicist**	IAR				
	Natural Science			1		1
	Physics		12	1		1
			12	2		2
196.263	**Pilot/Airplane**	IRC				
	English		1			
	History		1			
	Management		2			
	Marketing		1			
	Math/Computer Science			1		1
	Sociology		1			
			6	1		1
079.101	**Podiatrist**	SIR				
	Biology		3			
	Natural Science		1			
			4			
— —	**Podiatry Student**	—				
	Biology			2	1	3
				2	1	3

DOT	JOB TITLE	HOC	1960-1974	1975-1980 M	F	T
375.263	**Police Officer**	SRE				
	Accountancy		1	1		1
	Economics		4			
	Education		1			
	English			1		1
	History		5	5		5
	Management		4	7		7
	Marketing		2	1		1
	Math/Computer Science		1			
	Political Science			1		1
	Urban Studies		1	1		1
			19	17		17
189.117	**Private-Business Owner** ..	ESC				
	Accountancy		10	2		2
	Biology		2			
	Chemistry		2			
	Economics		7			
	Education		1			
	English		8		1	1
	History		12	1		1
	Management		13	1		1
	Marketing		10	2		2
	Math/Computer Science		3			
	Physics		2			
	Psychology			1		1
			70	7	1	8
163.267	**Production-Distribution Manager**	ESC				
	Biology			1		1
	English		1			
	History		2			

DOT	JOB TITLE	HOC	1960-1974	1975-1980 M	F	T
	Management		1			
	Marketing		4			
	Natural Science		1			
	Political Science		1			
			10	1		1
189.117	**Product Manager** .... ESC					
	Accountancy		5	1		1
	Chemistry		4			
	Economics		3			
	English		2			
	History		3			
	Management		8	4		4
	Marketing		9	1	3	4
	Math/Computer Science		2			
	Natural Science		2			
	Political Science		1			
	Psychology			1	1	2
			39	7	4	11
183.117	**Production Manager** ...... ESC					
	Accountancy			1		1
	Biology		2			
	Chemistry		3			
	Economics		2	1		1
	English		1			
	History		3			
	Management		14	8	1	9
	Marketing		4	2		2
	Physics		1			
	Political Science		1			
	Sociology				1	1
	Urban Studies		1			
			32	12	2	14

DOT	JOB TITLE	HOC	1960-1974	1975-1980 M	F	T
070.107	**Psychiatrist** .... (see Medical Doctor)	ISA				
070.107	**Psychoanalyst** .... (see Medical Doctor)	ISA				
045.107	**Psychologist**	SIA				
	Biology		1			
	Economics		2			
	History		4			
	Marketing			1		1
	Modern Languages		1			
	Natural Science		1		1	1
	Psychology		11	1	3	4
	Sociology		4			
	Urban Studies				1	1
			24	2	5	7
165.067	**Public-Relations Practitioner**	AES				
	Economics		2			
	English		8	1	1	2
	History			1		1
	Management		5	3		3
	Marketing		4		1	1
	Math/Computer Science		1			
	Modern Languages				1	1
	Political Science		1	1		1
	Psychology		1			
	Sociology		2			
	Urban Studies				1	1
			24	6	4	10

DOT	JOB TITLE	HOC	1960-1974	1975-1980 M	F	T
162.157	**Purchasing Agent**	ESC				
	Accountancy		1		1	1
	Chemistry		1			
	Economics		3			
	Management		12	1	1	2
	Marketing		3	3		3
	Political Science			1		1
	Sociology		1	1		1
	Urban Studies		1	1		1
			22	7	2	9
012.167	**Quality-Control Engineer**	ERI				
	Chemistry		1			
	Economics		1			
	Management		1	1		1
	Marketing			1		1
	Natural Science		1	1		1
			4	3		3
070.101	**Radiologist** .... (see Medical Doctor)	ISA				
250.357	**Real-Estate Agent/ Broker**	ESC				
	Accountancy		2	1		1
	Biology		1			
	Chemistry		1			
	Economics		1			
	History				1	1
	Management		4	1	2	3
	Marketing		2	1		1
	Political Science		1	1		1
	Sociology		1			
	Urban Studies		1			
			14	4	3	7

DOT	JOB TITLE	HOC	1960-1974	1975-1980 M	F	T
045.107	**Rehabilitation Counselor**	SIA				
	Biology		1			
	Economics		1			
	English		1			
	History		1			
	Management		1			
	Natural Science				1	1
	Psychology		4			
	Sociology		1			
			10		1	1
189.117	**Research-and-Development Director**	ESC				
	Art History			1		1
	Biology		2	2	2	4
	Chemistry		6			
	Education		1			
	History		1		1	1
	Management		4		1	1
	Marketing		5			
	Math/Computer Science		2			
	Physics		2			
	Psychology		2			
	Sociology		1			
	Urban Studies		1		1	1
			27	3	5	8
160.167	**Revenue Agent**	CES				
	Accountancy		22	3		3
	Chemistry		1			
	Classics		1			
	Economics		4			
	History				1	1
	Management		3			

DOT	JOB TITLE	HOC	1960-1974	1975-1980 M	F	T
	Marketing		1			
	Physics		1			
	Political Science		1			
			34	3	1	4
290.447	**Sales Clerk**	ESC				
	Accountancy		1	2		2
	Art History		1			
	Chemistry		1			
	Classics			1		1
	Economics		7			
	Education			1		1
	English		3			
	History		5			
	Management		14	5	1	6
	Marketing		20	6		6
	Math/Computer Science		2			
	Modern Languages		1			
	Natural Science			1		1
	Physics		1			
	Political Science		2			
	Sociology		1	1	1	1
	Urban Studies		1			
			60	17	2	18
163.167	**Sales Manager**	ESC				
	Accountancy		2	2		2
	Chemistry		2			
	Classics		2			
	Economics		8			
	Education		1			
	English		8	1	1	2

DOT	JOB TITLE	HOC	1960-1974	1975-1980 M	F	T
	History		7	1		1
	Management		24	5		5
	Marketing		27	11	1	12
	Math/Computer Science		1			
	Modern Languages		1			
	Philosophy		1			
	Political Science		1			
	Psychology		1			
	Sociology		1			
	Urban Studies		1			
			88	20	2	22
279.357	**Sales/Service Representative**	ESC				
	Accountancy		2	2		2
	Biology		5	1	1	2
	Chemistry		6	1		1
	Economics		28	1		1
	Education		1		1	1
	English		9	2	1	3
	History		23	5		5
	Management		36	19	3	22
	Marketing		41	10	3	13
	Math/Computer Science		4			
	Modern Languages		5		3	3
	Natural Science		3	2		2
	Political Science		3	2		2
	Psychology		1			
	Sociology		8	1		1
	Urban Studies				1	1
			175	46	13	59
020.167	**Securities Analyst**	IAS				
	Biology		1			
	Economics		5			
	Management			2		2

DOT	JOB TITLE	HOC	1960-1974	1975-1980		
				M	F	T
	Marketing		2			
	Political Science		1			
			9	2		2
186.167	**Securities Trader**	ESC				
	Accountancy		1			
	Economics		2	1		1
	History		3			
	Management		2	1		1
	Marketing		1			
	Sociology		1			
			10	2		2
189.167	**Security Officer**	ESC				
	Accountancy			1		1
	Economics		1			
	History		1	1		1
	Management			1		1
	Natural Science			1	1	2
	Political Science		1	1		1
	Sociology		1			
	Urban Studies		1			
			5	5	1	6
— —	**Seminarian**	—				
	History		2	1		1
	Marketing		1			
	Modern Languages		1			
	Philosophy		1			
	Political Science		1			
			6.	1		1

DOT	JOB TITLE	HOC	1960-1974	1975-1980 M	F	T
600-800	**Skilled Trades**	RIC				
	Accountancy			2	1	3
	Biology		1			
	Classics		2			
	Economics		2			
	Education		3	2		2
	English		1	1		1
	History		6	2		2
	Management		10	10		10
	Marketing		7	1		1
	Math/Computer Science		8			
	Natural Science		2			
	Philosophy		1			
	Political Science		1	1		1
	Psychology		1			
	Urban Studies		1	1		1
			46	20	1	21
188.117	**Social-Welfare Director**	ESC				
	Economics		1			
	English		1		1	1
	History		2			
	Modern Languages		3		1	1
	Political Science		1		1	
	Psychology		1			
	Sociology		1			
	Urban Studies		1		3	3
			10	1	5	6
195.107	**Social Worker**	SIC				
	Accountancy		1			
	Art History		1			
	Biology		1			

DOT	JOB TITLE	HOC	1960-1974	1975-1980 M	F	T
	Economics		2	1		1
	Education		2			
	English		7		1	1
	History		7	1		1
	Management		3	2		2
	Marketing		3		1	1
	Math/Computer Science		4			
	Modern Languages		2		2	2
	Philosophy		4			
	Political Science		6			
	Psychology		1		5	5
	Sociology		23	2	4	6
	Urban Studies		5		6	6
			72	6	19	25
054.067	**Sociologist**	SIA				
	Management			1		1
	Sociology		1			
			1	1		1
375.167	**Special Agent/FBI**	SRE				
	Accountancy		6	1		1
	Economics		4			
	Education		2	1		1
	History		1			
	Management		2			
	Modern Languages		1			
			16	2		2
076.107	**Speech Therapist**	SIR				
	Psychology		1			
			1			

DOT	JOB TITLE	HOC	1960-1974	1975-1980		
				M	F	T
020.067	**Statistician**	IAS				
	Economics		1			
	Management		1			
	Marketing			1		1
	Math/Computer Science		1			
	Sociology				1	1
			3	1	1	2
251.157	**Stockbroker**	ECS				
	Accountancy		1	2		2
	Economics		2			
	English			2		2
	History		2			
	Management		2	5		5
	Marketing		5			
	Math/Computer Science		1			
	Sociology		1			
	Urban Studies			1		1
			14	10		10
185.167	**Store Manager**	ESI				
	Accountancy		1	1		1
	Classics		1			
	Economics		1			
	History		4	1		1
	Management			5		5
	Marketing		3	1	1	2
	Math/Computer Science		2	1		1
	Modern Languages		1			
	Philosophy			1		1
	Political Science		1			
	Psychology			1		1
	Sociology		1			
			15	11	1	12

DOT	JOB TITLE	HOC	1960-1974	1975-1980 M	F	T
070.101	**Surgeon** .... (see Medical Doctor)	ISA				
012.167	**Systems Analyst/Electronic Data Processing**	ERI				
	Accountancy		8			
	Biology		1			
	Chemistry		1			
	Classics		1			
	Economics		8	2		2
	English		4			
	History		2			
	Management		23	2		2
	Marketing		9	1		1
	Math/Computer Science		32	1		1
	Modern Languages		1			
	Natural Science		1			
	Physics		2			
	Psychology		1			
	Sociology		4			
	Urban Studies		1			
			99	6		6
003.167	**Systems Engineer**	IRE				
	Art History		1			
	Economics		2			
	History		1			
	Management		3			
	Math/Computer Science		1			
	Philosophy		1			
	Physics		3			
	Psychology		1			
			13			

DOT	JOB TITLE	HOC	1960-1974	1975-1980 M	F	T
160.162	**Tax Accountant**	CES				
	Accountancy		18	10	1	11
	Economics		1	1		1
	Education			1		1
	Marketing		1			
			20	12	1	13
160.167	**Tax Administrator**	CES				
	Accountancy		6	2		2
	Economics		1	1		1
	English		1			
	Management				1	1
			8	3	1	4
110.117	**Tax Attorney**	ESA				
	Accountancy		6			
	Economics		1			
			7			
090.227	**Teacher/College**	SIA				
	Accountancy		2			
	Art History		2			
	Biology		9	1		1
	Chemistry		8			
	Classics		5			
	Economics		7			
	Education		1		1	1
	English		24			
	History		13			
	Management		3	1		1
	Marketing		1			
	Math/Computer Science		20			
	Modern Languages		14	1		1

DOT	JOB TITLE	HOC	1960-1974	1975-1980		
				M	F	T
	Physics		3			
	Psychology		9			
	Sociology		10	1		1
	Urban Studies		3			
			134	4	1	5
092.227	**Teacher/Elementary School**	SAI				
	Art History				1	1
	Biology		1	1	1	2
	Classics		3		1	1
	Economics		8	2	1	3
	Education		81	4	60	64
	English		21	2	2	4
	History		30	5	3	8
	Management		3			
	Marketing		2	1	1	2
	Math/Computer Science		5	1		1
	Modern Languages		5	1		1
	Natural Science		2		1	1
	Political Science		2	1		1
	Psychology		2		2	2
	Sociology		6		3	3
	Urban Studies		1			
			172	18	76	94
091.227	**Teacher/High School**	SAE				
	Accountancy		7			
	Art History		3			
	Biology		17	5	3	8
	Chemistry		5			
	Classics		7			
	Economics		14			
	Education		7	8	8	16
	English		86	2	3	5

DOT	JOB TITLE	HOC	1960-1974	1975-1980 M	F	T
	History		72	7	2	9
	Management		17	2	3	5
	Marketing		17	1		1
	Math/Computer Science		61	4	6	10
	Modern Languages		34		1	1
	Natural Science		10	3	2	5
	Philosophy		3			
	Physics		7	1		1
	Political Science		10			
	Psychology		2	1	2	3
	Sociology		10	3	1	4
	Urban Studies		1			
			390	**37**	**31**	**68**
099.227	**Teacher/Other** .... SIR					
	Accountancy		1	1		1
	Biology		3	1		1
	Chemistry		2	1		1
	Classics		1			
	Economics		2			
	Education		15	1	21	22
	English		16	1	4	5
	History		21	1		1
	Management		4	1	2	3
	Marketing		4		1	1
	Math/Computer Science		13		2	2
	Modern Languages		10	1	1	2
	Natural Science		2		1	1
	Physics		1			
	Political Science		2			
	Psychology		2	2		2
	Sociology		9		1	1
	Urban Studies		1	1	1	2
			109	**11**	**34**	**45**

DOT	JOB TITLE	HOC	1960-1974	1975-1980 M	F	T
094.227	**Teacher/Special Education** .... SAI					
	Education		1	2	4	6
	English		1			
	History		1			
	Marketing			1		1
	Math/Computer Science		1			
	Modern Languages		1			
	Psychology			1		1
			5	4	4	8
159.147	**Television/Radio Personnel** .... AES					
	Accountancy			1		1
	Economics		1			
	English		1			
	Modern Languages		1			
	Psychology			1		1
	Sociology		1			
			4	2		2
184.117	**Traffic Analyst/ Manager** .... ESC					
	Accountancy		1	1		1
	Art History				1	1
	Economics		2	1		1
	English		1		1	1
	History		2	1		1
	Management		5	3		3
	Marketing		1	2	1	3
			12	8	3	11
166.227	**Training Specialist** .... SEC					
	Economics		1			
	Education				1	1
	English		2			

DOT	JOB TITLE	HOC	1960-1974	1975-1980 M	F	T
	History		5			
	Management			1		1
	Marketing		1			
	Math/Computer Science		1			
	Political Science		1			
	Sociology		1			
			12	1	1	2
137.267	**Translator** .... ASI					
	Management		1			
	Modern Languages		1		1	1
			2		1	1
184.117	**Transportation Manager** .. ESC					
	Biology				1	1
	Economics		1			
	History		1	1		1
	Management		4	2		2
	Marketing		1	1		1
	Natural Science			1		1
	Sociology			1		1
	Urban Studies			1		1
			7	7	1	8
252.157	**Travel Agent** .... ECS					
	Education		1		2	2
	English		1			
			2		2	2
186.117	**Trust Officer/Bank** .... ESC					
	Accountancy			1		1
	Economics		7			
	Management		4			

DOT	JOB TITLE	HOC	1960-1974	1975-1980 M	F	T
	Marketing		1		1	1
	Math/Computer Science		1			
	Political Science		1			
			14	1	1	2
199.167	**Urban Planner**	ICR				
	Economics		2			
	History		1			
	Marketing		1			
	Natural Science				1	1
	Political Science		2			
	Sociology		4		1	1
	Urban Studies		1	1		1
			11	1	2	3
070.101	**Urologist**	ISA				
	(see Medical Doctor)					
073.101	**Veterinarian**	IRS				
	Accountancy		1			
	Biology		1		1	1
	Natural Science		1			
			3		1	1
045.107	**Vocational Counselor**	SIA				
	English		1			
	Political Science			1		1
	Psychology		2	1	1	2
	Sociology		1			
	Urban Studies		3		1	1
			7	2	2	4

DOT	JOB TITLE	HOC	1960-1974	1975-1980		
				M	F	T
131.067	**Writer/Fiction and Nonfiction**	ASI				
	English		2			
	Political Science		1			
	Sociology		1			
			4			
131.267	**Writer/Technical**	ASI				
	Economics		1			
	English		3	2		2
	Marketing		1			
			5	2		2

ABOUT THE AUTHORS

Lawrence R. Malnig earned his B.A. in French at Brooklyn College, his M.A. in Italian and Spanish at Columbia University, and his Ph.D. in Counseling Psychology at New York University. In 1951, he founded the Counseling Center at Saint Peter's College and since that time has had an abiding interest in the psychological needs of students, and in the outcomes of their education. With L. Augustine Grady, S.J., and Dr. Thaddeus V. Tuleja, he published the first survey of the Saint Peter's College alumni titled *Peacocks On Parade* which won national recognition. His more than 25 articles in newspapers, and in popular and professional magazines, include *Anxiety and Academic Prediction; Uptight Students;* and *Teen-Ager: Rebel With A Cause.* He has served on the editorial boards of The Catholic Psychological Record and The Vocational Guidance Quarterly. In addition to campus counseling and career-options research, Dr. Malnig conducts a private practice in psychotherapy and is Psychological Consultant in Communication and Administration to diploma and collegiate nursing schools. In his Ridgefield, New Jersey, community, he has served on the Board of Education and The Mayor's Environmental Committee. He is a member of the Board of Trustees of Elizabeth Seton College in Westchester County, New York.

Anita Malnig, a 1971 graduate, is herself a statistic in this book. After majoring in English Literature, she began her writing and editing career at the Golden Book Division of Western Publishing Company. She edited *Children's Playcraft* and *Children's Digest* for Parents Magazine Enterprises and served as children's book editor for Random House and Children's Television Workshop. She has published five of her own books and taught a course in book publishing in the New York University Continuing Education Program. Ms. Malnig, a consulting editor for a children's computer magazine, is also writing a series of nature books. She lives and works in San Francisco.

A special word of thanks to James C.G. Conniff, whose expertise did much to make this book the useful instrument we want it to be.

An Introduction to
ECOLOGY
AND
POPULATION
BIOLOGY

Thomas C. Emmel
UNIVERSITY OF FLORIDA

W · W · NORTON & COMPANY

New York · London

W. W. Norton & Company, Inc., 500 Fifth Avenue, New York, N.Y. 10110
W. W. Norton & Company Ltd., 25 New Street Square, London EC4A 3NT

Library of Congress Cataloging in Publication Data

Emmel, Thomas C
  An introduction to ecology and population biology.

  Includes bibliographical references.
  1.   Ecology.   2.   Population.   3.   Man—Influence
on nature.   I.   Title.
QH541.E45   1973   574.5′24   72-14170
ISBN 0-393-09371-9 (pbk.)

Illustration credits appear on page viii.

PRINTED IN THE UNITED STATES OF AMERICA

5 6 7 8 9 0

CONTENTS

ILLUSTRATION ACKNOWLEDGEMENTS   viii

PREFACE   ix

1. POPULATIONS AND ECOLOGY   1

    Why Study Ecology and Population Biology?   1

    The Levels of Organization of Ecology   2

    Evolution and Orderliness in Ecological Systems   5

    Summary   11

2. SOME BASIC PRINCIPLES OF ECOLOGY: ELEMENTS AND ENERGY   12

    Biogeochemical Cycles in Ecosystems   12

    How Man May Change Biogeochemical Cycles   21

    Energy Flow in Ecosystems   24

    Summary   37

3. SOME BASIC PRINCIPLES OF ECOLOGY: INTERACTIONS OF ORGANISMS   38

    Predation   39

    Symbiosis   49

    Competition   57

    Summary   61

4. THE ORGANIZATION OF POPULATIONS   63

Properties of a Population   63
Dispersion   64
Social Organization and Dispersion   67
Population Dispersal   71
Summary   75

5. POPULATION GROWTH AND REGULATION   78

Density   78
Growth   80
Biotic Potential   84
Population Growth Form   84
Population Regulation   87
Population Fluctuations   92
Summary   97

6. THE ECOLOGY OF COMMUNITIES   99

Differentiation in a Community   99
Lake Communities   100
Dominance in a Community   101
Productivity and Associated Concepts   103
Succession   104
Major Climax Formations   107
Climax Communities: Their Importance   119
Summary   120

7. ENVIRONMENTAL ALTERATION   121

Fire   122
Agricultural Clearing   124
Defoliation and Bombing   126
Urban Expansion   129
Clear-cutting of Forests   131
Public Works Projects   132
Summary   135

8. POLLUTION   136

Water Pollution   136
Air Pollution   141

Effects of Air Pollution 143
Solid Waste Pollution 145
Pesticides and Pollution Problems 148
Biological Control 153
Summary 156

9. POPULATION GROWTH IN MAN 157

The Population Explosion: Nature of the Problem 157
Population Growth in Primitive Societies 160
Population Growth in Modern Societies 164
Contraception and Family-Planning Programs 169
Abortion 172
Sterilization 173
Prospects for the Future 174
Summary 175

ADDITIONAL READING 176
GLOSSARY 178
INDEX 183

Illustration Acknowledgements

All uncredited photographs are by the author.

FRONTISPIECE: NASA. FIG. 1-2: Redrawn from Heinrich Walter, *Die Vegetation der Erde* (Jena: Veb Gustav Fischer-Verlag, 1964) after Beard in T. W. Richards, *The Tropical Rain Forests*, Cambridge, 1952. FIG. 1-3: Redrawn from Elna Bakker, *An Island Called California* (Berkeley and Los Angeles: University of California Press, 1971). FIG. 1-4: Redrawn from Orlando Park, *Ecology* 19 (1938): 219. Copyright by The Ecological Society of America. FIG. 2-1: Redrawn from Frank B. Salisbury, *Science* 136 (1962): 17–26. Copyright 1962 by the American Association for the Advancement of Science. FIG. 2-2: After Fig. 1, "The carbon cycle in the ecosystem" from *Environmental Insight* by Robert M. Chute (Harper & Row, 1971), p. 45. FIG. 2-9: A, B, D: Charles L. Hogue. E: Redrawn from Elna Bakker, *An Island Called California* (Berkeley and Los Angeles: University of California Press, 1971). FIG. 2-10: Redrawn from Elna Bakker, *An Island Called California* (Berkeley and Los Angeles: University of California Press, 1971.) FIG. 2-12: Data from H. T. Odum. FIG. 2-13: Redrawn from Arthur S. Boughey, *Ecology of Populations*, © 1968, The Macmillan Company, New York. FIG. 3-1: Redrawn from Francis E. Lloyd, *The Carnivorous Plants*, © 1942, The Ronald Press Company, New York. FIG. 3-2: Original painting by Anthony Angell. FIG. 3-3: Original painting by Byron B. Wolfe. FIGS. 3-4, 3-5: From R. W. Ficken et al., *Science* 173 (1971): 936–939. Copyright 1971 by the American Association for the Advancement of Science. FIG. 3-6: A, B: Charles L. Hogue. FIG. 3-9: A: Julian P. Donahue. B, C: Charles L. Hogue. FIG. 3-10: B: Julian P. Donahue. FIG. 3-11: Julian P. Donahue. FIG. 3-12: Redrawn by permission of the publishers from *Life: An Introduction to Biology* by George Gaylord Simpson, Colin S. Pittendrigh, Lewis H. Tiffany, © 1957 by Harcourt Brace Jovanovich, Inc. FIG. 3-13: After Gause, 1934. FIG. 3-14: Redrawn from Robert MacArthur and Joseph Connell, *The Biology of Populations* (New York: John Wiley & Sons. Inc., 1966). FIG. 4-3: Redrawn by permission of the author from Irven DeVore, *Primate Behavior* (New York: Holt, Rinehart and Winston, Inc., 1965). FIG. 4-4: Redrawn from Archie F. Carr, "Orientation Problems in the High Seas Travel and Terrestrial Movements of Marine Turtles," *American Scientist* 50 (1962). FIG. 4-5: From Carr and Hirth, *American Museum Novitates* no. 2091 (1962). FIG. 4-6: Redrawn from U.S. Fish and Wildlife Service material. FIG. 5-3: Redrawn from H. G. Andrewartha and L. C. Birch, *The Distribution and Abundance of Animals*. Copyright © 1954 by the University of Chicago Press. FIG. 5-5: Lynx and hare redrawn from the book *Palmer's Fieldbook of Mammals* by E. Laurence Palmer. Copyright © 1957 by E. Laurence Palmer. Published by E. P. Dutton & Co., Inc., and used with their permission. FIG. 5-6: Fox and lemming redrawn from the book *Palmer's Fieldbook of Mammals* by E. Laurence Palmer. Copyright © 1957 by E. Laurence Palmer. Published by E. P. Dutton & Co., Inc., and used with their permission. Graph after Chitty, 1950. FIG. 6-2: After Fig. 9, "A diagram of forest succession from annual weeds to mature forest" in *The Ecology of Man: An Ecosystem Approach* by Robert Leo Smith (Harper & Row, 1972, p. 15). FIG. 6-3: Redrawn from Elna Bakker, *An Island Called California* (Berkeley and Los Angeles: University of California Press, 1971). FIG. 6-8: Charles L. Hogue. FIG. 6-10: Charles L. Hogue. FIG. 6-11: Charles L. Hogue. FIG. 7-3: Gordon H. Orians. FIG. 7-4: Charles L. Hogue. FIG. 7-5: James Rose. FIG. 7-6: David Ehrenfeld. FIG. 8-1: Chuck Woods, IFAS, University of Florida. FIG. 8-2: Top: Los Angeles County Air Pollution Control District Photo. FIG. 8-3: Rondal Partridge. FIG. 8-4: Chuck Woods, IFAS, University of Florida.

PREFACE

Environmental and population crises have awakened widespread public interest in *ecology*, a word that prior to the 1960s seemed to refer solely to a little-known backwater area of biology. Now thousands of people are daily involved in making ecological decisions, from buying phosphate-free detergents to joining conservation organizations to turn their concern for the environment into political action. Yet, because this public interest in ecology has developed so recently, few of us have had the opportunity to obtain a broadly informative introduction to the subject.

This book was written for the educated general public and for students who want a good basic understanding of their environment, the need for preserving it, and the value of the natural populations that depend on it. The first half of the book develops an understanding of basic ecological principles and how they are involved in natural populations of plants and animals. After this preparation the remaining chapters apply these principles to problems of the human population, including population growth and the wide spectrum of environmental pollution and landscape alteration.

This book came to be written purely and simply because no concise elementary presentation of ecology was available. In the comprehensive biological sciences courses taken by several thousand undergraduates yearly at the University of Florida, a primary problem has been to find a text that would emphasize the ecological approach without becoming need-lessly detailed, would treat the salient aspects of population biology without bogging down in theoretical models, would emphasize man, and would be written in a style and depth appropriate to a course enrolling both science and non-science majors. While many good books of collected readings were available, a text of appropriate length built around the theme of ecology and population biology seemed hard to find. Thus this book emerged from both educational need and practical experience in teaching ecology to students with no previous college course in biology. But it is intended equally for all concerned readers who want a better biological under-standing of the need for environmental conservation and pop-ulation control.

I am indebted to many colleagues, students, and friends who have assisted in the evolution and writing of this book. I particularly wish to thank Michael M. Sligh of the University of Florida for his constant encouragement and careful edi-torial assistance on the manuscript. Three fine secretaries, Eu-genia Kelly, Mary H. Sligh, and Ruth F. Smith, have worked long and diligently in typing the manuscript. In preparing this book, I have also appreciated the careful assistance and patience of Kenneth B. Demaree, Mary Pell, and the editorial staff of W. W. Norton & Company. To all, I am most grate-ful.

THOMAS C. EMMEL

Gainesville, Florida
November 1972

An Introduction to
ECOLOGY
AND
POPULATION
BIOLOGY

The planet earth is a spaceship with limited supplies and a defined ecology. It is the only body in our solar system capable of supporting life as we know it. Will we render it uninhabitable, or learn to take care of the ecology of our ship in time?

1
POPULATIONS AND ECOLOGY

Why Study Ecology and Population Biology?

Ecology as a word and as a concern has come into its own in the 1970s. The average person today has heard more about "ecology" than any other area in biology. Daily he is inundated with the flow of newspaper and periodical articles, news broadcasts, and advertisements, all telling him the latest on the ecological crises or potential environmental catastrophes facing his community or even his world. Atomic blasts under a remote Aleutian island, oil spills off a coastal beach, mercury in the consumer's swordfish, DDT on his lettuce, strontium-90 in his milk, a sea-level canal in Panama that may allow poisonous sea snakes to move from the Pacific Ocean into pleasant Caribbean tourist beaches—all clamor for the intelligent citizen's attention, evaluation, and action where possible. Yet ecology is probably the most complex and least understood area of biology today, while being the biological discipline most important and relevant to the future of our world. Thus one purpose of this book is to provide an overall, rigorous, yet easily understandable introduction to ecological concepts and the flow of life, energy, and materials in the natural world.

1

Since the environmental dangers to the well-being of the human species are in large part the result of population increase, we must be especially concerned with the ways in which populations of organisms, particularly man, grow and function. In particular, how are they limited or left unregulated by natural as well as man-caused factors? Thus a second goal of this book is to familiarize the reader with the basic principles involved in the biology of natural populations of plants and animals, and then to apply these lessons and analyses to human population problems, including population growth and the broad spectrum of environmental pollution and landscape alteration. Familiarity with these points should give the reader a clearer view of the importance and immediacy of the population problems and ecological decisions facing us, and we may hope that your generation will provide the wise conclusions and actions necessary to preserve and improve human life and society as we have come to know it.

With these goals in mind, let us now look into the basic organization of ecology as a science and the biological systems it encompasses.

The Levels of Organization of Ecology

Ecology is the study of the interrelationships between organisms and their environment. It thus deals with nearly all levels of organization of life on earth, from the individual animal or plant to the whole community of organisms living in an area to the effects on these organisms of the climatic and even geologic factors that make up their physical surroundings. In the ultimate and broadest sense, ecologists (students of ecology) are involved in "building an understanding of the role of living things in the structure and function of the universe." * In practice, ecologists tend to specialize in one

* Robert M. Chute, *Environmental Insight* (New York: Harper & Row, 1971), p. 43.

particular level of organization in their research: the individual, the population, the community, or the ecosystem.

Autecology is the study of the individual organism. This is the smallest working unit for an ecologist, and the investigator is interested in what the individual requires and tolerates, its way of life, its functioning in the environment throughout all stages of its life cycle.

Population ecology is the study of populations of organisms. A population consists of all the individuals of a species living in an area. Population ecologists wish to explain the behavior of populations—their stability, rapid increase, or decline. In the southeastern United States, water hyacinths are far too numerous on the rivers and lakes, causing navigational and recreational problems for man, while Ivory-bill Woodpeckers are on the verge of extinction. Cockroaches live by the millions in old student housing on many university campuses, while the wilderness-loving Whooping Cranes number less than forty individuals. People in the United States expend great amounts of money to kill hyacinths and cockroaches and save Ivory-bills and Whooping Cranes. The reasons for these opposing situations of explosion and extinction are not only interesting from the practical and aesthetic viewpoints, respectively. They teach lessons that may be applied to man's current population explosion (man was a species that exhibited near stability in population size until about 1600 A.D).

Community ecology is the study of biotic communities. A biotic community is composed of all the organisms of all species living in a particular area. A pond community, for instance, with its plant and animal inhabitants, may contain a very complex set of biological interrelations which, when studied in detail, provide invaluable information on the flow of energy and chemical elements through organisms and eventually to man.

An **ecosystem** includes both the biotic community and the physical environment in an area. The Mojave Desert in southern California is a fairly simple terrestrial ecosystem, with rather few plant and animal species, high insolation (amount of sunlight), and a limited amount of rainfall (normally less than ten inches) each year. On the other hand, a

Fig. 1-1. The Mojave Desert in southern California (top), a relatively simple and orderly ecosystem with few species of organisms, and a tropical rain forest, a place of great diversity yet intricate orderliness in an evolutionary and ecological sense.

tropical rain forest, which receives some 150 to 200 inches of rain per year, is the most complex terrestrial ecosystem in existence, with thousands of plant and animal species found in a single square mile (Fig. 1-1). Both the desert and the tropical rain forest ecosystems will remain in the same general condition over hundreds of years if undisturbed by natural disaster, man, or climatic changes. A home garden or an orange grove, though, is a very artificial ecosystem that is highly dependent on man for its continued existence. Why do these man-created ecosystems differ so greatly in stability from natural ecosystems? Why are gardens and orange groves more desirable to man? Why won't they persist if man does not continue to maintain them? We will look at some of the answers to such questions in the remainder of this chapter and Chapter 2.

Evolution and Orderliness in Ecological Systems

An ecosystem's component organisms and the factors making up the physical environment are organized into a system that is analogous in many ways to the organization of an individual organism. The interrelation between organs in the body, or components of an ecosystem, is not haphazard. It has a definite history of development, a particular spatial orientation, an involvement of time in operation of the system, and an involvement of specific energetic sequences (food is consumed, processed, and the molecules re-utilized). Thus ecosystems are characterized by four major kinds of orderliness: **evolutionary, spatial, temporal,** and **metabolic** orderliness.

Evolutionary Orderliness

The species of plants and animals living in a given region are the most recent products of organic evolution. Each is adapted or adjusted to the particular environment it lives in through **differential reproduction,** which results in what we call **evolution,** that is, change in a species' characteristics, even the development of new species. Differential reproduction simply means that the best adapted individuals of a species tend to leave more offspring on the average than do less well adapted genetic variants. We call this result "natural selection" or "survival of the fittest individuals." When we consider the whole biotic community in an ecosystem, we see that the plant and animal species have not evolved independently of each other. Instead of a miscellaneous collection of kinds of organisms, the species composition of an ecosystem is *ordered.* There has been a coevolution of the plant and animal components of an ecosystem; mutual adjustments of species have taken place through natural selection. Thus the biotic parts of the ecosystem form a cohesive whole because they have shared a common recent evolutionary history, adjusting to each other and to the special set of environmental factors prevailing in that terrestrial or aquatic area.

Spatial Orderliness

An ecosystem does not contain a miscellaneous assortment of adaptively unrelated species; nor are these species distributed in a casual manner. The placement of individuals is specific for different species. Each animal or plant lives in a particular place, which may be in soil, above soil, in the tops of trees, in flower heads, in the shallow margin of a pond, or under rocks. This spatial arrangement is determined by each species' **ecological niche,** which is simply a way of life unique to each species. The niche includes the species' physical **habitat** (the place where the organisms live) and **adaptive strategy** (how the species acquires energy and makes its living). The problem of defining the concept of niche has been a subject of much debate among ecologists, but almost all agree that it is more than just a place on a shelf, that is, a physical space inhabited by the organism. It involves the organism's activities as well.

Spatial orderliness is frequently manifested as **stratification** in an ecosystem; the living organisms in an aquatic or terrestrial community seem to be arranged in vertical layers. In a deciduous forest, for example, one passes through wholly different sets of species as one goes from the soil up through the lower-story vegetation to the uppermost forest canopy. The extent of this stratification becomes quite complex in tropical rain forests (Fig. 1-2), where the number of species is greatest. Even animal communities often exhibit stratification in their physical distribution among foraging areas or nest sites (Fig. 1-3).

Temporal Orderliness

Organisms in an ecosystem are not randomly active through the 24-hour day; instead, each species has a particular time of maximum activity. This often permits many more species to exist in an area than if all species carried on their activities at one particular time or if their activity periods commonly overlapped. In **daily periodism** an organism's principal activities, such as feeding and moving about, are limited to certain hours in the 24-hour day; some activities may be at night and others in the daytime. A particular type of daily periodism is **nocturnal** or **diurnal periodism,** in which the activities of the organism take place only at night or only in the daylight hours (Fig. 1-4). On a longer time scale, **lunar periodism** is characteristic of many marine communities especially. Microscopic animals and plants called plankton will migrate vertically in the ocean depths in accord with the phase of the moon. **Breeding** or **reproductive seasons** are common examples of temporal orderliness in biotic communities: species utilize particular times of the year to reproduce (in the case of animals, usually when the maximum amount of food is available for rearing young).

Metabolic Orderliness

In an ecosystem, transformations of energy and materials follow definite, orderly paths. Materials are cycled in **biogeochemical cycles.** This term simply refers to the cycling of chemical elements through the organisms in a biotic (living) community and their physical environment. Few chemical elements are permanently lost from the community; hence transformations of matter are said to be cyclical. Energy is

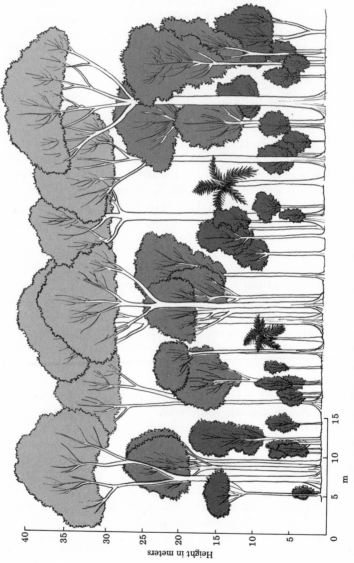

Fig. 1-2. Stratification in a tropical rain forest, as seen in vertical transect.

Height in meters

0   5   10   15   20   25   30   35   40

m   5   10   15

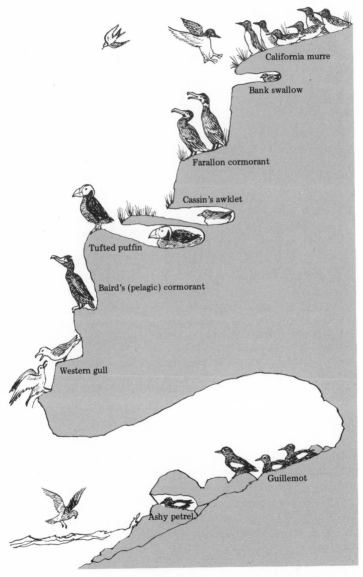

Fig. 1-3. Typical nest-site preferences of some California seabirds, showing niches and stratification of species in a rookery.

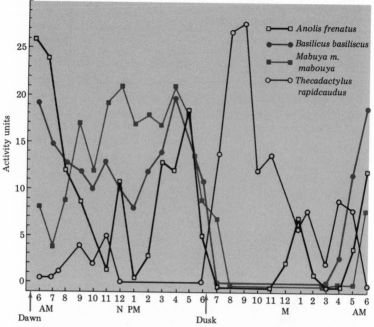

Fig. 1-4. The daily activity patterns of four Panamanian forest lizards. One species is a nocturnal gecko (*Thecadactylus rapidcaudus*); the other three species are diurnal. *Anolis* is an arboreal lizard similar to the Carolina "chameleon" sold in pet stores. *Basiliscus* is a large lizard that dwells along stream banks. *Mabuya* is a ground-dwelling, forest skink lizard. Each lizard species utilizes a different portion of the 24-hour day for its principal period of activity.

also transferred in orderly sequence within ecosystems. However, this transfer is *not* cyclical, because some energy is lost at every step and at the end of a chain of transfers. We shall consider these problems in more detail in Chapter 2. An understanding of these natural cycles will make the cycling and accumulation of such non-natural chemicals as pesticides immediately comprehensible. When we understand the relationships between these man-made chemical substances and natural cycles, we can better grasp their importance to man's present and future well-being.

Summary

Ecology is the scientific study of the interrelationships between living organisms and their environment, the physical world around them. It bears on every aspect of our lives, but is becoming more and more a vital topic to consider as our current population crisis grows in magnitude and our environment is further changed by man's actions. Ecology may be studied on the level of the individual, population, community, or ecosystem. Ecosystems, composed of biotic communities and their physical environment, exhibit evolutionary, spatial, temporal, and metabolic orderliness. The concepts of differential reproduction (natural selection), coevolution, ecological niche, habitat, adaptive strategy, stratification, and various types of periodism in activity are all necessary for an understanding of the structure and functioning of a biotic community.

2
SOME BASIC PRINCIPLES OF ECOLOGY: ELEMENTS AND ENERGY

In this chapter we consider in detail how chemical elements and energy flow through the ecosystem. Understanding these natural cycles thoroughly will help us understand such problems as how pesticides circulate in an ecosystem, the effects of mercury pollution, or the measures needed to capture more energy for food to feed man's expanding population on earth.

Biogeochemical Cycles in Ecosystems

Of the ninety-odd elements known to occur in nature, about forty are known to be required by living organisms. They are essential to maintain life. These chemical elements tend to be used over and over again, or to be *cycled*. They circulate in the **biosphere** (a term used to refer to all the living organisms on earth) in characteristic, more or less circular paths from environment to organisms and back to the environment again. Thus biogeochemical cycles involve pathways of ele-

ments moving repeatedly between inorganic forms and organic molecules. A summary of the biogeochemical cycles on
our planet earth is given in Figure 2-1. It can be readily seen
in this figure that there are several possible locations in the
environment where elements may end up in inorganic form,

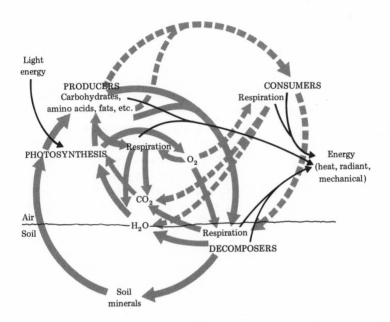

Fig. 2-1. Biogeochemical cycles on earth. Cycles of carbon, oxygen, hydrogen, soil minerals, and energy through the living organisms of the earth's biotic communities are indicated (nonbiological
transformations are not shown). Solid lines show essential transformations between producers and decomposers. Broken lines indicate
that consumers are not theoretically essential to a cycling of elements. Dotted lines show energy transfer from input as light energy to expenditure. Forked lines indicate that not all energy is
lost through respiratory processes, but that some may enter the external environment via other metabolic and physical functions of
the organism. Producers on earth are the photosynthesizers—the
chlorophyll-containing plants. Consumers include the animals and
many parasitic and saprophytic plants. Decomposers are primarily
microorganisms, although it is sometimes technically difficult to
draw a line between them and certain consumers. Water is indicated at the soil-air boundary because it usually enters metabolic
reactions by first being taken up through plant-root systems.

and indeed the rate and "perfection" [*] of the cycle depend on which portion of the environment acts as a **reservoir** for the element. The cycles in which the element is returned to the environment as rapidly as it is removed by living organisms are said to be more perfect cycles than those in which part of the material is locked up in inaccessible chemical forms or geological formations for extended times.

Gaseous Cycles

These are more nearly "perfect" than other biogeochemical cycles in that the elements circulated do not become inaccessible to organisms over long periods. The gaseous cycles are the **carbon, nitrogen, oxygen,** and **hydrogen cycles.** These elements are moved about in tremendous amounts, with the earth's atmosphere serving as the main inorganic storage reservoir. While the four elements having gaseous cycles are only 10 percent of the forty essential elements, they constitute about 97.2 percent of the bulk of protoplasm (living matter) and cycle the most easily. We will examine two of these cycles briefly.

The **carbon cycle** (Fig. 2-2) is a good example of a "perfect" cycle. Carbon dioxide in the atmosphere (and dissolved in water) forms the principal inorganic reservoir of carbon. The photosynthetic reactions of green plants incorporate carbon dioxide from the air with water from the soil and through a series of chemical rearrangements produce organic compounds called **carbohydrates,** which include carbon atoms as a basic molecular "backbone." If the green plant should die, these organic compounds are broken down by the actions of decomposer organisms such as bacteria. As a waste product resulting from the respiration of decomposer organisms, carbon dioxide is immediately released back to the atmospheric reservoir. Should the green plant be eaten by an herbivorous or omnivorous animal, the carbohydrates and other carbon-containing molecules from the plant will be bro-

---

[*] Perfection in an ecological sense refers to the completeness of the cycling process, i.e., an element moving uniformly through all stages of the biogeochemical cycle without being held up for long periods at any point.

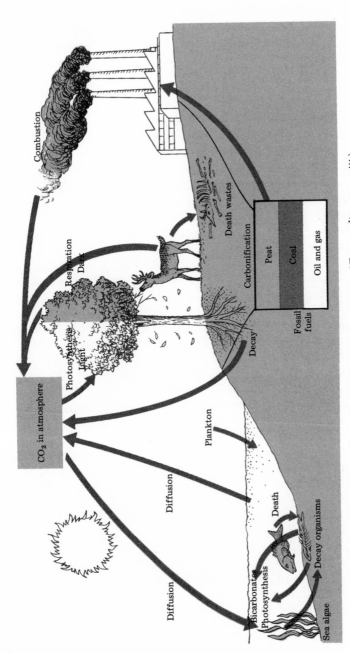

Fig. 2-2. The carbon cycle in an ecosystem. (*For credit see p. viii.*)

ken down in the animal's digestive system and body cells, and will eventually be synthesized into still different carbon compounds. Carnivores feeding on the flesh of these animals will break down and assimilate the compounds and re-use the carbon atoms in new organic molecules. In the end, though, respiration in these animal cells results in carbon being breathed out to the atmospheric reservoir in the form of carbon dioxide. Alternately, decomposer organisms break down the cellular organic molecules upon the death of the animal, releasing carbon dioxide to the atmosphere. Under certain conditions in past eras of geologic time, the carbon present in plants and animals was preserved in fossil fuels such as peat, coal, oil, and gas, and in rock formations such as limestone. Burning of the temporary fuel reservoirs and weathering of limestone return carbon to the atmosphere.

We can see by referring again to Figure 2-2 how important each part of the carbon cycle is. Should the green plants be destroyed, carbon would be unable to move from the inorganic atmospheric reservoir of carbon dioxide to organic compounds in protoplasm. If the decomposers in a biotic community were eliminated, organic matter from dead plants and animals would accumulate rapidly and the vital carbon atoms would be locked up, destroying the cycle.

The **nitrogen cycle** is another very complex, but more or less perfect, gaseous cycle (Fig. 2-3). About 78 percent of the atmosphere is nitrogen gas (N_2), the largest gaseous reservoir of any element. In its gas form, nitrogen is useless to most organisms. However, certain **nitrogen-fixing bacteria and algae** found in soils and wet habitats can convert inorganic N_2 into forms, especially **nitrates,** that are immediately usable by plants. Many of these nitrogen-fixing bacteria live in intimate association with **legume** plants (members of the pea family), in little **nodules** on the roots of clover, alfalfa, or other legumes (Fig. 2-4). The bacteria fix ° nitrogen from the air by combining it with oxygen in the form of nitrates (NO_3), which the host plant or adjacent plants can absorb through their root tissue for use in protein synthesis. It has been estimated that for the biosphere as a whole one to six pounds of

° To fix in a chemical sense means to form a solid from the gaseous form.

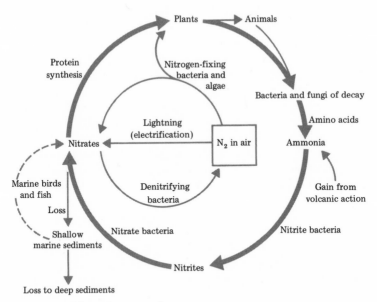

Fig. 2-3. The nitrogen cycle.

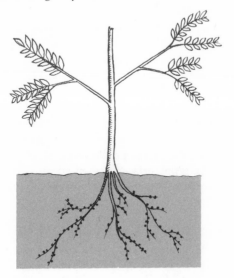

Fig. 2-4. Nodules containing nitrogen-fixing bacteria on roots of a legume plant.

nitrogen per acre per year are fixed from the air. In very fertile areas with a heavy concentration of legumes and nitrogen-fixing bacteria, up to 200 pounds of nitrogen per acre may be fixed! In water and moist soil, such as in oriental rice paddies, blue-green algae often perform the essential function of nitrogen-fixing. Increased yields result from adding extra algal cultures to these rice fields.

In the tissues of the plant whose roots absorb nitrates, the nitrogen atoms are used principally to synthesize amino acids, which are built into proteins. Several more organic rearrangements follow if the plant's protein molecules are passed through the digestive tracts and body cells of herbivorous animals and then (when herbivores are eaten) into the bodies of carnivores. When the plant or animal dies, decomposing bacteria and fungi cause the body to decay so that the nitrogen-containing amino acids are broken down, releasing ammonia gas (NH_3). **Nitrite bacteria** can convert this poisonous ammonia into simple nitrite (NO_2) molecules, and still other bacteria (**nitrate bacteria**) in the soil can add a third oxygen atom to nitrites to produce nitrates. At this point, we have gone full cycle, because plants in the area now have a usable form of nitrogen again. Note (Fig. 2-3) that nitrogen may be removed from the nitrates in the soil by **denitrifying bacteria** and returned to the atmospheric reservoir, from which it can be released again by either nitrogen-fixing bacteria or **electrification** by lightning. In the latter case, the energy of a lightning bolt passing through the atmosphere binds nitrogen and oxygen together into nitrates, which precipitate onto the soil from the air during electrical storms.

Thus the air is the greatest reservoir and safety valve of the system. Nitrogen is continually entering the air by the action of denitrifying bacteria. Nitrogen is continually returning to the cycle through the action of nitrogen-fixing bacteria or blue-green algae and through the action of lightning. Loss from the cycle occurs at the nitrate stage, when erosion and leaching of soils by rain wash nitrates into rivers and eventually into the ocean basins. Here they may be returned rather promptly to terrestrial ecosystems if marine birds and fishes that return to land or are brought there by man have fed on organisms utilizing nitrates from the shallow sediments near the shore. If nitrates in the shallow marine sediments are not absorbed by eelgrass, phytoplankton (microscopic free-floating plants), or other marine plants, they are gradually lost to deeper marine sediments where they re-enter the nitrogen cycle only upon the later geologic uplift of these sedimentary beds.

Sedimentary Cycles

These are said to be "imperfect" cycles because the constituent elements end up in sedimentary rock, a reservoir from which recycling is very slow. We have seen that carbon, nitrogen, oxygen, and hydrogen, constituting about 97.2 percent of the bulk of protoplasm, cycle quite easily because the principal reservoir in such elemental cycles is the gaseous form in the atmosphere. The rest of the approximately 36 elements comprising 2.8 percent of plant and animal tissues tend to go literally downhill in terrestrial ecosystems. Once they have been removed through erosion and other means of downhill transport, they have no immediate way of returning and hence their cycles extend across long periods of geologic time.

The **phosphorus cycle** is an excellent example of a sedimentary cycle (Fig. 2-5). Phosphorus is a necessary element in the hereditary material DNA, in other vital cellular molecules, and in the structure of bone in vertebrate animals. The principal reservoir for the cycle is phosphate rock formed in past geologic ages, although excrement deposits (guano) by fish-eating sea birds and fossil bone deposits contribute substantial phosphate in certain areas of the world. Erosion by rainfall and the runoff of streams dissolves phosphate out of these reservoir sources, forming a phosphorus "pool" in the soil. This makes phosphorus available to plants, which absorb it through their roots for use in cellular syntheses. Animals of ʌin phosphorus from plants; upon death or through normal excretion of waste products from the body, they return phosphorus to the dissolved phosphorus pool.

However, in the dissolved state much phosphorus is lost by downhill transport into shallow marine sediments. Some of this phosphorus is returned to land by sea birds who deposit

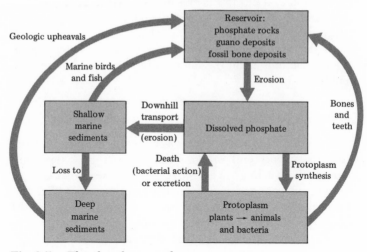

Fig. 2-5. The phosphorus cycle.

excrement on the shores and by migratory fish such as salmon and steelhead who carry phosphorus in their bones far inland on their return to fresh-water spawning grounds. These birds and large predatory fish have fed on smaller fish and other marine organisms, which in turn have fed on microscopic plankton. These plankton have incorporated phosphorus into their bodies from the shallow coastal sediments and estuarine waters where their early development normally takes place. But the majority of phosphate compounds is carried and lost to deep marine sediments by underwater currents and geologic subsidence and brought back to terrestrial reservoirs only through major geologic upheavals millions of years apart. The lack of sunlight for photosynthesis in the ocean depths, the low temperatures, and the high pressure there all prevent the extensive growth of plankton. Thus phosphorus on the deep ocean floor is simply not recycled before being covered by additional sediment and lost to the living world.

It appears to many experts that the present means of returning phosphorus to the cycle may soon be inadequate. There is no extensive upwelling of sediments currently in much of the world, and the transport function of formerly huge colonies of sea birds is not as extensive today as in past ages because of the depletion of many of these populations. Man does mine extensive amounts of phosphates from the earth, especially from central Florida, but the excessive use of these phosphorus materials as artificial fertilizers causes rapid loss through erosion and hence reduces the cycling effect still further.

How Man
May Change
Biogeochemical Cycles

One might think that the activities of man could have little effect upon such massive world-wide cycling of elements as goes on in the biogeochemical cycles just discussed. Up to recent times, this appeared true. Man did little to change the cycles except on a local scale; extensive deforestation and clearing might lower the rate of carbon or nitrogen cycling, or legume crops might be planted in rotation with more commercially valuable crops such as corn or cotton to restore nitrogen levels in the soil. However, we are now coming to realize that long-term effects on this almost inconceivably massive cycling may be occurring in ways we did not expect. A prime example of man's alteration of a major biogeochemical cycle is found in the carbon cycle.

Normally, the amount of CO_2 in the atmosphere is in equilibrium with dissolved CO_2 in fresh and salt water. Movement of the gas by diffusion from the air reservoir into the aquatic reservoirs equals the rate of diffusion of CO_2 back into the air from the water. From the CO_2 in the air or in water carbohydrate compounds are made by the interaction of sunlight and chlorophyll molecules in photosynthesis. Again, the amount of carbon tied up in protoplasm in this manner is in dynamic equilibrium with the CO_2 in the gaseous reservoir state. But over the past several hundred years man has been burning fossil fuels such as coal and oil at higher and higher rates. We are currently adding some six to nine *billion tons* of carbon per year to the atmosphere through the combustion of fossil fuels. Not too surprisingly, this is changing the composition of the earth's atmosphere. Let us look at the following data collected on the composition of the atmosphere since 1860:

Year	Carbon Dioxide Content of Air (parts per million)
1860	283 ppm of CO_2
1900	290 ppm
1960	330 ppm

In 100 years, the carbon dioxide concentration has increased an average of 47 molecules out of every million total molecules in the air. Currently we are burning between six and nine billion tons of fossil fuels per year, which would be sufficient to increase the amount of carbon dioxide in the air by 2.3 ppm per year. The measured rise of about 0.7 ppm, however, indicates that about two-thirds of the carbon dioxide released from fossil fuels is being dissolved in the sea or is increasing the total **biomass** (living weight of organisms) of land vegetation.

Even with this considerable increase, you might say CO_2 still represents only 0.03 percent of the atmosphere. Besides, more CO_2 would surely increase the rate of photosynthesis in green plants, which in turn would rapidly produce more useful oxygen. However, the amount of CO_2 in the air is critically important in maintaining the earth's temperature. Carbon dioxide, along with water vapor in the atmosphere, is translucent to the sun's electromagnetic radiation in the wavelength spectrum of visible light, but not to the longer infrared wavelengths. When solar energy (light) warms the earth's surface each day, infrared radiation (heat) is emitted back from the terrestrial sphere (Fig. 2-6). But CO_2 and water droplets do not allow these infrared wavelengths to escape, thus producing the so-called "greenhouse effect" on the earth's temperature. (In a greenhouse, the glass roof allows visible light to enter but traps the infrared radiation emitted from the interior surfaces and plants, causing a rise in temperature.) In the last hundred years there has been a 1.8° F rise in the mean temperature of the earth. This correlates precisely with the increasing amount of carbon dioxide in the air. This temperature trend, if continued, could potentially lead to the melting of the polar ice caps, which would raise sea levels drastically, to some 330 feet above present levels. Such states as Florida and most of the coastal areas around the world would be completely inundated. This predicted environmental effect gives us some idea of the importance of switching the energy sources of such major fossil-fuel consumers as power generating plants to atomic or fusion energy,

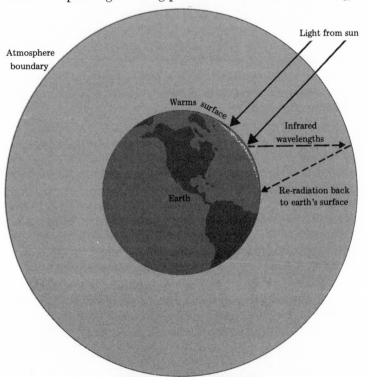

Fig. 2-6. The "greenhouse effect." Carbon dioxide and water vapor in the earth's atmosphere are translucent to the sun's electromagnetic radiation in visible wavelengths of light. These wavelengths heat the earth's surface and infrared wavelengths ("heat") are radiated back into the atmosphere. Carbon dioxide and water vapor, however, acting like glass in a greenhouse roof, do not allow these to pass. Hence the temperature of the atmosphere rises from the trapped infrared radiation.

provided that any environmental problems associated with these processes can be properly controlled.

Energy Flow in Ecosystems

Laws of Thermodynamics

In ecosystems energy is transferred in an orderly sequence, but energy flow is unidirectional, not cyclical. Only materials cycle. Some useful energy is lost as heat at every step in a chain of events, and two descriptive physical laws apply to this situation. These are the First and Second Laws of Thermodynamics.

The **First Law of Thermodynamics** deals with the conservation of matter and energy, and states that *energy cannot be created or destroyed but only changed from one form to another.* An example is given in Figure 2-7: visible light energy can be changed by the process of photosynthesis in green plants into chemical energy in the form of chemical bonds in the glucose sugar molecule. When the plant later uses this glucose molecule for food by breaking it up in the process of cellular respiration, the chemical energy present in the molecular bonds is released as heat, a third form of energy. Note that one form of light energy, infrared radiation, can result in heat energy too. The energy in the diagram is never destroyed, only changed from one form to another.

The **Second Law of Thermodynamics** states that some

(Infrared)

Light energy   Photosynthesis   Respiration   Heat energy

Chemical energy
(chemical bonds in organic molecules)

Fig. 2-7.   Some relationships among three forms of energy.

useful energy (energy available for doing work) is converted into heat energy at every transformation of energy. This heat energy escapes into the surrounding environment. When you slide a box along the floor, some of the work you are putting into pushing the box is being used up as heat energy due to friction. In the same way, when you use energy stored in muscle cells to contract your arm muscles, some of the useful energy is lost as body heat from the arm's surface skin. In other words, energy transformations in the biological as well as physical worlds are less than one hundred percent efficient. Since heat energy cannot be used easily to do work, more energy must be supplied to a biological system from outside the organism to counterbalance the inevitable loss of energy as heat. In fact, the universe as a whole is running down; it is tending towards a state of maximum **entropy,** a condition of random disorganization where all energy will be transformed into heat energy at a uniform temperature. In order to continue to function, organisms must continue to receive new supplies of energy in the ecosystem. Ultimately this energy comes from outside our earth in the form of light energy from the sun. The passage of energy through an ecosystem may be diagrammed as:

Energy has to be added constantly to the ecosystem via solar radiation. Plants convert this light energy into chemical bond energy during the process of photosynthesis, but much of the original energy is lost as heat (shortly in this chapter, we shall see just how inefficient this conversion into chemical energy really is). When plants are eaten by herbivorous animals these chemical bonds are broken and then reformed into new molecular bonds within the animals' cells. More energy is lost as heat at this stage too. When carnivores eat the herbivores, still another sequence of breaking and reforming of chemical bonds occurs, and further heat energy escapes unused by the carnivore.

Given these principles of energy transfer, how can we more precisely describe energy flow between the component species of an ecosystem? The simplest form of this flow is through the **food chain.**

The Food Chain Concept

A food chain simply transfers food energy from a given source through a series of species, each of which eats the one before itself in the chain. This repeated series of eating and being eaten is always initiated with green plants, which receive their energy from the sun. A very simple food chain is:

grass⟶cow⟶man

heat energy lost   heat

At each transfer a large proportion of the potential energy present in the chemical bonds of the food species is lost as heat. This limits the number of steps in a food chain, usually to four or five. In the aquatic ecosystem at Silver Springs, Florida, for example, one of the longer natural food chains is:

algae⟶ midge (fly)⟶ bream ⟶bass
(microscopic   larvae   (fish)
green plants)

We shall see shortly and in more detail how the amount of energy at each step limits the number of links in this chain.

A final attribute of food chains is that the shorter the food chain (or the nearer the organism is to the beginning of the chain), the greater the available energy that can be converted into biomass (living weight) and utilized in cellular respiration. In a two-step food chain of more of the potential energy initially available per pound of corn reaches man than if the corn is first fed to pigs and the swine are then eaten by man, as in this three-step food chain:

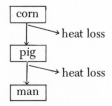

Normally we visualize food chains of the **predatory** type, where smaller organisms are eaten by larger organisms, which in turn are eaten by still larger species. Some food chains involve larger organisms being eaten by smaller species; these are the **parasitic** food chains. An example would be a deer fed upon by internal roundworms or external ticks, or a man with malarial parasites in his blood. A third special term, **saprophytic,** is given to a food chain where dead organic matter is fed upon by fungi such as mushrooms and finally bacteria. (Saprophytes are any plants that feed on dead and decaying matter.)

If we had only a series of isolated food chains to deal with in nature, the transfer of energy in an ecosystem would be very simple indeed. However, we find in any biotic community that these food chains are interlocked in a complex pattern of feeding relations that we call a **food web.**

The Food Web Concept

A food web is simply the total set of feeding relationships in a biotic community. With many interlocking food chains the community will remain stable even if one or more of these relations is altered. At Silver Springs, for instance (Fig. 2-8), we see that if one of the food species (e.g., the bream) for the bass should become rare or absent (through heavy predation by another organism, seasonal migration out of the area, and so forth), the bass are not forced to die or move out. They can feed more on the other species (mullet, caddisfly larvae, water beetles) that are in the same nutri-

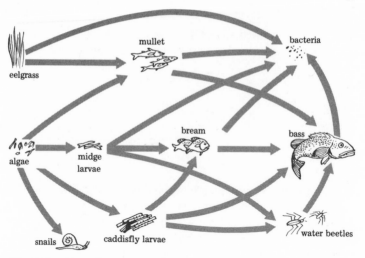

Fig. 2-8. Part of an aquatic food web at Silver Springs, Florida.

tional relationship to them as the bream. Obviously, then, a food web introduces a strong element of *stability* into an ecosystem. The more components involved, the more stable the system will probably be.

The Trophic Level

All organisms that share the same general source of nutrition are said to be at the same **trophic level.** This feeding level concept implies that these organisms obtain food through the same number of steps from plants in a food chain. The first trophic level (Fig. 2-9A) in ecosystems comprises the **producers,** organisms that photosynthesize (convert light energy from the sun into chemical-bond energy)—in other words, green plants. The **herbivores,** animals that eat plants, are the second trophic level (Fig. 2-9B). (Because herbivores are the first organism level to feed on other organisms, their trophic level is sometimes called the primary consumer trophic level.) The **carnivores,** animals that feed on herbivores, are the third trophic level (Fig. 2-9C) or secondary consumer trophic level. The **top carnivores** are animals that feed on other carnivores; they represent the fourth and sometimes even the fifth trophic levels (tertiary or quaternary consumers). The **decomposers** (Fig. 2-9D), organisms that feed upon dead organic matter, consume plants and animals from all trophic levels. They perform the instrumental role of breaking down dead plant and animal bodies, reducing them finally to inorganic soil material. Their action breaking down the fallen trunk of a pine tree (Fig. 2-9E) illustrates the sequential scheme that decomposition often follows. Large tunneling insect species such as beetles begin the gross breakdown of the wood structure. These are followed by carpenter ants, and eventually termites find the decomposing wood suitable for their tunnels. Fungi grow in the ever moister wood. Eventually bacteria perform the ultimate decay functions and reduce all the material into organic molecules, which can dissolve into the soil.

You are already probably thinking from the above discussion that a species *can* occupy more than one trophic level. Man does it daily in most parts of the world, eating meats and grains simultaneously. A bear (*Ursus*) feeds on plant material such as berries and roots (producers) and then may catch animal prey such as mice or ground squirrels (herbivores). This bear is in the second and third trophic levels simultaneously.

Returning to our original overall problem of energy transfer, we may now ask: what is the pattern of energy flow in an ecosystem in terms of these trophic levels? The general observation we can make in every ecosystem is that out of the tremendous quantities of solar energy falling on an area each year, only a tiny fraction of the light energy is actually utilized by the plants and animals living there. On the average in ecosystems around the world, more than 98 percent of the available light energy from the sun is lost and less than 2 percent is trapped by plants and stored as chemical-bond energy. At each successive transfer between trophic levels, more energy is lost via respiration and heat. This happens in aquatic ecosystems as well as terrestrial systems (Fig. 2-10). The inexorable principles which we saw expressed in the laws of thermodynamics insure that plants and animals simply are not able to utilize all the energy available to them. Figure 2-11 summarizes this general pattern in a crudely quantitative way. This can be done much more accurately by

A

Fig. 2-9. A. The first trophic level: producer organisms in a tropical rain forest in Costa Rica. B. The second trophic level: herbivores on the African plains. C. The third trophic level: predatory spider (carnivore) feeding on a tropical heliconiine butterfly. D. The fate of all trophic levels is shown in this photograph of a decomposer at work—a tropical fungus on a dead fly. E. Reduction of a fallen pine log to inorganic soil by a succession of various decomposer organisms.

B

C

D

Long-horned beetle holes

Bark beetle engraving

Woodpecker holes

Carpenter bee galleries

Termite and carpenter ant work

Dry rot fungus

As time progresses

Wood reduced to powder

E

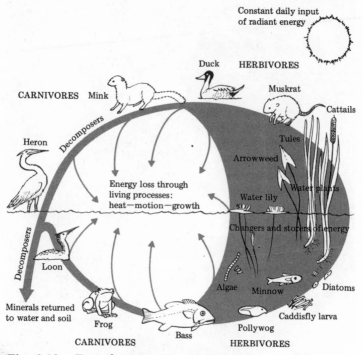

Fig. 2-10. Typical energy flow patterns through a freshwater marsh.

Fig. 2-11. Diagrammatic representation of energy loss in a typical ecosystem on earth. Sunlight enters from outside the system and most light energy passes through, with less than 2 percent trapped by photosynthesis.

calculating the ecological efficiencies of these trophic levels, which we shall now consider.

Quantifying Energy Flow in Ecosystems

We would like to be able to determine for any ecosystem, whether an agricultural field crop or a mountain forest, how much of its potential food supply each trophic level is using. In other words, how efficient is a particular level in exploiting the total amount of food available to it? This is a very practical kind of ecological question because if we know how efficient a level is in a particular environment (say, the corn plants in an Iowa field), we may be able to manipulate the environment in certain ways to increase that efficiency for the ultimate benefit of man.

Ecological efficiencies are calculated as the ratios between energy flow at different points along the food chain. An ecologist named Howard T. Odum did a classic study on the Silver Springs, Florida, ecosystem in which he measured how many units of energy were captured by each trophic level over a year's time. The results of his study are depicted in Figure 2-12. At this particular latitude and locality, Odum found that 1,700,000 kilocalories (units of energy *) were falling on each square meter of Silver Springs over a 365-day year. Of this amount, only 20,810 kcal of energy were captured by green-plant producers through photosynthesis in each square meter per year. Less than 2 percent of the available solar energy was trapped by chlorophyll molecules ($\frac{20,810}{1,700,000}$ kcal by our definition of the ecological efficiency of the producer level). Over the course of a year, herbivores consumed and utilized some 3,368 kcal out of the 20,810 kcal available in the plant material in each square meter: a 16 percent efficiency (84 percent was lost to the environment). And we can continue up through the pyramid diagram, determining the efficiency of energy utilization for each trophic level. Do note in particular that the decomposers are quite ef-

---

* One kilocalorie (kcal) represents the amount of heat required at a pressure of one atmosphere (sea level) to raise the temperature of one thousand grams of water one degree centigrade.

Fig. 2-12. The ecological efficiencies of the trophic levels at Silver Springs, Florida.

ficient. Feeding on all trophic levels, they utilize some 24 percent of the original potential energy available in the chemical bonds of the producer plants.

Table 2-1 summarizes the efficiency of energy transfer at various trophic levels in three aquatic ecosystems. Note the very *low primary efficiencies* in the plants, on the order of 1 percent or less. Apparently very low efficiencies are necessary for maximum output by plants. Photosynthetic plants have only a few hours of high sunlight intensities to operate in each day; so apparently rapid growth per unit time (with accompanying waste of energy) is more valuable for survival than maximum efficiency in the use of fuel (solar energy). Plants in suitable areas *could* grow more slowly and be more efficient in trapping and using energy, but they do not. Perhaps this is because of high competition with other plants (in the tropics) or short growing seasons (in the temperate zone and deserts).

Also note that there is generally *increasing efficiency* in higher consumer groups. Plants cannot move much to capture

TABLE 2-1. EFFICIENCY OF ENERGY TRANSFER
AT VARIOUS TROPHIC LEVELS
IN THREE AQUATIC ECOSYSTEMS
(AFTER ODUM, 1959)

	Trophic level energy intake efficiency (percent of available energy that a trophic level acquires)		
Trophic Level	*Cedar Bog Lake, Minn.*	*Lake Mendota, Wisc.*	*Silver Springs, Fla.*
Photosynthetic plants (producers)	0.10	0.40	1.2
Herbivores (primary consumers)	13.3	8.7	16.0
Small carnivores (secondary consumers)	22.3	5.5	11.0
Large carnivores (tertiary consumers)	not present	13.0	6.0

sunlight; hence great amounts of light energy never hit the leaves or photosynthetic cells. Herbivores can move around to feed, and the searching behavior of predators greatly increases their chances of finding suitable prey.

Ecological Pyramids

We have seen that in a food chain there is energy loss at each transfer, and that this involves a regular sequence of trophic levels. This picture of trophic structure can be summarized graphically in the form of an **ecological pyramid** (Fig. 2-13). The first or producer level forms the base, and successive levels form the tiers which make up the apex. Ecological pyramids or food pyramids may be of three general types:

1. the *pyramid of numbers,* in which the number of individual organisms is depicted for each trophic level;

Fig. 2-13.   An ecological food pyramid in the sea.

2. the *pyramid of biomass,* based on the total dry weight or caloric value or other measure of the total amount of living material in each trophic level;

3. the *pyramid of energy,* in which the rate of energy flow and/or productivity (rate of production) of successive trophic levels is shown.

Why should a pyramid be used to depict energy relationships in a community? First, of course, whether we are dealing with nature or geometry, many small units are required to equal one large unit. One larger animal needs to feed on many smaller ones of a lower trophic level in order to secure sufficient energy for its own metabolic requirements. Second, there is a loss of energy at each step in a food chain. Thus there is simply less energy available to the higher trophic levels and they cannot reach the same abundance.

Summary

Biogeochemical cycles maintain a constant movement between physical environment and biosphere of the approximately forty chemical elements known to be essential to life. Gaseous cycles, with the atmosphere forming the chief reservoir, are said to be perfect cycles because the elements involved (carbon, nitrogen, oxygen, or hydrogen) do not become inaccessible to organisms over long periods. Sedimentary cycles are imperfect cycles because the elements involved end up in sedimentary rock, a reservoir from which recycling is very slow. Man's recent activities are causing significant changes in natural cycles such as the carbon cycle.

Energy flow in ecosystems, unlike the flow of elements, is unidirectional and not cyclical. Energy (as heat) is constantly lost in the process of transfer of energy, as expressed in the First and Second Laws of Thermodynamics. A food chain is a simple representation of this flow of energy through the feeding relationships of a series of species. A food web, composed of many interlocking food chains, more accurately represents the pattern of energy relationships in a community. All organisms that share the same general source of nutrition are said to be at the same trophic level; these trophic levels in a community are the producers, herbivores, carnivores, top carnivores, and decomposers. Ecological efficiencies are a method of quantifying energy flow between trophic levels. They show that higher trophic levels tend to be more efficient than lower ones at utilizing available energy. Trophic structure may be graphically represented by an ecological pyramid, which can refer to numbers, biomass, or energy present at each trophic level in the community.

3
SOME BASIC PRINCIPLES OF ECOLOGY: INTERACTIONS OF ORGANISMS

Great fleas have little fleas upon their backs to bite 'em,
And little fleas have lesser fleas, and so *ad infinitum*.

Augustus de Morgan (1872)

Organisms, whether they live in a terrestrial or aquatic community, interact with each other constantly. As we saw in Chapter 2, many of their contacts result in energy flow through the ecosystem. On a long-term basis, these interactions result in ecological and evolutionary changes in one or more of the species involved. The three basic types of interspecific relations in a biotic community are **predation, symbiosis,** and **competition.** Understanding the ecological outcomes of these relationships will help us see how communities are structured; then, in the following several chapters, we will study the organization and dynamics of the populations of the individual species that make up a biotic community. In other words, we will move from the global scale of biogeochemical cycles in ecosystems to energy flow in a particular ecosystem to community relationships and finally to the organization of a population. Let us now consider the basic interspecific relations.

Predation

Predation may be defined as the behavior of capturing and feeding on another organism with the latter being consumed wholly or in part. This has a negative effect on the growth and survival of individual members of the population who are being eaten. The two components of a predation system are the predator and the prey species. The **predator** is a free-living organism that feeds on other living organisms, usually of another species. Intraspecific predation, more commonly called cannibalism, is almost always associated with conditions of overcrowding in a population. The **prey** is an organism that is eaten by a predator. Both carnivorous and herbivorous animals are predators (the latter eat plants as prey).

We are usually more concerned with animals in thinking about predation, but, surprisingly, there are also predatory plants. Among these are such unique species as the Venus' Fly-trap (*Dionaea muscipula*) and the aquatic bladderworts, which capture living prey in a leaf that closes like a steel trap. The Sundews (*Drosera* species), found in many boggy parts of the United States, have sticky secretions at the tips of many bright red hairs standing above the paddle-shaped terminus of a leaf. When unwary insects land to investigate the bright color and glistening droplets, they become firmly stuck and the sensitive hairs turn inward, enfolding the prey in the center of the leaf blade. The plant cells of the trap then secrete digestive enzymes that break up the bodies of the prey. The chemical molecules that formerly composed the prey are then absorbed into the cells lining the trap.

Pitcher plants use the pitfall method to capture their prey. An unwary insect descends into the deep vertical trap cavity and finds hundreds of downward-pointing hairs blocking its return. It eventually falls into the fluid in the bottom of the trap, dies, and its proteins are digested by both plant-secreted enzymes and bacterial action. The lassoing fungi in water or wet soil are able to trap nematode worms unwary enough to pass through a loop of fungus cells. Examples of some of these predatory plants are shown in Figure 3-1. Carnivorous plants, however, are relatively rare in the plant

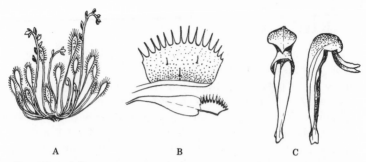

A   B   C

Fig. 3-1.   Some carnivorous plants found in the United States. (A) A Sundew (*Drosera*), which preys on tiny insects by catching them with sticky globules on the ends of the hairs on its leaves. (B) The trap and the trap with leaf petiole of a Venus' Fly-trap (*Dionaea muscipula*), native to North Carolina. The three trigger hairs on the inner surface of each trap lobe will cause the trap to snap shut in about 0.3 seconds when touched by an insect prey. (C) A pitcher plant (*Darlingtonia californica*) from the West Coast. This particular species has a hood covering most of the open mouth of the "pitcher."

kingdom and we may mainly regard them as curious anomalies and evolutionary specialists rather than as a major kind or class of predator.

Animal predators are commonplace to us. Hawks (Fig. 3-2) and other predatory birds are still seen even in suburban areas of the United States. Man is as much a predator as a house cat or dog, though we usually do not see our food killed and processed when we purchase it. Plains Indian tribes were well known among frontiersmen in western North America as expert hunters who could bring down even a three-thousand-pound buffalo with bow and arrow (Fig. 3-3). Today our predation is done for us by the slaughterhouse and the farmer harvesting his vegetable or cereal crops.

We tend to picture predation as harmful to the prey species. Though on an individual basis we can say predation is destructive in character, over the long term it is almost always beneficial to the prey population as a whole. Later we shall consider in detail the ways in which predation helps regulate population sizes in both animals and plants. For now let us note that the effect of predation interaction on the

Fig. 3-2. A sharp-shinned hawk with a freshly captured sapsucker.

Fig. 3-3. Man was a direct predator during almost all of his tenancy on earth.

prey population will differ in degree depending upon how long the species have been associated with each other. A predator-prey relationship of recent origin usually has severe negative effects on the prey population; in other words, large numbers of the prey species are killed by the predator. New predator-prey relationships can occur when there is a major alteration in the ecosystem (often produced by man), or when a predator or prey species is first introduced into a region. Either event sets up a new frame of reference for the organisms concerned. The species in that ecosystem begin adjusting and determining a novel set of biological relationships and relationships to new physical environmental factors. Species that were not previously preyed upon by a particular predator may now become the chief source of food for it.

In a predator-prey relationship that has existed for a long time, **coevolution** (essentially simultaneous evolutionary adjustments in each of several species) minimizes the negative effects on the prey. In other words, if adjustments in the interaction were *not* made by natural selection over the course of time, one or both of the populations would probably become extinct. The prey would be eaten into extinction and the predator species would die of starvation unless alternate prey species became available. Instead, in continuing predator-prey relationships we generally have a dynamic balance between predator and prey. Adjustments in such factors as the birth rates and dispersal of each minimize the disturbance of the system and continue the status quo.

Several widely observed aspects of animal coloration have arisen through natural selection in response to predator-prey interactions. In addition to sharp claws, canine-like teeth, rapid reactions, and other prey-capturing adaptations, many vertebrate predators have color lines leading forward from the eye that apparently function as aiming sights. These circles and lines are found about the eyes of predatory birds, mammals, reptiles, amphibians, and fish (Fig. 3-4). Besides their role as lines of sight in tracking and capturing prey, dark eye marks also reduce glare in bright open habitats. Light circles around the eyes probably function as light-gathering devices (Fig. 3-5). Man has adopted these principles in the sphere of athletics by applying dark grease or charcoal smears just below the eyes of players to reduce the glare caused by sunlight or artificial lighting.

Another evolutionary result of predation pressure is **protective coloration,** where the prey comes to resemble some

Fig. 3-4. Eye lines serve as sighting and aiming devices for predators in catching prey. (A) Simple eye line of the partially insectivorous blue tit (*Parus caeruleus*). This is the most common type of eye line in vertebrates. The eye line in this species is wider than it is in other avian examples. (B) Combined eye circle and eye line of the yellow-throated vireo (*Vireo flavifrons*). (C) Raised yellow feathers above the eye line in a white-throated sparrow (*Zonotrichia albicollis*); these may cast light along the line of sight. (D) Red-necked grebe (*Podiceps griseigena*) showing eye line slanting downward. Such a line also occurs in some other fish-eating birds. (E) Long-billed curlew (*Numenius americanus*) showing direction of eye line forward of center of pupil to bill tip. (F) Teardrop mark of the pickerel (*Esox americanus*) associated with downward dashes at prey. (G) Rearward pointed eye line of the European woodcock (*Scolopax rusticola*), probably used to sight predators coming from behind. Associated with 360° vision plus front and back binocularity. (H) Head of the arboreal vine snake (*Oxybelis aeneus*) showing eye line and groove.

Fig. 3-5.   Figures showing facial markings with adaptive functions other than predatory sighting alone. (A) Facial patches and stripes associated with reduction of glare in very bright habitats. (B) Here eye lines may hide eyes and further decrease visibility to potential predators by interrupting the beast's outline; also, the pattern may decrease glare on the line of sight toward clumps of grass in the animal's usually bright open habitat, and the pattern may be important as a social signal. (C) Here there is no sighting line; stripes are probably mainly for disruption of the head pattern (hiding the eye) and for aiding species recognition. (D) Alcids and penguins are very highly specialized for catching fish. The lines about the eyes and heads of virtually all birds of these two groups could not be for sighting on prey; they probably serve in intra- and interspecific recognition. (E) Male (top), female (middle), and first-year male (bottom) American redstart (*Setophaga ruticilia*), showing development of differences for recognition of sex, species, and age as well as a complex eye line and eye circle associated with feeding.

object in its environment, thereby deceiving potential predators. Protective coloration has profound ecological as well as evolutionary implications, for many more prey species can be packed into a community if each is protectively colored in some way, reducing the impact of predation upon the individual species. Several examples of types of protective coloration are shown in the accompanying figures.

In **cryptic coloration** (Fig. 3-6) the prey resembles or mimics some inanimate object or background. This type of protective coloration is commonly found among insects, such as walking sticks, "stick" caterpillars of geometrid moths, leaf-like katydids, or beetles that resemble bark or rocks.

In **Batesian mimicry** the prey resembles a toxic, venomous, or unpalatable species found in the same region. The tasty or at least harmless prey is the **mimic** and the species dangerous to potential predators is the **model** in a Batesian mimicry complex. Behavior is an important component of the mimicry, as otherwise the deception provided by similar external structure, coloration, and pattern would not convince the predator that it was seeing an unsuitable prey.

The monarch butterfly (*Danaus plexippus*) is a common species in most parts of the world and is distasteful to birds, lizards, and other predators. The adults are large slow-flying butterflies with bright and showy red-orange coloration bordered with black (Fig. 3-7). The adult is poisonous because of the diet of its caterpillar. As it feeds upon the leaves of the milkweed foodplants, the larva incorporates into its body poisonous compounds called cardiac glycosides. When the larva pupates and the body tissues reorganize inside the chrysalis (pupa) to form the adult, these compounds are not broken down but are built into the tissues of the adult monarch. When the adult emerges from the pupa, it is recognized as a distasteful insect by predators with previous experience of the species. In the United States, the monarch is the model in a Batesian mimicry complex with the viceroy butterfly, a good mimic. The viceroy belongs to an unrelated group of butterflies, but the adult has evolved to fly and look almost exactly like the monarch. Thus, although it is edible (the viceroy larva feeds on willow and similar non-poisonous plants), potential predators such as birds will shy away from it, mistaking the adult for a monarch adult.

Several kinds of **repelling coloration** exist, where the coloration of the prey warns predators of its genuinely noxious qualities. In **Mullerian mimicry,** for instance, all potential prey species in a mimicry complex are distasteful and share a common warning color pattern and behavior (Fig 3-8). This is a survival advantage to each of the prey species because

Fig. 3-6. Protective (cryptic) coloration shown by: (A) boa constrictor on rain forest floor; (B) a tropical *Hamadryas* butterfly on a tree trunk; (C) a walking-stick insect in Colorado; and (D) two poor-will nestlings (family Caprimulgidae) in bare "nest" on forest floor in Costa Rica.

C

D

Fig. 3-7. Batesian mimicry complex in the eastern United States: the Monarch (*Danaus plexippus*) is the distasteful model and the Viceroy (*Limenitis archippus*) is the edible mimic.

Fig. 3-8. Mullerian mimicry complex in the Neotropics (Costa Rica): all four specimens are different species of distasteful *Heliconius* butterflies (*H. hewitsoni, pachinus* [left]; *sarae* and *doris* [right]). On structural grounds it is believed they are not at all closely related species, but have converged solely in color pattern.

the predators in the area will learn to associate distasteful-ness with that pattern without trying all the species. A preda-tor has only to try one species of yellow- and black-banded wasps to know that it will be severely stung by an insect that looks like the species it attempted to capture as prey. In **warning coloration,** on the other hand, the bright colors and markings of the individual prey species simply advertise its noxious qualities to any potential predator (Fig. 3-9). Bum-blebees and brightly colored caterpillars, especially those bearing red or yellow patches, are frequently encountered ex-amples of warning coloration.

Another more ecologically intricate interaction between predator and prey is found in **aggressive mimicry.** Here the predator deceives the prey by its coloration and behavior. Ambush bugs (members of the insect order of "true bugs," Hemiptera) that live in flowers look like part of the flower; therefore it is easy for them to attack unsuspecting bees and flies coming for nectar. Some female fireflies imitate the mating flashes of females of other species and then capture and eat the males of the species that come in response to the mim-icked flash pattern.

Symbiosis

Symbiosis refers to a long-term interspecific relationship in which two species live together in more or less intimate asso-ciation. This is not a social system but an ecological associa-tion involving some transfer of energy or adaptive benefit. Symbioses are of three general types: **commensalism, mutual-ism,** and **parasitism.**

Commensalism occurs when one species benefits from the association but the other species is not significantly affected. Cockroaches benefit quite a bit from living in close proximity to man but humans are rarely harmed or benefited by having them in their homes. They may be aesthetically displeasing commensals to their human hosts, but they hardly eat enough to affect man's energy intake. In the American tropics and subtropical Florida, Old World cattle egrets have become

A

Fig. 3-9. Warning coloration: (A) a bright red beetle (*Tetraopes*) on a milkweed leaf; (B) a bright yellow and black striped moth larva with irritating hairs; and (C) a brilliant red "poison arrow" frog (*Dendrobates*) of the Costa Rican rain forest. South American Indians boil the skins of frogs of this genus to produce a deadly poison.

B

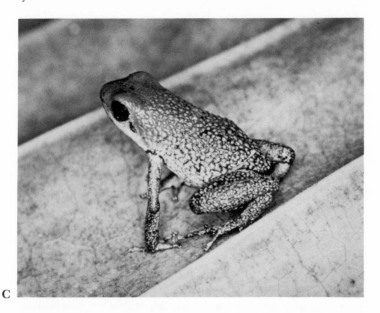

C

well established during the last two decades. These birds
feed in pastures very close to cattle, eating the insects that
the cows scare up while grazing. As far as is known, the cattle are not benefited or harmed (e.g., by diseases the birds
might carry from herd to herd) by the presence of the egrets.
However, in the African tropics to which the cattle egret is
native, it probably serves as a warning sentry for the grazing
mammals, alerting them to possible predator danger by sudden flight. A more intimate commensal-host relationship is
that of epiphytic plants, such as arboreal orchids and bromeliads, with the trees on whose limbs and trunk surfaces they
grow. These so-called "air plants" gain support (a physical
substrate on which to grow) above the ground in a favorable
light level, and spend their entire life spans there. But they
neither benefit nor harm their host, unless the weight and
wind resistance of the epiphytes become so great that the
structure of the tree is weakened.

In mutualism both species in the relationship benefit. Lichens, for instance, are mutualistic associations between one-
celled photosynthetic algae and chlorophyll-lacking fungi.
The algae, through photosynthesis, provide sugars as food for

both species while the fungal hyphae (thread-like bodies) collect and hold moisture and mineral nutrients that both symbiotic partners can use. Pollination of flowering plants by insects is perhaps the commonest example of mutualism (Fig. 3-10). Bees depend on flowers for food in the form of nectar and pollen, and the flowering plants depend on bees or other pollinators to carry their male reproductive cells (sperm in the pollen grains) specifically to the female parts of other flowers of the same species. In Africa there is a small mammal species called the honey badger or ratel that has a mutualistic relationship with birds called honey-guides. The honey-guide will fly along in front of the ratel to lead it to a bee nest that the bird has discovered, and after the ratel has torn open the nest for the honey, the bird will feed on the wax of the honeycomb.

Domesticated plants and animals usually enjoy a mutualistic relationship with man. Man cares for them and insures their continued reproduction (without which they would soon die in competition with wild species) while he depends on them for his own existence. In their original wild state, these plants and animals were perfectly capable of survival, but artificial selection by man during the course of domestication has bred out many of these adaptive traits in exchange, as it were, for traits yielding higher food production. The three great prehistoric centers of domestication have yielded most of our commonly cultivated species during the last ten thousand years. From southwest Asia we obtained wheat, cattle, sheep, goats, barley, and rye; from southeast Asia rice, pigs, and chickens; and from our New World tropics we have corn, beans, potatoes, squash, and turkeys, as well as other crops of economic value such as tobacco. In Africa today considerable attention is being directed toward the possibility of domesticating some of the larger antelope species to breed on a large scale for meat production. This possibility is of particular import because essentially we have not added any new species to our assemblage of domesticated plants and animals for the last several thousand years. Thousands of years ago, men everywhere subsisted by hunting game animals and gathering wild plant products. Today man really only predates significantly on fish and a few other wild species in the oceans, and

A

Fig. 3-10. (A) A checkerspot butterfly (*Euphydryas anicia*) pollinates Colorado sunflowers during its visits for nectar, an example of mutualism; (B) A purple sunbird (*Nectarinia asiatica*) pollinates the flowers of *Capparis aphylla* in India while it sips nectar, a less familiar example of a mutualistic interspecific relationship.

B

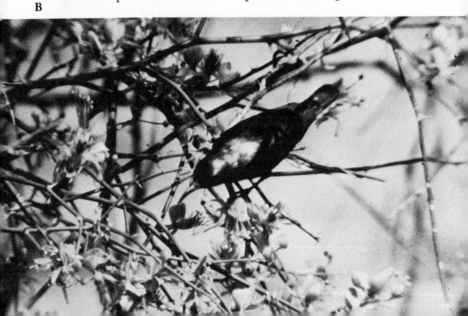

modern agricultural techniques have made gathering (of blueberries, for example) more a novelty than a necessity. The domestication of certain plants and animals in a mutualistic association with man allowed man to break the continuous cycle of hunting and gathering that he had previously been forced to follow. Hence we can truly say that our large cities and advanced civilization today were made possible by this rather recently established mutualism.

In parasitism one species, the **parasite,** is benefited while the other species, the **host,** is harmed. Parasitism, like predation, is frequently an important factor in controlling natural populations. But despite the similarity of function and definition there are significant differences between parasitism and predation. Parasites are much smaller than their hosts, living as they do on a portion of the host's energy intake. A predator is almost always larger than its prey. Parasites live on, in, or near the host (Fig. 3-11), whereas predators associate closely with the prey only when actually feeding on them. Parasites will kill their host only very slowly or not at all;

Fig. 3-11. Cocoons of a parasitic braconid wasp on a sphinx moth larva (*Manduca quinquemaculatus*).

predators kill their prey quickly and consume it immediately. The most efficient parasite is one whose presence is hardly noticeable to the host; should it kill its host before parasite reproduction the parasite would die without leaving any offspring and a species with this habit would rapidly become extinct.

Ectoparasites live on the body surface of the host and possess modifications for secure attachment to the host species. Examples include ticks, lice, fleas, and bedbugs. **Endoparasites** live inside the host, frequently in the digestive tract. Consequently they exhibit adaptations for resisting the internal movements and defensive measures of the host's body. For example, tapeworms and flukes must have outer skins that will protect them against digestive secretions and cellular enzymes. The life cycle of endoparasites frequently includes intermediate hosts between the egg and adult parasite stage, as in the Chinese liver fluke life cycle, where snails and fish host larval fluke stages (Fig. 3-12). The fluke larva is passed to man when he eats an intermediate fish host. In man the fluke becomes an adult and produces great quantities of eggs, which pass out of the human body in the feces. The eggs hatch and the new larvae infect snails, starting the cycle again. Later larvae leave the aquatic snails to infect fish. Occasionally in nature one encounters the phenomenon of **hyperparasitism,** where one parasite will live in another parasite which in turn is living in a host. An example would be a wasp larva parasitizing a fly larva that is parasitizing a moth caterpillar.

These three basic types of symbiosis—commensalism, mutualism, and parasitism—are all profoundly important interactions in biological communities. Without the mutualistic association between nitrogen-fixing bacteria and legume plants, for instance, the nitrogen biogeochemical cycle would be far slower and would no doubt have limited the expansion and evolution of life on earth to a lower level than we have today. In company with predation, certain of these symbioses exercise important density-limiting functions on populations of other species. Let us now look at another complicated set of interactions within and between species; we may term it competition.

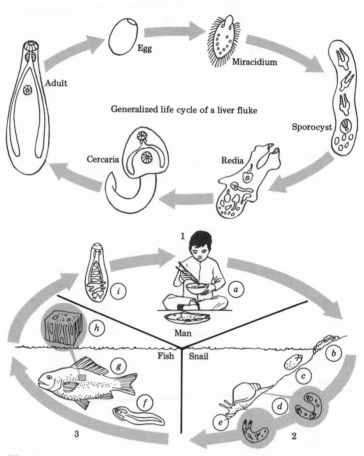

Fig. 3-12. The extreme complexity of some parasitic relationships is exemplified by the life cycle of the Chinese liver fluke (*Clonorchis sinensis*). The life cycle involves more than one host (man, snail, and fish), and there is much asexual budding, which increases the total reproductive potential. *Top figure:* the succession of developmental stages in the life cycle. The adult releases eggs which hatch as miracidium larvae. This larval type becomes a sporocyst which buds, internally, a large number of redia larvae. These new larvae in turn bud, internally, a large number of cercariae, tadpole-like larvae which develop into adult liver flukes. *Bottom figure,* the succession of hosts. *1.* Man: (*a*) Eggs are liberated in human feces (*b*) reaching fresh-water ponds, where the miracidium larvae (*c*) swim about and, on contacting a snail, enter it. *2.* Snail:

Within the snail the miracidium develops into a sporocyst (d) that, in turn, liberates rediae (e). The rediae enter the snail's liver; here they themselves reproduce, and some of these eventually produce cercariae (f). 3. Fish: The cercariae leave the snail and swim free in the pond, eventually entering a fish in whose muscles they encyst. The infective cycle is completed when the fish is eaten by man; the cysts germinate and the adult fluke parasitizes man.

Competition

Competition in an ecological sense is a struggle between organisms for food, space, mates, or any other limited resource. In intraspecific competiton the struggle is between individuals of the same species. This experience is common to all species whose numbers are increasing in a limited environment; in a later chapter we will treat it as one of the central factors regulating population growth. In interspecific competition the struggle is between the populations of two species. The basis for such struggles has been expressed as **Gause's Principle,** which states that two species cannot occupy the same niche simultaneously. If two species that occupy the same niche (way of life) come together in space and time, as a general rule there are three possible results.

Extinction

In this outcome, one species becomes **extinct** (locally) because its competitor was more successful at monopolizing available resources such as food or space. G. F. Gause formulated his principle after studying competition between two species of *Paramecium,* tiny one-celled aquatic animals in the phylum Protozoa. These can be grown in laboratory culture vessels of limited size where the *Paramecia* compete for food (bacteria), oxygen, and other requirements. They reproduce themselves by splitting in two (binary fission) as often as several times a day. When grown alone in containers in the laboratory, the numbers of *Paramecium caudatum* increase more slowly than *Paramecium aurelia* (Fig. 3-13). Eventually each species reaches the capacity of that environment to support the population, and growth levels off to a population size characteristic of the species. When grown together in the

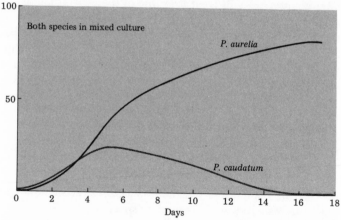

Fig. 3-13. (*Top*) The growth of each of two species of closely related *Paramecium* when grown alone. *Paramecium aurelia* and *P. caudatum* exhibit normal sigmoid growth in controlled cultures with a constant food supply. (*Bottom*) Effect of competition between *Paramecium aurelia* and *P. caudatum* when grown together; the latter species is eliminated.

same containers, *P. aurelia* increases more slowly than it did alone and *P. caudatum* grows poorly and eventually becomes extinct (Fig. 3-13, bottom). Three facts may be noted in this competitive situation: (a) normal growth rate was experienced by each species when first combined, as long as food was not limited in relation to the size of the population; (b)

the population of *P. caudatum* declined to extinction eventually because of competition from *P. aurelia;* (c) when food
became limited and competition was acute, *P. aurelia* grew
more slowly than when cultured alone, but it gradually attained the normal population size. *P. aurelia* was the more
successful competitor because it was adapted to rapid growth
and hence could trap a greater percentage of the limited
available energy (bacterial food) in each generation.

Competitive Exclusion

In **competitive exclusion** one species is forced out of part
of the habitat when it comes together with its competitor, but
it continues to survive in other adjacent portions of the habitat. An experimentally verified case of competitive exclusion
is seen in the vertical distribution of two species of barnacles
along the coast of Scotland. *Balanus* barnacles normally live
on coastal rocks below the mean high mark of the lowest tide
each lunar month; thus these barnacles are always covered
with water for part of each twenty-four hour period. *Chthamalus* barnacles live on rocks in the splash zone above the
mean high neap tide mark (Fig. 3-14). This distribution suggested competitive exclusion as an explanation, but experiments had to be made to eliminate the possibility that the
species are restricted in their distribution not by competition
but by inability to adapt to other parts of the shoreline habitat. So the biologist J. H. Connell removed *Chthamalus* barnacles from splash zone rocks and found that the *Balanus*
species still would not live there. When he removed *Balanus*
from underwater rocks, however, he found that *Chthamalus*
did move down and survive below the water line. Thus competitive exclusion is involved in limiting the distribution of
Chthamalus wherever both of these species occur together;
the young *Balanus* simply grow more rapidly than the young
Chthamalus in the lower zone and vigorously over-grow or
pry off their competitors.

Character Displacement

Where two potentially competing species occur **sympatri-**

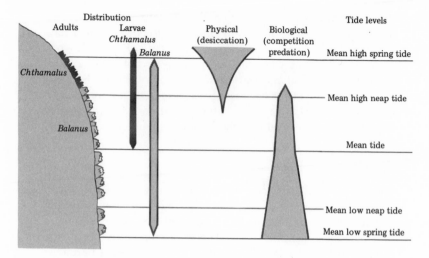

Fig. 3-14. Competitive exclusion effect of competition between two species of barnacles. Although there is a broad area in which the larvae of both species settle, competition eliminates most of the overlap by the time the adult stage is reached, *Chthamalus* being largely restricted to the zone above the level of the mean high neap tide (neap tides are the lowest tides of a lunar month) and *Balanus* to the zone below this level.

cally (together), they have greater differences in their feeding adaptations (such as bill size in birds) than in areas where they do not coexist. Each species has evolved characteristics that lessen competition with other species for food resources and hence promote reproductive success. This divergence of characters in areas of overlap is called **character displacement.** In birds, for instance, bill sizes will differ distinctly between related sympatric species, and one species with a long thin bill will feed on large insects while another with a short thick bill will feed on seeds. These differences minimize the competition that would result if both species were similar enough to feed on the same prey. Where these bird species occur alone (**allopatrically**), the beak size of each will often be similar, adapted for generalized feeding on a variety of food items. A hypothetical example of character divergence, this adaptive consequence of the influence of competition in areas of sympatry, is shown graphically in Figure 3-15.

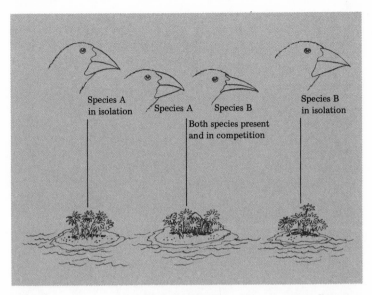

Fig. 3-15. Character displacement effect of competition between two hypothetical species of finches on an island chain. Where species A or species B is found alone on an island, the beaks are generalized in shape and hence are adapted for feeding on a whole variety of food sources. A local evolutionary change in beak size occurs when both species are found on the same island, allowing each species to specialize on different food resources.

Summary

Three basic types of interspecific relations in a biotic community are predation, symbiosis, and competition. The predator and prey populations in a long-established predation relationship are usually in a dynamic balance that benefits both species. A common evolutionary result of predation pressure is protective coloration in the prey species. Symbioses involve long-term intimate association with some transfer of energy or adaptive benefit. In commensalism, one species (commensal) benefits while the other (host) is not affected by the association. Both species benefit in mutualism. In parasitism one species (parasite) benefits and the other (host) is harmed. Competition represents a mutual struggle, either intraspecific or interspecific, for a limited resource. Gause's Principle states that two species cannot occupy the same niche simultaneously. Hence interspecific competition usually results in extinction of one species, competitive exclusion, or character displacement.

4
THE ORGANIZATION
OF POPULATIONS
Properties of a Population

Populations are like the individual organisms that constitute them in that they are living, have a definite structure and orderly functioning, and grow and die. Many of the principles of ecology that we have considered in the preceding chapters apply to the population level of organization as much as to communities or ecosystems, and we shall begin our consideration of population biology in this chapter with an overview of the organization of these biological units.

Before continuing, though, let us first define what we are talking about: a **population** is a group of organisms of the same species living in a particular space. We cannot be much more specific than that, for populations vary greatly in size and character depending upon the species of organism involved and the limits of the space it occupies. For example, we frequently consider the species of man (*Homo sapiens*) to be a population over the whole earth or a population as small as that of a tiny mountain village; either application of the term "population" is technically correct. Of course, until the development of modern transportation, people on different continents and even people separated by natural geographic barriers on any one continent composed reasonably isolated populations.

Some of the properties of a population are unique to the aggregation and are not characteristic of the individuals in the group. Under the general category of organization, a population can show **dispersion** (distribution), **dispersal** (moving out from a center of origin), and **density** (degree of crowding), while the growth of a population includes its **natality** (birth rate), **mortality** (death rate), **age distribution** (percentage of the population in each age class), **biotic potential** (maximum possible growth rate under ideal conditions), and **growth form** (the manner and speed of population growth). Each of these properties influences the ecological status and evolutionary future of a population, and when we understand their normal role it becomes easier to see how environmental pollution and other changes wrought by man can radically affect natural populations of organisms. It also clarifies the role of similar properties in the population biology of man himself. Let us look at these particular population parameters in more detail now.

Dispersion

Dispersion is simply the internal distribution pattern of individuals within a population. Organisms in a population may be distributed according to three general patterns: **random, uniform,** or **clumped** (Fig. 4-1).

Random Dispersion

Random distribution—individuals scattered over an area without any regularity or any degree of affinity for each other—is relatively rare in nature. It occurs only where the environment is very uniform, with resources spread evenly throughout the area of the population's distribution, and only when the species has neither a tendency to aggregate because of social attractions nor a tendency to repel one another. Since we usually find a non-random dispersion of resources in nature, organisms are almost never random in distribution. Solitary predatory spiders living on a forest floor uniformly

Fig. 4-1. The three basic patterns of dispersion of individuals in a population: (A) random, (B) uniform, and (C) clumped.

covered with similar leaf litter and with uniform moisture conditions will, however, show random dispersion.

Uniform Dispersion

This type of distribution is more regular than random dispersion, yet no aggregation of individuals occurs. Uniform distribution is not infrequent in nature and may occur where competition between individuals for resources is severe or where positive antagonism promotes even spacing. This type of distribution occurs in island nesting colonies of sea birds, where nests are often spaced apart by the length of the mother birds' neck-to-bill-tip reach! But it is more common among plants than animals. The creosote bush and other desert plants of southwestern North America compete intensely for the little annual moisture that falls. The roots of many species actually secrete antibiotics that inhibit the growth of seeds or neighboring plants within the radius of their root systems.

Clumped Dispersion

Clumped dispersion is defined almost by elimination: it is irregular, non-random distribution of individuals in the population. Clumping of varying degrees represents by far the most common pattern of dispersion of organisms in a population area. This clumping distribution may vary in intensity and even be present only at certain times of the year or of the organism's lifetime. The clumps or aggregates themselves may be scattered uniformly or at random throughout the area of distribution, depending upon the distribution of resources or degree of social interaction between the sub-groupings within the population.

The reasons why clumping is common are not hard to understand. Individuals respond to local habitat differences within the population's area of distribution, seeking out or surviving optimally in habitats with the best combination of environmental factors (temperature, light, minerals, water, etc.), which are rarely distributed uniformly. At certain seasons of the year weather conditions may promote aggregation. During the dry seasons, populations of most wildlife species in Everglades National Park in south Florida will aggregate around "gator holes," depressions in watercourses that have been made by alligators, where water will stand long after the open flat marshlands have dried up. The degree of sociality of a higher animal species is important in determining aggregations within a population. Many mammals and birds feed and function best as groups, and hence social attraction promoting clumping is adaptively advantageous to them. Reproductive processes require at least one male and female cohort to aggregate, and depending upon the type of reproductive pattern characteristic of the species, the grouping may involve any number from a pair of organisms to a whole colony of breeding individuals.

The above points are some of the obvious reasons for animal and plant aggregation, but what of the ultimate evolutionary reasons for most clumping behavior? In a positive sense, we can observe that aggregation often increases the *survival* of the individuals in the group. Individuals found in clumps tend to have a lower mortality rate than isolated individuals. The group offers *protection* against attacks by predators, and will frequently *modify* the microclimate or microhabitat where they live in such a way that unfavorable climatic periods do not affect the grouped individuals as much as they do solitary organisms. Sufficient heat is generated within a beehive to allow the colony to survive cold night temperatures that would kill any isolated bees. The chief negative aspect of aggregation is that it almost inevitably *increases competition* for light, nutrients, food, or space.

Social Organization and Dispersion

As we have noted, the degree of sociality of an animal species will affect the distribution of the members of a population. Three principal types of social organization that affect dispersion are **territoriality, social hierarchies,** and the existence of actual **societies** in which all individuals of a population live.

Territoriality

Most vertebrates and higher invertebrates commonly live their whole lives in a definite area. This area of normal activities is called a **home range.** This is where the animal searches for food, searches for mates, rears its young, and so forth. If all or part of this area is actively defended, the defended portion is termed a **territory.** An individual (or a pair or a family group) will defend such an area against intrusion by any other individual. This naturally results in a *spacing out* of the population, frequently in direct relation to the resources (especially food supply) of the environment other than mere physical space. We can see a nice example of this effect of territorial behavior in Howler Monkey (*Alouatta villosa*) populations inhabiting the lowland forests of the New World tropics. A small population group of these monkeys travels around as a unit, maintaining a "core" of territory against all other Howler groups. It does this by communal howling in the early morning hours, which warns other groups of Howlers of their presence near a defended territory (Fig. 4-2).

The advantages of the dispersion resulting from territorial isolation are threefold: (1) interindividual competition is reduced; (2) energy that would be spent in antagonistic fighting if all individuals were close together is conserved during critical periods such as the mating season; and (3) overcrowding and exhaustion of the food supply is prevented.

Fig. 4-2. Spacing of individuals by group territories, in this case territories of three troops of Howler Monkeys in the tropical deciduous forest of Costa Rica. The home ranges of the three bands actually overlap; only the "core" territory areas are shown. Dots represent the howler monkeys in each troop. At dawn all the males howl vociferously for about an hour (see inset) and each troop can determine the position of the neighboring groups without actual physical contact or fighting. The result is a well-spaced series of populations that do not exhaust the resources of the environment.

Social Hierarchies

A social hierarchy is simply a series of dominance-subordination relationships in a population. You may have heard this concept referred to as a "pecking order," since step-like series of dominance relationships are commonly observed among chickens and other barnyard fowl. The most aggressive individual is at the top of the pecking order and is free to peck all the other birds. The least aggressive individual is at the bottom and may be pecked by all the birds above him in the social hierarchy. In a closed system like a flock of ducks on a farm, it may be hard to see how this social relationship could extend to dispersion. But in the wild, such hierarchies frequently result in the expulsion of a certain subordinate segment of the population, which is forced to move to new ranges. In African baboon troops, small sub-dominant groups containing both males and females split off from the main troops when these latter units run by dominant adult males grow quite large (Fig. 4-3). In deer, elk, or antelope herds at rutting season, a dominance hierarchy of males is established, with the most powerful males each obtaining control over their own harem of females. Juvenile and mature subordinate males are forced by the dominant males to disperse into adjacent areas of the population's home range. After the mating season, the herd reforms.

Societies

Sometimes organisms form highly organized societies in nature, outside of which an individual cannot survive. It may seem confusing to define a population for species where a colony or society contains one reproductive pair and all the other individuals are sterile workers. The social insects, such as termites, ants, wasps, and bees, are good examples of society-dependent organisms where a "population" of the species may properly refer to all colonies within a particular region. The colonies are spaced out in the environment according to the availability of resources necessary to maintain them. Each colony is actually a genetic extension of one reproductive pair; that is, all the non-reproductive workers and other castes arise from this pair's genetic contribution through the queen's production of millions of eggs during her lifetime. As many as several million sterile individuals may work together to maintain a reproductive pair in a colony. Because new colonies are founded by specially produced reproductive adults leaving the mother colony several times a year and settling nearby, a population's dispersion really includes all the colonies in such an area. Colonies that are too close to each other risk extinction as a result of competition for food. Hence in an adaptive sense there is strong selection for an adequate dispersion of colonies. The emerging new queens have to fly a sufficient distance away from their "home" colony or the society they will found by egg-laying will soon be lost through competition from the older, larger, and better-established colonies in the overall population.

Fig. 4-3. The positions of group members during movement of a baboon troop at Nairobi Park, Kenya. Dominant adult males accompany females with small infants and a group of older infants in the group's center. A group of young juveniles is shown below the center and older juveniles above. Other adult males and females precede and follow the group's center. Two estrous females (dark hindquarters) are in consort with adult males. New troops are probably formed by splitting off a sub-dominant groups when the original troop becomes quite large.

Population Dispersal

All our discussion on dispersion (the pattern of distribution of organisms *within* a population) has assumed normal individual movement on a local scale. Now we may consider the problem of population dispersal in a wider sense, which is the movement of individuals into or out of the population area. This takes three forms: **immigration, emigration,** and **migration.**

Immigration is one-way movement into an established population area or an uninhabited area from neighboring areas. This is normally successful for the immigrants only when the population into which they are merging is undercrowded in relation to its available resources. *Emigration* is one-way movement out of a particular population, and commonly occurs when overcrowding results from excessive reproduction or an environmental stress such as drought. *Migration* is the periodic departure and return of individuals to and from a population area. We are often filled with wonder and excited intellectually at the remarkable feats of animal migration recorded in the annals of natural history and ecology. It is well worth considering in detail several of these migratory scenarios, where careful biological investigation has indicated the functioning of emigration and migration as dispersal factors shaping population growth and density.

The green turtle, *Chelonia mydas,* is found in oceans around the world and originally became famous because of its use by London soup chefs and for victualing ships. Populations are genetically isolated by their habit of mating and egg-laying at widely separated sites, even though much of the intervening time is spent on communal feeding areas. One such population lays its eggs on the beaches of remote Ascension Island in the middle South Atlantic, located over 1200 miles from the eastern coast of South America (Fig. 4-4). Yet in the extraordinary life history of the turtle, this site is visited by any one female only at two- or three-year intervals. During the many intervening months she feeds with the other adults along the shores of Brazil. When it is time for her to

Fig. 4-4. Map of the middle South Atlantic, showing the position of remote Ascension Island, where green turtles (*Chelonia mydas*) nest, and the eastern coast of Brazil, where the turtles disperse on feeding grounds and spend most of their lives. (*Data provided by Archie Carr.*)

lay her eggs, she swims 1200 to 1400 miles from the mainland to the tiny (six by seven miles) oceanic island, apparently navigating by celestial or olfactory clues on the high-seas portion of the journey. Appearing at the Ascension Island nesting grounds in April with hundreds of other females and males from the Brazilian coast, she makes her way ashore. She lays about 115 eggs in a pit she digs in the sand and then leaves the beach, not to return for another several years (Fig. 4-5). During this visit she mates with a male in the offshore surf, fertilizing the developing eggs that will be laid two or three years hence. When the eggs hatch about 60 days after oviposition, the tiny hatchling turtles rapidly navigate across the beach to the sea and swim off into the Equatorial Current, which they apparently follow downstream to the bulge of Brazil. There they grow up on a diet of turtle grass in the rich offshore feeding grounds, and repeat the cycle of return with the adults to Ascension Island when they mature some years later. When they return, over 80 percent of them will "home" to the exact island beach on which they had emerged.

To explain this remarkable sequence of migratory behavior one must emphasize its ecological benefits. By utilizing the warm shallow waters of the Brazilian coast and Caribbean for feeding purposes, the sizable population of thousands of green turtles that must come together at the time of reproduction is able to disperse over a broad area and thus reduce grazing pressure on the turtle grass. If all these turtles remained permanent residents of a restricted area along the Brazilian coast, nesting and feeding in the same site, probably only a small population could be supported by the marine environment. By nesting briefly on remote beaches the species is protected from predation pressure on both the eggs and young turtles. This sudden influx of possible prey on the beaches is too brief and too infrequent to allow predators to develop evolutionary specialization on the vulnerable stages

Fig. 4-5. Female green turtle nesting at Ascension Island. Digging has been completed and laying begun. The more pronounced and more angular emargination of the shell over the neck of the Ascension turtle is typical of this population.

in the turtles' life cycle. In sum, periodic migratory behavior and the cycle of adult concentration (breeding) and dispersal (feeding) seems to increase population stability and hence survival of the green turtle.

In the arctic lemmings, however, emigration is a response to overcrowding and no return movement occurs. Periodically these small rodents increase tremendously in numbers, and in northern Europe they have been known to march by the millions across the land, devouring everything edible in their path. Upon reaching the coast, many die by drowning. Predators become so satiated by the immense numbers of prey that they are ineffective in controlling these outbreaks. It is only the migratory behavior that accomplishes the population reduction necessary to bring the lemming numbers down to the level that the environment can support. We shall consider population regulation in these interesting mammals in more detail in the next chapter. Meanwhile, we may merely note that the ecological advantage of population regulation through emigration is that the remnant of animals left behind will be able to continue to breed and form the nucleus of the next generation, without the fatal environmental stress of continued overpopulation.

Migratory waterfowl are classic examples of organisms that utilize long-distance movement as an adaptive response to seasonal abundance of food. In the late spring of the year these ducks and geese fly north to the arctic, where they mate, nest, and raise their young. When these young are able to fly in late summer, the adults and young leave the nesting grounds together and fly several thousand miles south to the tropics where they spend the winter.

As a result of studies of bird-banding data on ducks and geese, Frederick Lincoln, a biologist with the U.S. Fish and Wildlife Service, discovered and reported in 1935 the existence of four great migratory flyway systems in North America. Later work has shown that most if not all of the other American migratory birds follow the same routes. Each flyway is a vast geographic region with extensive breeding grounds and wintering grounds connected with each other by a system of migratory pathways. A particular flyway has its own populations of birds, which use the same route every fall and spring. During the nesting season, the northern breeding grounds are shared in many areas by birds of the same species but belonging to different flyways. The extent of the Pacific Flyway across the North American continent is illustrated in Figure 4-6.

The tropical wintering grounds provide adequate food for the migratory adults as long as they are there only part of the year. Competition with resident species for food and space would, however, limit a waterfowl population that bred in the tropics. Thus during the breeding season these migratory birds take advantage of the several months' abundance of food in the arctic and the ample territorial space there in which to rear their young.

Of course, beyond social organization and various evolutionary drives for adaptive migratory behavior, we must recognize that the dispersal of an organism is greatly influenced by natural barriers. These may be ecological barriers, such as unsuitable habitats, or broader geographic barriers like mountains to a desert species or a large body of water to a strictly terrestrial species. Also, the **vagility** (inherent ability for movement) of an organism will greatly affect dispersal. The capacity of most birds to fly long distances greatly exceeds that of most butterflies, for example. In all of this discussion, we must remember that the movement of the **disseminules** ° of individuals, such as seeds, eggs, larvae, and spores, are just as significant ecologically in establishing the dispersion of a species as the movement of the mature adults themselves. Ultimately, the ecological meaning of dispersion and dispersal is found in the growth and regulation of the population unit itself.

Summary

A population is a group of organisms of the same species living in a particular space. Such an aggregation possesses prop-

° Disseminules are any stage of the life cycle of an organism which is capable of being dispersed, but this term usually refers to the immature stages.

Fig. 4-6. The Pacific Flyway for migratory waterfowl in North America.

erties unique to the group, such as dispersion, dispersal, density, natality, mortality, age distribution, biotic potential, and growth form. In this chapter we considered the first three characteristics under the category of population organization. Dispersion, which is the internal distribution pattern of individuals within a population, may be random, uniform, or clumped. Clumping, the most common type, is caused by non-random local habitat differences, social attraction, and reproductive processes, although aggregation almost inevitably increases competition between the individuals involved. Territoriality, social hierarchies, and colonial species or societies are principal types of social organization that affect dispersion. Movement into or out of the population area involves three kinds of dispersal behavior: immigration, emigration, or migration. Natural barriers, adaptive behavior, and the vagility of the species greatly affect dispersal.

5
POPULATION GROWTH AND REGULATION

For everything there is a season,
and a time for every matter under heaven:
  a time to be born, and a time to die;
  a time to plant, and a time to pluck up what is planted;
  a time to kill, and a time to heal;
  a time to break down, and a time to build up . . .

Ecclesiastes 3: 1–3.

Population growth is the increase in number of individuals comprising an aggregation. As we shall see shortly, it is not necessarily the result of more births than deaths, but may be caused by increased survivorship, movement into the area of new organisms of the species under consideration, or other factors. Growth of a population without increase in emigration or removal by other means does cause an increase in **density,** which is simply the size of the population within a particular unit of space.

Density

Population density is usually measured and expressed as the number of individuals per unit area (or volume). We may measure the **crude density,** that is, the number (or biomass) per unit of *total* space, including all environment within the described boundaries. Alternatively, the ecologist may measure the number (or biomass) of organisms of a species per unit of *habitat* space. That is, the area that is actually suitable for a species to live in may be much smaller than the total space, which might include rocks, ponds, or other unsuitable habitats. In this case the measurement is known as the **specific** or **ecological density.** It states the number of individuals in the area or volume actually available to be colonized by the population. Naturally, there is always some amount of space within a population's dispersion that simply cannot be occupied because it is used by other organisms or because of physical features of the environment. Thus the specific density is a preferable measurement.

A common difficulty is that one can measure this density (crude or specific) at a time when the population is changing in size, and the estimate may not mean too much. Especially in the lower plants and animals, such as algae and soil insects, with short generation times, population size can change *very* rapidly. Under such conditions many means of population measurement will give grossly underestimated or overestimated figures. Accurate measurement may also be very difficult because of the large area the population is inhabiting or the irregular distribution of individuals. Thus ecologists frequently find an **index of relative abundance** a more useful statistical reference than an absolute density figure. To obtain it, rather than counting the number of mealybugs per acre in two different groves, for example, one counts the average number of mealybugs per orange tree in each area. The statement that there are 5,000 mealybugs per orange tree in grove A versus 20 mealybugs per tree in grove B is a much better indicator of the relative severity of infestation than calculating a "guesstimate" of the numbers per acre, when tree hosts may be of different ages and sizes in the two areas or more widely spaced in one than the other.

Of course, whichever measurement of density is used, it must be recognized that populations are rarely static in size and that there is usually an input of new individuals into a population by births and immigrants as well as a loss by deaths and emigrants. The resulting trend in numbers we call positive or negative **population growth,** depending on whether input exceeds loss, and it inevitably influences density. The component factors involved in population growth will now be examined, and then we shall take up the subject of the regulation of population growth and size.

Growth

Involved in the overall growth of a population are three major factors: natality, mortality, and survivorship. These determine the pattern of increase (or decrease) for a population.

Natality

The natality or **birth rate** of a population is simply the increase in the population due only to the normal rate of reproduction. The maximum possible natality, of course, is rarely reached because the ideal conditions that would be the prerequisite of maximum production of new individuals do not exist in natural situations. Ideal conditions would exert no ecologically limiting influences, and thus reproduction would be limited only by physiological factors, such as the maximum egg production possible per unit of time. Therefore we will normally use "natality" to refer to the observed population increase from reproduction under a particular set of ecological conditions. Unlike the maximum possible natality for a species adapted to a certain area, this actual birth rate is not a constant, but will vary with the size and composition of the population as well as physical environmental factors.

Natality is usually expressed in mathematical notation as

$$\frac{\Delta N}{\Delta t} \quad \text{or} \quad \frac{\text{number of new individuals produced in population}}{\text{change in time}} \, °$$

This indicates the production of new individuals per unit of time. The natality rate for a flock of hens producing 90 new chicks per month would be approximately 3/day (90

° The Greek letter *delta* (Δ) in mathematical notation means "change in" the quantity following the delta.

chicks ÷ 30 days). Demographers, specialists in the study of human populations, usually express natality or birth rate as the number of live births per one thousand members of the population per unit of time. Here one divides the total number of new babies for the year by the size of the population at the midpoint of the stated time period to find the number of births per person. One then multiplies this figure by 1,000 to get the number of births per thousand persons. Thus, during 1971 there were approximately 3,769,000 live births in the United States. At mid-1971, the country's population was estimated to be 207,100,000. Therefore the birth rate for the year 1971 was 3,769,000/207,100,000=0.0182. Since this is the rate per person in the population, we multiply 0.0182 by 1,000 and see that the United States birth rate was 18.2.

Mortality

The mortality or **death rate** of a population refers to the number of individuals dying per unit of time. The minimum possible mortality equals the population loss under ideal or nonlimiting conditions. That is, even under the best environmental conditions, individuals will die of old age, at a point determined by their **physiological longevity.** The actual observed mortality is the rate of loss of individuals under given environmental conditions where predators, accidents, competition, and other factors share in causing deaths. This actual mortality is what we normally consider the mortality rate of a natural population.

While the death rate for most species is expressed as number of organisms dying per unit of time, e.g., 85 deer dying per year in the population inhabiting a particular forest, demographers describe mortality in human populations as the number dying per one thousand members of the population per year. In 1970, for example, the death rate for the United States was 9.6 people per thousand individuals in the total population.

Survivorship

The percentage of individuals living at various ages is the **survivorship** in a population. This is usually expressed in a survivorship curve: the surviving percentage per thousand born is plotted from the maximum of 1,000 alive at birth to the death of the last individual at the maximum life span for the species. Sample survivorship curves representing four types of situations are illustrated in Figure 5-1.

In a population of starving adult fruit flies in a laboratory bottle (curve A), most of the *Drosophila* live out the potential life span. After this long period of a nearly horizontal survivorship curve, all the flies begin dying at once, causing a precipitous drop in survivorship near the point of maximum life span under starvation conditions. This survivorship pat-

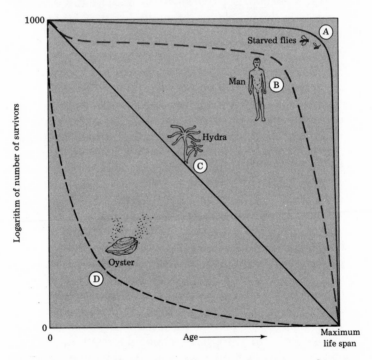

Fig. 5-1. Four different types of survivorship curves, depicting the number of individuals still living at various times after birth. (A) Survivorship of a population of starved adult fruit flies starting with emergence from pupae. (B) Survivorship of a population of man. (C) Survivorship of a *Hydra* population. (D) Survivorship of a group of 1,000 oysters from the time of hatching of the larvae to end of adult life span.

tern is very rare in nature since environmental factors normally kill some fraction of a population early in life.

The situation represented by curve B, with an initial drop in survivors and then a period of good survival until death of individuals in old age, is representative of man and many other larger animals. If the organisms survive infancy, with its relatively high death rate, they have a good chance to live out almost the entire maximum life span for the species in that region.

When the mortality rate at all ages is constant (curve C), one sees a survivorship curve like that of the population of *Hydra*, a freshwater coelenterate. Fledged birds also show this type of survivorship: mortality at any age after fledging (acquisition of flight feathers) is equally probable.

If, on the other hand, most individuals die early in life and the survivors of that period then have a comparatively low death rate, we have a curve (curve D) similar to that of the oyster. Tremendous numbers of oyster larvae die soon after hatching because of the hazards they meet as they are moved by the currents through their marine environment. These tiny larvae are particularly vulnerable to predation and are very likely to land in places where they cannot survive, when they settle on the bottom to begin life as sessile adults. Thus the survivorship curve for the population drops rapidly at first. The few larvae that attach to a satisfactory substrate will survive well.

Obviously, the pattern of survivorship for a species' population depends on the extent of environmental pressures on each age group. Should all environmental restraints be absent, one would expect a typical survivorship of 100 percent until the maximum life span had been reached. In this case, we would expect to see the maximum possible rate of increase for the population, since all individuals in each generation would survive to reproductive age. Though this rarely if ever happens, the concept of this **biotic potential** is useful because it allows us to estimate the extent of operating ecological restraints (**environmental resistance**).

Biotic Potential

The biotic potential is simply the growth rate inherently possible in a population under ideal conditions. Thus this maximum growth rate is equivalent to the maximum natality less the minimum mortality, with no restraints such as lack of food, predation, parasitism, or competition for space. Since these growth-restraining factors are normally present in natural situations, we actually find and measure only the *realized* rate of increase. The difference between the biotic potential, as measured under ideal conditions in the laboratory or from estimating total egg production, and the realized rate of increase is a measure of the environmental resistance present —that is, all the limiting factors in the environment acting on this particular population.

As a result of the interaction of the biotic potential and environmental resistance, populations tend to have a characteristic pattern of increase or **population growth form,** which we will now now consider in detail.

Population Growth Form

When conditions are nearly ideal, a population may increase very rapidly indeed, at a rate approaching its biotic potential. In 1879–1881 a total of 435 striped bass were released in San Francisco Bay after transport from the Boston area. Striped bass were not native to this Pacific marine environment, and their natural enemies and other limiting factors were apparently absent. By 1899 more than one million pounds of striped bass were being harvested *per year* from San Francisco Bay. This explosive population increase represents one extreme of population growth form, the **J-shaped** or **Exponential Growth Curve.**

J-shaped or Exponential Growth Curve

In species or situations where this type of growth form is

permitted, population density increases rapidly, in exponential or compound interest fashion (Fig. 5-2). The more individuals are added to the population, the faster it increases, because all those that are added also breed and hence increase the total growth rate of the population. The process is similar to bank interest compounded daily, the interest being added to the principal balance and thus providing a larger base on which to calculate the interest for the next time period. This exponential J-shaped growth rate may stop abruptly as environmental resistance becomes effective more

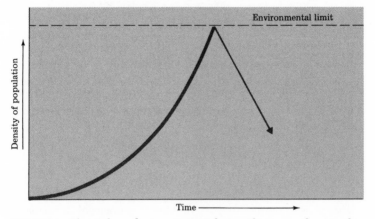

Fig. 5-2. The J-shaped or exponential growth curve of a population. After an initial establishment phase, the population increases exponentially until the environmental limit causes a population crash.

or less suddenly. The population then suffers a crash in numbers, regardless of population density. This kind of population growth pattern is characteristic of insects with short life spans, such as thrips, and most annual plants. The population grows very rapidly during a period of favorable weather (spring and summer), and then crashes rapidly when the weather changes in the autumn. Over several years, seasonal changes in a population of adult thrips living on roses show regular population peaks in the summer, with the crashes each fall occurring when cold weather comes (Fig. 5-3).

Fig. 5-3. Seasonal changes in a population of adult thrips living on roses in Australia.

S-shaped or Sigmoid Growth Curve

A more frequently encountered pattern of population growth is the S-shaped or sigmoid growth form, where growth starts slowly, accelerates rapidly in exponential form, and then decelerates and continues thereafter at a more or less constant level (Fig. 5-4). This growth curve is characteristic of larger organisms with longer life cycles and lower biotic potentials. Here, population growth is slow at first, in the **establishment** or **positive acceleration** phase. Then population increase becomes rapid, as in populations exhibiting J-shaped or exponential growth curves; this is the **logarithmic** phase. Somewhere in this period, an **inflection point** in the curve is reached where the population growth rate no longer continues to accelerate, but begins to decelerate. This **deceleration** phase is a slowdown of population growth caused by the gradual increase of the environmental resistance present in the system. The deceleration continues until a more or less equilibrium level is reached and maintained. This upper level, beyond which no major increase can occur, represents

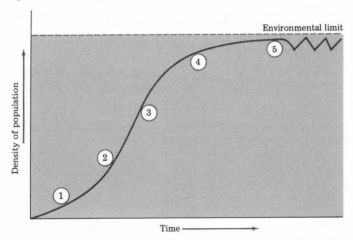

Fig. 5-4. The S-shaped or sigmoid growth form of a population. The indicated points along the curve are (1) the establishment of positive acceleration phase; (2) the logarithmic increase phase; (3) the inflection point, where the growth rate begins to slow down; (4) the deceleration phase; (5) the maximum population size or carrying capacity.

the size at which the population limits itself. Such a limiting size is often called the **carrying capacity** of the environment.

How is this carrying capacity determined? What factors control the maximum size to which a population can grow in a particular ecological setting? To consider these questions we must look at the ecological components of population regulation.

Population Regulation

As we have noted in discussing the two major types of growth form, limiting factors of some sort, which we have loosely called "environmental resistance," always slow or stop population growth. These factors can be of many kinds, but they are commonly grouped into two categories: **density-independent** and **density-dependent factors.** Any factor, whether limiting (negative) or favorable (positive) to a population, is

density-independent (in terms of the total population) if its
effect is constant regardless of the number of individuals in
the population. It is said to be a density-dependent factor if
the effect on the population varies with the density. Let us
consider some examples of these components of environmental resistance.

Density-independent Factors

These factors exert the same effect on the population regardless of the number of individuals present. Climatic factors
such as seasonal changes in photoperiod (daily amount of
sunlight), rainfall, and temperature are almost always density-independent in their effect. Generally, such factors are
most important in governing the population growth of small
organisms (such as insects or plankton) with short life cycles
and high biotic potentials. Weather and other physical environmental factors such as soil or water temperature are quite
important in determining the length of favorable periods of
annual growth for such organisms. They generally lack stability in their population size, which changes radically through
the seasons.

The yearly abundance of the small sap-sucking insect
Thrips imaginis in Australia is frequently cited as a classic example of density-independent population regulation. The
biologists H. G. Andrewartha and L. C. Birch and their coworkers found that the thrips populations on flowers reach a
minor peak of abundance in the southern winter (August), increase dramatically as late spring approaches (September to
December), and then become very scarce until the next August. This is because in southern Australia flowers are abundant in spring but not during the long dry summer or in the
growing period of the cool winter. With so many flowers, the
abundant food and living space provide an unlimited environment for expansion of the thrips populations. They never
have a chance to become excessively abundant on individual
flowers because the long dry summer comes first and the
thrips must leave the dying blooms, usually dying themselves
in the search for new flowers. So there is not an absolute
shortage of food, only a seasonal change in the accessibility

of food. Hence the rather regular seasonal changes in the abundance of thrips each year (Fig. 5-3) depend upon the influence of the climate and upon the level of the thrip population at the start of the principal growing season.

Other density-independent effects may be caused by heavy rains, drought, human destruction of habitat, or even pesticide use. Nesting and hatching success as well as survival of young quail, ring-necked pheasants, rabbits, and other birds and mammals may be greatly affected by the timing of heavy rains, cold snaps, or even by lack of moisture. Muskrats and beavers are forced to migrate overland when drought dries up marshes or ponds and their burrow and lodge entrances are exposed. Flooding of their home environments, of course, can result in the same disruption of normal activities. During such overland movements, foxes, coyotes, and minks can easily attack the muskrats and young beavers. When man destroys extensive areas of natural habitat, as through clear-cut logging, draining of prairie potholes, and cultivation practices, the result is serious reduction or extinction of native animal populations regardless of their density. The widespread use of pesticides has caused dramatic declines in wildlife populations independent of the number of individuals present at the time of spraying. Robin populations in sprayed areas of Wisconsin dropped 69 to 98 percent below those in unsprayed areas. Their earthworm diet was responsible; the earthworms had built up a concentration of DDT from feeding on leaves that decayed in the soil beneath elm trees sprayed to control Dutch elm disease. The degree of mortality caused by the poison was independent of the size of the robin populations.

Density-dependent Factors

These factors exert effects varying proportionately to the size of the population. Density-dependent factors are responsible for the steady-state population sizes seen in the upper-level portion of the sigmoid growth curve. These kinds of factors operate throughout population growth, not solely at one point in time. They normally begin to act well below the carrying capacity (causing the inflection point in the sigmoid growth curve) and intensify their effect as the upper population limit is approached. There, at the equilibrium density, the production of offspring exactly balances the loss of adults by death or emigration. Should the population size exceed the equilibrium density, the density-dependent factors exert a stronger effect and cause a greater rate of loss. This brake operates until the equilibrium density is reached again. Likewise, if the population size drops below the equilibrium density, the density-dependent factors will permit the population to increase. Since growth and reproduction require time, it is obvious that there will be a time lag between cause and effect, and hence the population size will oscillate about the equilibrium density. As a governor mechanism regulates the speed of an engine, so density-dependent factors regulate population growth, preventing overpopulation in most animal and plant species. Thus they, rather than density-independent factors, are said to be the factors primarily responsible for the achievement of a steady-state or mildly fluctuating density level at the carrying capacity of the environment.

Density-dependent factors are usually biotic in character, involving interactions with other organisms. **Intraspecific competition** is commonly an important regulating process in natural populations. Individuals of the same species compete for a resource in limited supply; under such conditions the population can accommodate only a certain maximum density. Food and space are normally the environmental resources in short supply. When the rate of reproduction is excessive and the equilibrium density is surpassed by new animals added to the population, competition for food or space will cause an increasing mortality rate, which accelerates as the population increases. The younger animals are usually most affected and hence the addition of new reproductive animals to the population is curtailed, eventually dropping the birth rate back to a level that yields an equilibrium density.

Density-dependent agents operating on a population may also include parasites, **pathogens** (bacteria, viruses, and protozoans) causing disease, and predators. Parasites and pathogens spread more easily from organism to organism in high-density populations of either plants or animals and hence tend to reduce the density of the hosts through mortality. Predators can find prey more easily in populations of high density and as long as they are not swamped by extremely high numbers of potential prey, they operate as a very efficient density-dependent factor.

Emigration also acts as a density-dependent process. At high population levels, emigration of a portion of the adults or young into unoccupied territory (when available!) can regulate the population density of the original area. Each year in black-tailed prairie dog towns of the Rocky Mountains, the adults of a family group will leave their home territory in a town and emigrate to the outskirts of the town to colonize a new area. In this species, the younger, inexperienced animals are able to remain behind in the center of the town in familiar territory while the mature, experienced prairie dogs take on the more dangerous task of establishing residence on the edges of the town. Over the years the population density in the town's center remains more or less constant.

Other processes operating in a density-dependent fashion include physiological and psychological control mechanisms. The social stresses caused by crowding have been shown to act on the individual through the endocrine system. As local populations of certain locust species increase in numbers, at a certain density crowding causes a hormonal change in the new young locusts, so that they develop longer wings and other morphological changes that will equip them for migratory movement. When this new generation matures, the whole series of local populations in an area will move off in flight *en masse,* migrating hundreds of miles in huge swarms. In vertebrates, these endocrine-induced changes are particularly associated with the pituitary and·adrenal glands. Increasing population density leads to inhibition of sexual maturation, lowered sexual activity, and inadequate milk production in nursing females. Stress caused by crowding also curtails the number of offspring produced per litter, through spontaneous abortion or absorption of tiny fetuses into the uterine walls in pregnant mammalian females.

In general, species controlled by density-dependent factors tend to be larger organisms such as birds or mammals or trees. They tend to have longer life cycles, usually more than a single year. Their rate of production of offspring is lower and thus they have lower biotic potentials and more stable population sizes than populations controlled principally by density-independent factors.

Of course, these various regulating factors we have been examining are *not* perfect, and no animal or plant population maintains a perfectly constant density over time. Population fluctuations are a basic fact of life. Before closing our consideration of population growth and regulation we should look briefly at the several classes of fluctuation in density.

Population Fluctuations

Periodicity in populations is commonly seen in **seasonal** or **annual** changes in density. These are often correlated with corresponding seasonal or annual variations in physical limiting factors such as temperature and rainfall.

In the temperate zones of the Northern and Southern Hemispheres, populations primarily respond to seasonal changes in temperature. One of the most noticeable responses in many species is **hibernation,** in which an animal greatly slows its metabolic processes and remains quiescent during the winter months. Frequently, the period of hibernation is spent in an underground burrow or den where the inactive animal is protected from disturbance and where a relatively constant environmental temperature may be maintained by trapping the escaping body heat. During the summers in desert or seasonally hot areas, some animals escape the heat by **estivation,** a state of reduced metabolism and activity similar to hibernation but carried out to survive a hot period rather than a cold period. Leafing of perennial trees and shrubs in the spring and leaf-drop in the fall are other seasonal responses to temperature changes in temperate climates.

In the tropical areas of the world, rainfall is commonly the key factor governing seasonal changes in population structure and functioning. Many organisms pass the tropical dry season in state of **diapause** or dormancy, hidden underground away from the desiccating temperatures and low humidities characteristic of this time of year. The first rains of the wet season give the cue for breaking of diapause and these organisms become active again. Annual plants spend the dry season in the form of dormant seeds. Leaf production and leaf-drop in tropical deciduous forests are tightly correlated with the alternation of wet season and dry season. Termite and ant swarming of reproductive adults (winged queens and males) from nests is often cued by rainfall.

Obviously, then, in both tropical and temperate environments population growth is keyed to favorable periods in the annual cycle. During periods of environmental stress in the course of a year the visible population density may drop drastically as the animals seek shelter for a dormant stage or a portion of the population dies.

Long-term oscillations in density, however, are not obviously related to seasonal or annual change and may involve remarkably regular cycles of abundance with many years between peaks and depressions. The best known cases are described from arctic mammals, but periodicity of this nature exists in certain birds, insects, and fish, and seed production in certain plants.

A classic case of a ten-year oscillation is that of the snowshoe hare and the Canadian lynx, a large relative of the more familiar bobcat. Since about 1800 the Hudson Bay Company in Canada has kept records of the number of pelts of fur-bearing mammals taken by trappers and purchased by the company each year. When these data are plotted over a long span of years (Fig. 5-5), it is apparent that the lynx reaches a population peak every nine to ten years (average of 9.6 years). These peaks of abundance are often followed by "crashes," or rapid declines in number, and the lynx becomes very scarce for several years. When numbers of pelts of the showshoe hare are plotted for the same time period, it is found that the hare follows the same general cycle, with a peak abundance usually preceding that of the lynx by a year or more. Since the lynx is largely dependent upon the hare for food in these arctic areas, it is obvious that the cycle of the predator is related to that of the prey. But the two cycles have not as yet been shown experimentally to be related by cause and effect.

Fig. 5-5. Changes in the abundance of the Canadian lynx and the snowshoe hare, as indicated by the number of pelts received by the Hudson Bay Company from 1845 to 1935. This is the classic case of long-term cyclic oscillation in population density.

A shorter, three- or four-year cycle of abundance is characteristic of many northern mice, lemmings, voles, and their predators such as the snowy owl and the arctic fox (Fig. 5-6). Lemmings live in the northern tundra of Europe (two species) and North America (two species), and become very abundant every three or four years, then crash to very low population levels within a single season. The populations of the predators likewise increase and then crash, following the

sudden decline of the lemming populations. The arctic foxes
compete for the remaining food following a lemming population crash and hence may starve, but the snowy owls respond
to the decline in lemming numbers by migrating far to the
south in search of food, occasionally even to North Carolina.
Bird watchers in the United States can count on this migration occurring every three to four years. The regulating factors causing the lemming population crashes appear to be
density-dependent in nature, involving pathogens, changes in

Fig. 5-6. The brown lemming (*Lemmus trimucronatus*) and its
two principal predators, the snowy owl and the arctic fox. The
graph shows the short-term, three-to-four-year peaks and lows of
the lemming cycle on Victoria Island (eastern end), Canada.

food quality and quantity, and physiological and psychological stress as well as predators. After such a crash, the lack of
predators and the low density of lemmings in relation to the
amount of available food and space allow the lemming populations to increase almost unchecked again for the next several years. Then the overcrowding again produces a sudden
population crash and another complete cycle has occurred.
Occasionally, dramatic emigrations occur to relieve exceptional
outbreaks, as has been mentioned earlier in discussing population dispersal (Chapter 4).

In some insect groups, long-term population cycles appear to be utilized as a successful strategy to avoid predation.
The seventeen-year cicada has a seventeen-year gap between
adult generations. In the year of an emergence, the adults
emerge synchronously in early summer and live only four to
six weeks. These insects come from nymphs that hatched
originally from eggs laid over a period of several weeks some
seventeen years earlier. Yet the developing nymphal stages in
the soil manage to keep track of the years and synchronize
their emergence from the ground to become adults at exactly
the same moment as the rest of the population. Until the cuticle (outer skin or integument) becomes hardened by exposure
to the air for several hours, the newly emerged adult cicada
is helpless (Fig. 5-7). However, because the population emergence is synchronized the predators in the area cannot destroy the millions of individuals that suddenly appear. Thus

Fig. 5-7. A periodical cicada, an insect with a seventeen-year life
cycle.

the seventeen-year cicadas overwhelm predators when they appear. The extreme length of the cycle makes it very difficult for a predator to get into a similar cycle and specialize in cicadas. What would the bird or wasp eat the other sixteen years?

It is also hypothesized that the long cycle enables the cicada to escape certain fungal pathogens present in the soil of Eastern deciduous forests. The spores of these molds may be unable to survive until the next emergence of the adults. Naturally, the other density-dependent factors operate during the years the cicada nymphs are underground. Intraspecific competition for nymphal food (the cicada nymphs feed on sap in tree roots) and annual predation on nymphs by moles and shrews probably play an important role in establishing the carrying capacity for this cicada in the areas it inhabits.

Summary

Population density refers to the number of individuals per unit of space and may be measured in several ways (crude density, relative or ecological density, and index of relative abundance). Growth of overall number in a population involves natality, mortality, and survivorship. The form of survivorship curves depends on the time in life when mortality factors act. Should all environmental restraints be absent, all individuals would survive to reproductive age at each generation and the population of that species would have reached its biotic potential (simply maximum natality less minimum mortality). The fact that natural populations do not increase at this maximum possible growth rate reflects the strength of the environmental resistance present. The result of the interaction of the biotic potential and environmental resistance is a characteristic pattern of increase in numbers called the population growth form. The two extremes of this form are the J-shaped or exponential growth curve and the S-shaped or sigmoid growth curve; the latter levels off at the carrying capacity of the environment. Population regulation is accomplished by a variety of density-independent and density-dependent factors. Commonly, one will find periodic fluctuations in population density relating to seasonal or annual variation in limiting factors of the physical environment. Relatively long-term oscillations that cannot be explained as easily are found in arctic mammals and other species.

6
THE ECOLOGY
OF COMMUNITIES

Individuals constitute populations, and populations in turn make up plant and animal **communities.** Thus a biotic community is an assemblage of populations of various species living in a particular region or habitat. It is the *living* part of the ecosystem. Communities have internal structure and regulatory processes just like the population and the individual organism. We have already touched upon many of these basic structural and energetic interrelationships in earlier chapters, without making special note that they are most significant on the level of the community. It is relatively meaningless to speak of energy and element flow, food webs, interspecific relationships, and so forth outside the context of the total biotic community. Thus in this chapter we will look specifically at several additional concepts of community ecology that will be of special importance in relating basic ecological phenomena to population growth in man and the resultant crises in environmental deterioration.

Differentiation in a Community

The word *community* can describe biotic assemblages that differ greatly in size, from the living organisms in a decaying log to the fauna and flora of a huge rain forest. **Major com-**

munities are those that, together with their physical habitat, form more or less complete and self-sustaining ecosystems. In such systems solar energy is the principal or only needed input from external areas. Such communities are relatively independent of adjoining communities because of their sufficient size and level of organization. **Minor communities,** on the other hand, are more or less dependent on neighboring aggregations of organisms for an input of energy. The decaying log or a temporary rain pool in a desert canyon represent minor communities with comparatively short but intense periods of biological activities.

The various plant and animal species that compose a community of any size have different ways of life. Hence community differentiation shows simultaneously on the horizontal plane, on the vertical levels, and temporally. **Horizontal differentiation** is the patchy or mosaic-like occurrence of species; we have already seen it in discussing the dispersion of populations (Fig. 1-3). **Vertical differentiation** shows in the different heights to which plants of various growth forms ascend and in the resultant "layering" of animal species living at these several levels in the community (Fig. 1-2). **Temporal differentiation** is exhibited by different species carrying on similar functions at different times in both daily and seasonal cycles (Fig. 1-4). Nocturnal owls and diurnal hawks both hunt small rodents, but their periods of activity do not overlap. These aspects of community differentiation are not unique to terrestrial communities. We may see the effects of environmental factors on distribution of aquatic life forms particularly well in ponds and lakes.

Lake Communities

Lakes are large, relatively still bodies of fresh water. They may be formed by glacial erosion, uplifting of mountains, deposition of debris in the beds of slow-flowing streams, or other geological activity. With dams on large rivers, man has created many new lakes for power, water storage, and agricultural irrigation.

Within any lake there are notable gradations of light penetration, temperature level, and oxygen content of the water. The depth to which light will penetrate is limited by suspended materials, such as silt particles; hence the extent of turbidity restricts the photosynthetic zone in the aquatic habitat. For this reason phytoplankton tend to occur in the upper levels of the lake. The annual cycle of seasonal changes in water temperature also affects the distribution of plant and animal life within the lake. As the surface layer warms up from more intense sunlight in the spring and summer, the difference in density between the surface water and the deeper, colder layers establishes a barrier against mixing. The nutrients in the sediment on the lake bottom are no longer lifted by upwelling of the deep water, and the more highly oxygenated surface waters do not sink. The overall result of this pronounced thermal stratification is to halt mixing of the nutrients, the dissolved oxygen, and the plankton near the surface with the deeper water. Hence most fish have to move upward in the lake during the midsummer period to gain sufficient oxygen and plankton. In the fall this thermal stratification disappears again and free mixing of the shallow and deep water can take place.

With erosion from surrounding slopes and input of sediment by rivers, smaller lakes tend to support relatively short-lived communities of aquatic life. The natural succession that takes place as the lake basin fills in eventually leads to a pond, a marsh, and finally a grassy depression in the landscape. Man's giant reservoirs in the American southwest, as well as in other parts of the world (for example, the Aswan Dam of the United Arab Republic), have an especially short lifetime because the particular rivers dammed to create the reservoirs carry large loads of silt.

Dominance
in a
Community

When one looks at a community of organisms from an ecological viewpoint, one or several species usually stand out as major influences on the composition and internal energy dynamics of the community. Such species are said to be **dominant** because of the *numbers* of organisms present, their *size*, or their *energetic* activities. Thus out of the hundreds of species in a California pine forest, we immediately notice the greater numbers of Ponderosa pines and regard that species, *Pinus ponderosa*, as the dominant organism in the community (Fig. 6-1). In a fifty-acre pasture in the eastern United States, we might find the following numbers of animals and plants present in the total area covered:

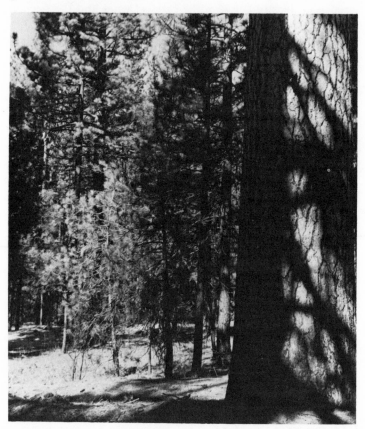

Fig. 6-1. A Ponderosa pine forest community in the western United States, showing *Pinus ponderosa* as the readily identifiable dominant species.

dairy cattle	50 individuals
turkeys	6 individuals
sheep	1 individual
bluegrass	45 acres
white clover	3 acres
oak trees	2 acres

Clearly, the dairy cow is the dominant species among the consumers and the bluegrass is dominant among the producers in this farmland community.

Productivity and Associated Concepts

We frequently want to know how much an area in a particular type of biotic community will produce. For instance, agriculturists use the concept of **productivity** to describe how many cattle can be raised per hundred acres of pasture. Wildlife biologists can likewise use it to describe the number of native antelope subsisting on a hundred acres of savanna in Kenya. Applied ecologists may then desire to compare the production of such man-maintained communities and natural communities. The concept of productivity provides a way to standardize such comparisons. Productivity is defined as the production of organic matter per unit of area over a particular time interval, usually a year. Productivities measured on an annual basis take into account the differences in organic matter present at various times of the annual cycle, and hence prevent the erroneous conclusions that may be reached from comparisons of two regions sampled at different seasons.

Sometimes, however, it is useful to know the number of individuals or the total biomass present in a community at one particular time. Such a measurement is termed the **standing crop** of that area. During the winter in temperate-zone localities, the standing crop would be small. But in the late spring and summer, as growth and reproduction take place, there is a very considerable increase in the amount of organic matter making up the biomass of the community. Similarly, in the tropics the forests have a lower biomass in the dry season than in the wet season when the trees produce more foliage in response to heavier rainfall.

Finally, ecologists speak of the carrying capacity of a community or area, a concept we have already mentioned in Chapter 5. This is the largest standing crop of a species that an area can support without deterioration of the habitat. Should the carrying capacity be exceeded through overpopulation, the various regulatory factors we have previously discussed will soon bring the standing crop below the critical level again.

Succession

Change in a biotic community is more or less constant. New species enter the area; old ones find conditions changing and must move or die out. The continual replacement of one community by another is called **succession,** and it terminates only when a **climax** stage is reached. The process of succession is partly a result of ever-changing climate and physical habitat in the region, and partly of the activities of the previous community's organisms. Lichens, for instance, are an excellent **pioneer** organism in the first organic community growing on a bare rock surface. Their secretion of organic acids breaks down the rock surface, making available enough nutrients and substrate ° for moss spores to germinate and establish a new rock community dominated by mosses. In turn, mosses trap more rainwater than do lichens and in general change the environmental conditions so much that many of the lichens die out. Thus a new stage in succession has been attained. Next, the rich bed of mosses may provide satisfactory conditions for the establishment of ferns. This series of steps or communities that develop in the process of succession is called a *sere* (Fig. 6-2).

After passing through relatively transitory communities (called **seral stages**), the sere ends in a **climax community**

° The substance or base on which an organism grows.

Fig. 6-2. Forest succession from annual weeds to mature forest. Note the increasing stratification as one seral stage advances to another. (*For credit see p. viii.*)

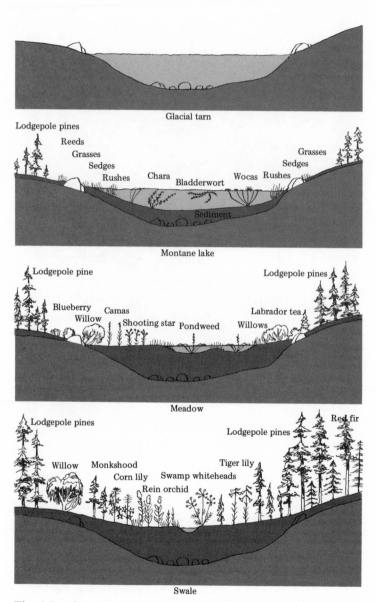

Glacial tarn

Montane lake

Meadow

Swale

Fig. 6-3.   Stages in primary succession from a lake to climax forest in the Sierra Nevada mountains of California.

that is best suited for the prevailing climate or soil conditions. If the succession that led to this climax stage began on an area such as newly exposed rock or sand not previously occupied by a biotic community, we have **primary succession** (Fig. 6-3). The first seral stage in primary succession is called a pioneer community. Should community succession proceed in an area where a community was removed (e.g., a plowed field or clear-cut forest), we have **secondary succession.** The process of secondary succession is usually quite rapid, as nutrients, soil bacteria, and other necessities are already present from the activities of earlier organisms. Thus weeds spring up in great numbers in a plowed field within a few weeks; they need not wait for the early stages of primary succession to prepare the soil substrate for the specific requirements of these evolutionarily higher flowering plants. Shrubs and, later, trees will follow the weed seral stage if the climate and soil are suitable. The whole trend in either primary or secondary succession is toward a stage with a complex community food web where less energy is wasted and there is high ecological efficiency at all levels of the food pyramid.

Major Climax Formations

The major climax community types of the world are called **biomes.** Biomes are general groupings of similar communities. These groupings are based upon the distinctive life forms of the important species in each community. Thus the great number of biotic communities around the world is reduced to a concise and mentally manageable set of nine or so biomes.

In terrestrial regions, dominant vegetational types are usually used to characterize biomes. The principal biomes of the world are:

Tundra	Grassland
Coniferous forest or Taiga	Desert
Temperate deciduous forest	Tropical savanna
Chaparral	Tropical deciduous forest
Tropical rain forest	

Tundra

North of the Arctic Circle extends a vast treeless region with a very short growing season (June–July), extremely low temperatures during the winter and cold temperatures even during the brief summer, and a permanently frozen soil (the **permafrost**) below the surface. This is the arctic **tundra** biome (Fig. 6-4). Under such harsh conditions only a few species of animals are found, but their populations often reach huge numbers. Human visitors to tundra areas often find mosquitoes to be overwhelmingly abundant organisms in the arctic summer.

Most of the mammals are burrowing species, such as lemmings and mice. Some of the larger mammals, such as caribou and musk ox, must migrate annually in search of food. These herbivores feed in the tundra zone only during the short time of production of grasses and lichens. Other migrants, especially the birds, depend for food upon smaller organisms that are only active during the warmer summer months.

Fig. 6-4. The tundra biome found north of the Arctic Circle and on mountain tops above timberline, here seen near St. Mary's Glacier in northern Colorado.

Plant life is represented by many lichen species, mosses, and low-growing flowering plants such as sedges, grasses, and hardy shrubs, growing in a tight mat upon the surface of the ground. Food chains and webs are relatively simple in the Arctic and for that reason they have been well studied by ecologists. There is a great amount of annual moisture in the tundra, but much of it is tied up in snow or permafrost or lost by evaporation. Thus relatively little water is available to tundra organisms.

Coniferous Forest or Taiga

South of the tundra, around the polar region of the Northern Hemisphere, one finds a broad band of evergreen coniferous forest, or **Taiga** (Fig. 6-5). In the Southern Hemisphere only a small area of coniferous forest exists. This results from the lack of land area, since the proper latitudes largely fall between the coast of Antarctica and the tips of the southern continents. The spruces, firs, pines, and other conifers of the Taiga are able to grow at these latitudes because of the increase in *available* annual moisture. This moisture increase in the Taiga as compared to the tundra results from warmer temperatures farther away from the poles. In these higher temperatures, large amounts of moisture cannot remain in frozen forms that cannot be absorbed by plant life, as in the tundra. Although the conifers are subject to long cold winters at these latitudes, they remain green all year and do not drop their leaves (needles) simultaneously. Yet the stresses of the subarctic winter bring photosynthetic production to a virtual halt. Flowering plants like willows and birches grow along streams and in pioneer habitats in the Taiga, and drop their leaves in the winter. Animal life in this biome is also relatively poor in species. Fur-bearing mammals such as bears, weasels, and martens are typical inhabitants. Predators are not as likely to be migratory in this biome as in the tundra since the prey species that inhabit the Taiga can be active above ground during the winter.

Temperate Deciduous Forest

Rainfall in this biome is sufficient to support broad-

Fig. 6-5. The coniferous forest (Taiga) biome in Colorado.

leafed shrubs and trees. The great hardwood forests of eastern North America (Fig. 6-6) and Europe are excellent examples of **temperate deciduous forest.** Since this forest type occurs in the temperate zone, the species are subject to considerable temperature fluctuations and a cyclic alternation of photosynthetic production, which is high in the summer months and low in winter. This biome was the cradle of European civilization, and historically most scientists, including those living today, have worked in it. For this reason, much of our ecological thinking is biased in the sense that it is based upon experience in the temperate zone rather than in the tropics. In some cases this has probably been quite beneficial. Linnaeus probably succeeded in establishing a binomial system of nomenclature for plant and animal species in the eighteenth century because of the *few* organisms he had around him in Sweden where he lived. Had he resided in tropical South America, the incredible abundance of different kinds of organisms might have overwhelmed him and prevented such a logical and adaptable taxonomic system from coming to mind.

Fig. 6-6. The temperate deciduous forest biome in western New York.

Chaparral

The Mediterranean climate of parts of southern Europe, southern Australia, and southern California is very dry for most of the year, with low total precipitation in the form of winter rains and occasional summer thundershowers. The low, shrubby vegetation in these areas has thick, evergreen leaves whose toughness and waxy coatings make them resistant to prolonged periods of drought. This **chaparral** biome

vegetation is also **fire-adapted;** that is, it depends upon periodic fast-burning fires to perpetuate itself and allow reproduction of the various species of shrubs at the expense of
trees. After a fire passes, with the first rains of the next
growing season the chaparral species sprout from their
stumps or from seeds lying dormant in the soil. However, if
fires do not race through the chaparral every ten to twenty
years, the community becomes overly mature and growth of
new seedlings is prevented by the densely growing older
plants. When a fire finally occurs, it will be extremely destructive because of all the accumulated fuel under the older
plants (old leaves, branches, etc.). Even the stumps and roots
of many shrub species will be killed by the intense heat.
When shrubs have been destroyed this way, tree seeds floating in from adjacent forest areas can germinate and grow in
the area before the chaparral can recover. Thus chaparral is
an example of a fire-maintained climax community.

Grassland

In the extensive temperate plains areas of North America, Eurasia, and Australia there is sufficient rainfall to support a heavy growth of herbaceous plants, especially bunch
grasses and spreading grasses (species with underground
stems). No trees are present except along watercourses. Burrowing rodents are common and often form extensive colonies. Large herds of grazing animals (including marsupials
such as kangaroos in Australia) were typically found in the
grasslands of recent times; today, many of these species have
disappeared or been nearly exterminated by man. Man has
also been interrupting the ecology of grasslands by cutting
through the sod with plows and other mechanical devices.
Today, little remains of the flora and fauna of the original
Great Plains and prairie areas of the eastern United States.
In fact, many of the grasses would probably have disappeared
under the farmer's plow long ago were it not for their acci-
dental preservation along railroad track right-of-ways. The
great herds of American bison were reduced by hunting to a
few individuals in Canada by the end of the last century, but
fortunately this remnant was bred to reintroduce the species to United States park areas.

Fig. 6-7. The desert biome, here represented by the Mojave Desert in eastern California.

Desert

The **desert** biome (Fig. 6-7) is worldwide in extent and is characterized by very low rainfall, a high evaporation rate, high diurnal temperatures, and low nocturnal temperatures. The plant species present are generally quite low in profile. Desert shrubs and other plants tend to have reduced, waxy, drought-resistant leaves. Some plants such as cacti have virtually lost their leaves and depend upon greatly expanded photosynthetic stems for **autotrophic °** food production. Primary production in a desert is low and hence primary consumption by animal life is low. Relatively few species of animals are active during the daytime or even live in the desert. Because of the cool nights, dew is a significant source of moisture for desert organisms, which lack the availability of surface water or frequent rain showers. Many desert plants

° Capable of producing its own food. An autotroph, like a typical green plant, does not have to depend on other organisms for food. It acquires carbon dioxide from the air and water from the soil, and from these inorganic molecules it makes, through photosynthesis, the sugar glucose, which can be used in its cells as food.

can absorb dew and translocate its moisture from their leaves
to their stems and roots.

Tropical Savanna

In some of the tropical areas of the world, one finds
grassland with scattered trees. This mixture of dry-adapted
herbaceous plants, shrubs, and occasional trees is called **tropical savanna.** In overall appearance (Fig. 6-8) it is like an
open park. Acacias in Africa and palms in South America are
the usual trees on the savanna. Rather large mixed herds of

Fig. 6-8.   Two views of the African savanna.

primary consumers characterize the savanna fauna. In eastern Africa, for instance, gazelles graze the lowest layers of the vegetation while giraffes feed on the tops of the thorny acacias. Large predators such as lions prey primarily upon such herds of herbivores. In tropical Australian savannas the primary consumer herds are marsupials.

Tropical Deciduous Forest

Where the rainfall becomes heavier on the margins of a tropical savanna and can support regular forest, one finds the **tropical deciduous forest** biome (Fig. 6-9). This biome is subjected annually to a dry season–wet season environmental cycle instead of the cold winter–hot summer regime of its temperate-zone counterpart. With uniformly warm temperatures all year, the growth of the trees and herbaceous plants of this tropical forest is affected only by seasonal distribution of the rainfall. Hence, in the annual dry season such forests lose most leaves and then leaf out again at the onset of the rainy season. In the considerable number of species in such a forest, most exhibit special adaptations for passing the dry season in much the same manner as temperate-zone species pass the winter.

Tropical Rain Forest

In the circumtropical biome of the **tropical rain forest,** rainfall tends to be more or less evenly distributed throughout the year. The mean annual temperature lies between about 68°F and 82°F, with very little seasonal fluctuation. In fact, the change from daytime to nighttime temperatures in a rain forest is greater than the annual mean temperature fluctuation. Neither temperature nor water is a limiting factor on plant or animal growth. Soil conditions do exercise some limitation on plant growth. Biotic interactions are very important as limiting factors; there are more different kinds of organisms in this region than in any other biome. Such unusual creatures as parrots, army ants, and tapirs (Figs. 6-10 and 6-11) are representative of the diversity of life in the tropical rain forest. Yet there are fewer individuals of any one species per unit area than in other biomes.

Fig. 6-9. The tropical deciduous forest biome during the dry season in northwestern Costa Rica.

Fig. 6-10. The tropical rain forest on the Osa Peninsula in Costa Rica, the richest and most diverse climax community on earth. Parrots and large army ants are typical inhabitants.

Fig. 6-11. A South American tapir, a large mammal found in tropical rain forests.

Fig. 6-12. Adaptive features of plants in a rain forest. (A) A bromeliad with a rosette of basal leaves forming a basin for rain water. (B) A "drip tip," the structurally modified end of a typical tree or shrub leaf in the rain forest.

A   B

Arboreal epiphytic plant life is particularly well developed in Central and South American rain forests. Orchids and "tank plants" of the family Bromeliaceae are exceptionally abundant. The latter plants catch rain water in the leafy basins formed by their rosettes of leaves (Fig. 6-12), and aquatic communities of insects, frogs, and other organisms develop in these pools. The rain forest canopy becomes essentially continuous in some places so that the forest floor receives little light; hence undergrowth is limited. Where the canopy is broken, the forest is much more complex and trees of various heights present a layered or storied picture. Long hanging vines called lianas cascade down from the canopy in such areas. Most plants are evergreen and may exhibit "drip tips" on the ends of their leaves, apparently an adaptive feature to speed runoff of rain water (Fig. 6-12). Because of the constant high humidity, a miniature plant community composed of mosses and fungi can develop on the surface of a broad, wet leaf of a tree or shrub within a short time. These tiny plants making their home on the surface of leaves are called **epiphylls.** Such epiphylls would cut down on the photosynthetic capability of that leaf (and hence of the shrub or tree) in the dim lighting of the understory of the forest. The drip tips of many plant species are a distinct advantage in protecting their leaves from the development of an overgrowth of epiphylls.

Climax Communities: Their Importance

Terrestrial climax communities tend to be more stable and have more diverse paths of energy flow in food webs than do intermediate seral communities. Hence they are generally the most productive of the natural communities in a sere. They are composed of the plants and animals best suited by evolutionary adaptation to the prevailing climatic and soil conditions of the region. Today, climax communities everywhere are being threatened by human activities. If a climax community is destroyed, we know that hundreds of years are necessary for succession to create another. Thus it becomes imperative for us to be fully cognizant of the risks involved in any major environmental alteration. We shall be looking at the results of some of these alterations in the next chapters.

Summary

A biotic community is an assemblage of populations of various species living in a particular area. Within this mixture of organisms one finds horizontal, vertical, and temporal differentiation. Dominant species stand out because of their numerical abundance, size, or energetic activities. The productivity of a community is measured by the production of organic matter per unit of area over a specified time interval, usually a year. The total biomass or number of individuals present at a particular point in time is the standing crop of a community. The carrying capacity of an area or community is the largest standing crop of a species that an area can support without ecological damage. The process of continual replacement of one community by another is called succession and occurs because the activities of the previous inhabitants change the environmental conditions. The series of steps or communities that develops during succession is called a sere. Primary succession begins with a pioneer community and ends in a climax community. Secondary succession proceeds in an area where a community was recently removed. The major climax community types of the world are called biomes and include tundra, Taiga, temperate deciduous forest, chaparral, grassland, desert, tropical savanna, tropical deciduous forest, and tropical rain forest. Climax communities are the most stable and most productive of the natural communities in a sere, and take hundreds of years to replace if destroyed by environmental alteration.

7
ENVIRONMENTAL
ALTERATION

We have seen that communities are assemblages of plants and animals sharing a common environment and operating as a closely interrelated unit. Despite the diversity of life on earth, the number of major kinds of communities is small; and after viewing these principal biomes in Chapter 6 we realize that each is the climax type for a particular set of environmental factors, being principally dependent upon available precipitation and annual temperature cycles. In each case, the climax community, arising through a series of intermediate communities, is the result of the succession process. We noted that when the sere reaches the climax stage, things become relatively stable; that is, energy flows are more balanced, the mature community is more diverse, and there is less chance of catastrophic changes in the biotic balance, should one species suddenly boom in numbers or become extinct.

With this review as background, why is succession so significant when we consider factors that endanger natural communities? Simply because most of the natural communities that are particularly threatened are the *climax* communities in that area. *When a climax community is destroyed, the only way to restore it is by the lengthy process of succession.* It may take hundreds or thousands of years for a sere to reach that final stage; thus once a mature community is altered, the damage is almost permanent on the time scale of human activity.

With this fact in mind, let us view a selected spectrum of factors that change, pollute, or otherwise threaten natural communities. Underlying perhaps *all* of these problems is the basic factor of the burgeoning population and technology of man, which we shall treat later in detail.

Fire

Fire is a natural phenomenon that can happen in almost any terrestrial ecosystem because of the accumulation of plant remains or plants that at some point in the year become combustible. Under these circumstances, lightning or acts of man can set off uncontrolled fires. But though these fires are destructive in the immediate sense, there is no reason to think of fire as an evil to be totally abolished by man's efforts from all ecosystems. In the United States our thinking on the place of fire in the natural forest has changed radically over the past hundred years.

Historically, great fire disasters in northern lumber towns and forests in the nineteenth and early twentieth centuries made the American public consider fire in natural communities inherently undesirable. American foresters trained in European schools imported the protective concepts that were useful in the intensely tended forests there. Thus for decades the U.S. Forest Service emphasized in a well-advertised campaign that fire was extremely bad for the forests of America. However, ecologists have recently shown that where fire has been a natural part of the forest environment, it is frequently necessary for effective forest management.

In the southeastern United States, for example, fire is necessary for successful reproduction in longleaf pine forests. The longleaf pine grows along the coastal plain from Virginia south to Florida and west to Texas. In their natural state longleaf pines are well spaced and there is a light cover of grasses on the forest floor. When these forests were first logged, reproduction of the longleaf pine was very poor. At first, ground fires were blamed; so fire was tightly controlled or totally prevented in such forest areas. Soon there was no reproduction of the pines at all. Upon investigation of the

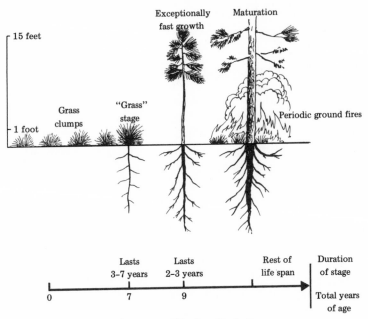

Fig. 7-1. The growth stages of the longleaf pine.

species' life history, the answer to this problem became evident (Fig. 7-1). For the first three to seven years after sprouting, the young longleaf pine consists of a long taproot, with a thick terminal bud, protected by a long tuft of needles, above ground. Grass fires sweep by too rapidly to harm such a bud. During the next two or three years, the pine grows exceptionally fast, to ten to fifteen feet in height, and thus raises its more sensitive new branch growth above the range of the normal grass fire. The development of a thick, fire-resistant bark protects the young tree from further ground fires. The periodic ground fires characteristic of southern forests are necessary to prevent the incursion of much less valuable hardwoods or other species of pine into the longleaf pine stands. Without the fires, the fire-susceptible hardwoods are able to grow relatively well and shade out the young longleaf pines. Thus fire is *necessary* to maintain the economically desirable climax community of longleaf pine. Today this is recognized by forest managers, and use of periodic controlled ground fires is a common practice.

Agricultural Clearing

Historically, the clearing of land for cultivation has been the major means of landscape alteration. But currently the United States, the Soviet Union, Ireland, and Japan, among other nations, have actually *reduced* their land area under cultivation. On the other hand, India and China, the most populous countries today, are already cultivating nearly *all* of their suitable land areas. The chief remaining biotic communities seriously threatened by agricultural expansion are the lowland coastal deserts found on most continents, and the tropical rain forests of the Amazon basin, southeast Asia, and Africa south of the Sahara.

Deserts can be very productive areas from an agricultural point of view. The chief limiting factor is the lack of fresh water, and it will remain limiting in these areas until desalinization of sea water becomes economically practical —probably around 1980.

Tropical rain forests (Fig. 7-2) present more of an ecological problem. There is no guarantee that it will *ever* be feasible to encourage large-scale agriculture there because **laterization** of the soil occurs when the forest is cleared. Despite the lush appearance of rain forests, their soils are usually thin and poor. When this soil is exposed to heavy rainfall by deforestation, silica and other soil minerals are leached downward and organic material is oxidized. If the thin topsoil is then eroded by the rain, a layer of aluminum and iron oxides is exposed, which in the air can form a hard, impermeable, red crust called **laterite.** Once formed, this crust appears to be relatively permanent and the vegetation that can grow there (including crop plants) is very sparse.

There is also considerable evidence that clearing large rain forest areas may raise temperatures and change climates. Feininger and other scientists working in northern South America have reported dramatic decreases in rainfall over large areas of the Amazon basin rain forest in Colombia during the past 26 years. The decreases have amounted to as much as 21 to 24 percent from earlier records of normal rainfall. A correlation exists between these changes and the fell-

Fig. 7-2. Clearing and burning tropical rain forest for cultivation in Costa Rica.

ing of vast tracts of rain forests in Colombia and neighboring countries. Feininger warns: "Should the decrease be widespread throughout the continent, the consequences could seriously retard the development of the tropical Latin American countries. . . ." [*]

[*] Tomas Feininger, "Less rain in Latin America," *Science* 160 (1968): 13–14.

Provided Latin American population levels are stabilized, many ecologists believe it may be best to follow the traditional Indian agricultural methods in Central and South America. These methods are usually called by the general term of **slash-and-burn agriculture.** The native typically clears a small area or areas of forest with axe and saw, allows the fallen logs to dry out, and then burns the plots. He plants a variety of crop plants, such as bananas, sugar cane, papayas, and cassava, in the same small field among the tree stumps. Several years later, when the nutrients in the soil are exhausted and erosion may be occurring, the farmer abandons his fields and moves on to clear another patch of forest and repeat the procedure. Meanwhile, secondary succession starts in his abandoned fields and eventually the young regenerating forest replenishes the soil nutrients. It still may take over a hundred years to restore a mature climax forest to the site, of course. This system will work as long as there is not an *excess number* of farmers operating in a particular area, increasing the probability of repeated use of the land before the forest has fully regenerated itself. Large banana plantations, exemplifying attempts at extensive clearing for agricultural purposes, have a high productivity in their first years, but not later. With prolonged use of the land for growing bananas alone, banana parasites (especially a root fungus) move in and destroy the plantings. Huge plantation holdings have been devastated by fungal parasites in Costa Rica, and the future of banana plantations in that famous banana-producing republic of Central America is in serious jeopardy. The only current way to fight the fungus, once established, is to abandon the fields and clear new areas some distance away; but this is a temporary holding action at best.

Defoliation and Bombing

Defoliant chemicals in considerable quantity are sprayed along roadsides and railroad tracks in this country to kill unwanted plant life. But nowhere in the world have herbicides been used in such quantities as in Vietnam during the late 1960s. In a massive landscape-altering program, approximately 13 to 14 million pounds of the defoliants 2, 4-D and 2, 4, 5-T (di- and trichlorophenoxyacetic acids), the *entire* production of these chemicals in the United States during 1967 and 1968, plus other compounds, have been sprayed on the Vietnamese forests by the U.S. military. The effect of these herbicides is to kill all vegetation from the ground up, rendering enemy units more visible in the thick natural forests and also destroying crops used as food. Agent Orange, a mixture of the n-butyl esters of 2,4-D and 2,4,5-T, was the most commonly used defoliant for general forest and brush clearing because it attacks a wide variety of broad-leafed plants. The C-123 sprayer aircraft can carry 1,000 gallons of the defoliant and spray their load in slightly over four minutes, flying just above the treetops at about 125 miles per hour (Fig. 7-3, top). Within several weeks, the forest is leafless and many or all of the trees may die, depending upon their susceptibility to the poison (Fig. 7-3, center).

Short-range changes in the sprayed biotic communities of Vietnam have already occurred. Nearly all flora and fauna are gone in the repeatedly sprayed areas. Forest fires have raged through the dead woods (living rain forests do not ordinarily burn), further exposing the soil to erosion and laterization. Near Saigon, a single forest fire destroyed nearly 100,000 acres of woods heavily treated with herbicides. Long-term changes are uncertain as yet, although mangrove swamps that had been heavily sprayed were still totally dead five years later. Mangrove trees help to stabilize coastlines and coastal waterways with their extensive root systems. Ecologists have noted dense bamboo stands, which prevent forest reproduction, developing in less heavily sprayed areas. Evidence also indicates an increase in the number of birth defects among babies of Vietnamese mothers who lived in sprayed areas.

Defoliation is not the only landscape alteration caused by warfare, of course. In Indochina, tremendous tonnages of bombs dropped on both forests and agricultural areas have resulted in craterization of the landscape (Fig. 7-3, bottom) on an immense scale, perhaps the largest excavation project

Fig. 7-3. Landscape alteration by defoliation and bombing in Vietnam. In the top photograph, C-123 are spraying Agent Orange defoliant (a mixture of 2,4-D and 2,4,5-T compounds) on a forest in central Vietnam. The center photograph shows a defoliated mangrove forest along the Saigon River; 100 percent of the trees have been killed by the application of Agent Orange. No regeneration has occurred in areas last sprayed over five years ago. The bottom scene shows B-52 bomb craters in agricultural country northwest of Saigon. Each crater is about 30 feet deep and 40 feet in diameter.

in mankind's history. The total cratered area throughout Indochina has been estimated to exceed the area of the state of Connecticut by 5,000 square miles. These craters are filled with water even late in the dry season, providing breeding sites for mosquitoes, ponds for aquatic snails that serve as intermediate hosts to parasitic worms that later infest man, and other pests. The total ecological and agricultural inpact of these bomb craters is yet to be measured, but it is likely to be great.

Urban Expansion

Today the worldwide phenomenon of urbanization (Fig. 7-4) is far more threatening to natural communities than is the expansion of agricultural clearing. The growth of urban areas will increase because of continued migration to cities, which increases the urban population, and high birth rates, which increase the total population. This increase in urban population, coupled with the trend towards spacious suburban residential development, is making continually greater demands on the available land around the urban fringe. In the United States alone, it is estimated that urban land area will increase from 21 million acres in 1960 to 45 million acres in the year 2000.

The increase in urbanized land is taken not only from surrounding terrestrial communities but also by filling in shallow marine bays. Land developers can purchase shallow areas of a bay and dredge up fill from adjoining bay bottom or bring in solid waste and soil fill from adjacent land areas. Prime examples of the dramatic extremes to which **dredge-and-fill** operations have been carried are seen in Tampa Bay in Florida, where 15 to 20 percent of the original water area has been filled in, and San Francisco Bay on the West Coast, with some 33 percent of the old bay filled. Such filling destroys principal spawning areas for a host of marine fish and invertebrates, destroys wintering places for migratory waterfowl, and may change the local weather patterns. San Francisco Bay is the most important stopping place for migratory waterfowl on the great Pacific Flyway. Approximately one million waterfowl winter on the Bay. If the filling trend continues at San Francisco (some 70 percent of the Bay is less than twelve feet deep and therefore easily fillable), these birds will lose their feeding and wintering grounds. Some meteorologists predict a sharp increase in summer temperatures (the cool summer fogs characteristic of San Francisco have already been noted to be less frequent now than formerly) and a drastic increase in smog. Not the least of the worries of San Franciscans who live or work in buildings constructed on

Fig. 7-4. Urbanization in a mountain valley of Peru: the city of Cuzco, 1970. Note the heavily terraced mountain slopes of the Andes behind the city; the people are using all available land either for cultivation or housing.

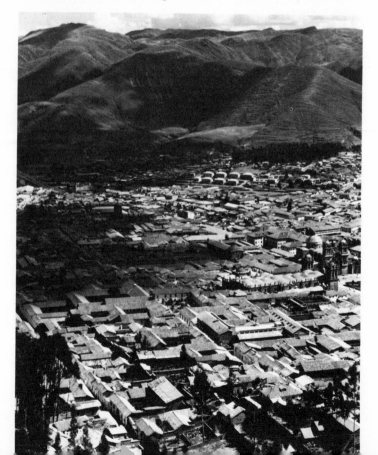

the unstable landfill should be the consequences of future earthquakes.

California and Florida are not ignoring the ecological problems of filling in bays. Many cities around bays have established so-called **bulkhead lines:** where no commercial filling and developing is allowed in a bay beyond a certain line (usually at the mean high water mark). Some counties have placed moratoriums on the sale and dredging of submerged lands, or passed laws requiring ecological surveys of bay areas before permits are granted for dredging, filling, or sale. The widespread public concern over the quality of the environment has been instrumental in bringing about these wise restrictions.

Clear-cutting of Forests

There are currently 182 million acres of national forests in the United States. These forest areas are administered by the U. S. Forest Service, an agency of the Department of Agriculture. Under a long-standing policy, formalized by a 1960 federal law, the 154 national forests are supposed to be maintained for multiple use, including timber, recreation, grazing, wildlife preservation, and watershed protection. In 1971, as a result of lobbying pressure from major western lumber companies, the President ordered the Forest Service to give top priority to private logging on this public land. To increase the immediate yield to the lumber companies, the Forest Service has increasingly authorized **clear-cutting,** an economical and efficient (100 percent yield) logging method that involves cutting of *all* trees in an area (the yield from selective cutting of mature trees is about 60 percent). Aside from the loss to recreation, grazing, and wildlife protection, perhaps the most dangerous result of clear-cutting (Fig. 7-5) is watershed degradation. A **watershed** is the area whose rainfall collects and drains downhill into a particular stream. The extent and character of the hillside cover of plant growth determines how fast the runoff is and how much sediment is picked up

Fig. 7-5. The ecological results of clear-cutting in a northwestern forest.

en route to the stream. Clear-cutting can cause a 7,000-fold increase in stream sedimentation and ruin breeding grounds for fish. Heavy snowmelt or rainfall on clear-cut slopes can cause rapid runoff and devastating downstream floods. These adverse effects of clear-cutting are of far greater economic cost to the whole human population of a region than is the expense incurred by lumber companies restricted to selective logging.

Public Works Projects

One of the major persistent threats to the natural environment is the giant public works project; ostensibly undertaken to "control" the environment and bend it to man's immediate needs, such projects often result in deleterious side effects that make the overall scheme an economic as well as an ecological loss.

In 1969 and early 1970 there was great controversy over plans to build a 39-square-mile jetport in Big Cypress Swamp, just north of the Everglades in south Florida. Not recognized by the planners was the ecology of surface water flow across the southern half of the state. This movement of water would be seriously disrupted by the runway construction for a jetport and associated commercial developments. Since the Big Cypress Swamp provides 38 percent of the water flowing south into Everglades National Park and the park is already suffering ecologically from years of drought in south Florida, the lack of water would irreparably destroy the basic ecology of this unique national preserve. Other powerful arguments, such as those concerned with expected air pollution and noise pollution, combined with this critical question of water supply, resulted in the defeat of this project by the aroused people of Florida.

Projects that may be desirable at one time in history are sometimes not accomplished then, but linger on in the minds of special interest groups and resurface later. A classic example is the U. S. Army Corps of Engineers' Cross-Florida Barge Canal. This mammoth project to cut a canal across the upper part of the Florida peninsula was proposed during World War II, with the intent of allowing barge and other coastal maritime traffic between the Atlantic Ocean and the Gulf of Mexico to avoid the threat of German submarines off southern Florida in the Caribbean. The war ended before the project could be initiated. In the late 1960s, the plan was revived and construction was begun by the Corps of Engineers, which also undertook an elaborate propaganda campaign, citing supposed economic benefits to be derived from cheaper shipping costs. Ecologists and conservationists soon discovered faults in the grossly favorable estimates used by the Corps, and challenged its supposed justifications and conclusions. Not only was the canal shown to be a potential disaster economically, but its proponents also failed to justify its construction in the face of the ecological damage it would have done. The proposed route would have created lengthy, biologically sterile channels in place of ecologically rich rivers, and destroyed more than sixty miles of natural communities adjacent to the canal, five major freshwater springs, and sev-

eral large and unspoiled lakes (Fig. 7-6). The Army Corps of
Engineers project was at last laid to rest by the personal in-
tervention of President Nixon.

One of the largest public works projects ever conceived
is the proposed Rampart Canyon Dam on the Yukon River in
Alaska. The reservoir created by this proposed dam would
flood 10,500 square miles and obliterate 400 miles of the
Yukon River in addition to more than 12,000 miles of its trib-
utaries and some 36,000 lakes and ponds of the Yukon Flats.
Instead of the diverse natural communities of the area, the
dam would substitute a huge and relatively sterile lake—
useless as a breeding site for the 1.5 million ducks and 12,500
geese that currently reproduce in this valley. These ducks
and geese, of course, fly south each fall to the main area of
the United States, where thousands of sportsmen and amateur

Fig. 7-6. The River Styx, a cypress swamp near the Oklawaha
River—former proposed site of the Cross-Florida Barge Canal project.

naturalists enjoy hunting them with gun or binoculars. More than 10,000 moose and other mammals such as caribou would have their habitat destroyed, a matter of considerable concern to the native peoples of the region, who depend on these animals for food. A salmon run along the Yukon that provides 800,000 fish per year for the local inhabitants would be lost. The sole purpose of the proposed dam is to generate huge quantities of electric power, which is not needed now and will not be needed in the next fifty years in Alaska. There are many other still unused power sources nearer the population centers of Alaska. Economically and ecologically, this proposed dam would be a disaster. But only an aroused and ecologically informed public can prevent a small body of narrow-sighted "development" or "dam-building" proponents from achieving such plans as these.

Summary

Landscape alteration may occur principally by fire, agricultural clearing, defoliation, urban expansion, clear-cutting, and public works projects. Periodic fire is a natural phenomenon that is actually necessary for the maintenance of certain climax communities. Agricultural clearing has become less of a threat to the environment today than in the past, although its expansion into the lowland coastal deserts and tropical rain forests of the world is anticipated. Defoliation caused by chemical sprays has caused severe ecological damage in Vietnam. Urban expansion, including the filling of bays, is destroying many natural communities. Clear-cutting of national forests is currently advocated by the lumber industry to increase timber yields. Giant public works projects that would harm great areas of our remaining natural environment are being constantly proposed. Prevention of environmentally harmful practices is usually accomplished only when the public protests with sound ecological and economic arguments in favor of an alternate course.

8
POLLUTION

Pollution of the environment simply means the introduction of an undesirable change in the particular features of concern, such as the constitution and quality of water, air, or soil. To a certain degree, the biological activities of all organisms cause some waste pollution in the environment, but man with his modern technology has increased his contribution by many orders of magnitude. In the natural world, decay organisms in the soil and water and the natural flushing action of massive water and air movements prevent the accumulation of organic or inorganic pollutants. When such cycles are upset either by a greatly increased quantity of pollution or by alteration of part of the natural restoration process, we have a major pollution problem, which often comes to our attention in unpleasant fashion.

The subject of pollution is almost endless and many excellent books have been written on its numerous facets. Some of these are listed in the Additional Reading section at the end of this book, for readers who are interested in studying this topic in more depth. Here we shall limit our consideration to the major types of pollution, with examples of some of the complexities and ecological factors involved.

Water Pollution

We seldom stop to consider the routine filtration and chemical treatment of urban water supplies today, but without this prophylaxis, disease organisms of many varieties (e.g., those that cause typhoid, paratyphoid, cholera, and various dysenteries) would be widespread pollutants among our human population. Pollutant materials or effects of other sorts are of much more concern than these disease organisms in today's society because we have had less success as yet in solving their particular pollution problems.

Change in the desirable characteristics of a water supply can occur in many ways. **Thermal pollution,** for example, is caused by the disposal of excess heated water into a body of water. This is usually done along rivers by power-generating plants and industrial factories that use water as a coolant. But in the construction of many large building complexes, also, the "solution" to the problem of hot water generated in the air conditioning system is to dump it into a nearby river or lake. Since most aquatic organisms have a body temperature at or near the temperature of the surrounding water and have a narrow range of temperature tolerance, the direct effect of a temperature rise is to change the rate of metabolic activity in using up food energy, which results in death. Since a rise in temperature of 18° F is sufficient to double the rate of many chemical reactions in plant and animal cells, it is easy to see why even a relatively small amount of thermal pollution is enough to cause lethal disruption in the organization of aquatic communities.

Storm drains often carry pollutants washed off paved streets directly into a water supply with no filtering or other treatment to which sewage is subjected. A major source of such pollution in our northern states is the salt used for de-icing streets during the winter. In the 1969–70 winter 77,000 metric *tons* of salt were used for de-icing in the densely populated Irondequoit Bay drainage basin near Rochester, New York. Investigators found that about 32,000 metric tons of salt went into the bay and the rest remained stored in the soil and ground water of the basin. The chloride concentration in this small bay (1 by 3.7 miles, with a maximum depth of 75 feet) has increased at least fivefold during the past two decades. The increase has been greatest at the bottom of the bay, and this has prevented complete vertical mixing of the bay's waters. The resultant lack of oxygen in the deeper waters could be expected to cause considerable reduction of the aquatic life in such areas (see page 101). The changing concentration of dissolved chloride could upset the internal salt balance of freshwater fish in the bay and the adjacent south side of Lake Ontario. During parts of the year the chloride levels exceed the U. S. Public Health Service recommended limit for human consumption. Since certain chlorine compounds are known to cause genetic mutation*, an increase of chlorine in water or food consumed by humans must be viewed with concern. Finally, the fraction of de-icing salt that is accumulating in the ground water may pose serious future problems for well water supplies in Rochester and other areas with similar de-icing programs.

Oil pollution has been a major public concern since the day in March 1967 when the giant tanker *Torrey Canyon* hit a reef off the Cornish coast of England and broke apart, releasing 117,000 *tons* of crude oil into the sea. Thousands of tons of oil drifted ashore in England and in France, on the other side of the English Channel. When the British found that the oil on the water could not be ignited, they sprayed some 12,500 *tons* of detergents on the oil spill to try to emulsify it (i.e., break the continuous oil sheet into tiny globules) and on the oil-covered coastal rocks to remove the oil that had already reached the shoreline. This course was not very successful either at sea or along the coast.

Ecologists investigating this disaster found that the chief immediate biological effect of the floating oil was to kill marine birds. When they landed on the surface or dived into the water for prey, the oil coated their feathers and destroyed the birds' ability to float. The death counts in two species alone were at least 20,000 murres (penguin-like birds) and 5,000 razorbills. The oil did not kill the intertidal zone life such as limpets and barnacles, or much of the plankton in the open sea. Detergents, on the other hand, turned out to be extremely toxic to the marine plankton and to the intertidal forms living on and around the English coastal rocks. The French did not use detergents; instead, they dropped powdered chalk on the floating oil. The chalk-oil complex sank to

---

* A genetic mutation is a change caused by a chemical, radiation, or other agent, in the hereditary material composing the chromosomes. It will be inherited by later generations and is usually harmful in effect.

the ocean bottom, preventing much of the oil from drifting into shallow coastal waters where it would do more harm to abundant marine life. The ecological lessons learned from fighting the Torrey Canyon oil spill have proved valuable in handling later spills from ships and sea oil-well platforms, and in passing federal and state legislation to prevent them.

Vessel pollution, involving discharge of wastes from ships into oceans, lakes, reservoirs, and rivers, is becoming an increasingly significant problem with growth in the number of merchant ships and the boom in recreational boating in the United States. **Dredging** operations in estuaries to improve ship channels or produce landfill create **silt pollution** on a grand scale.

Irrigation pollution occurs when agricultural water leaches out minerals or salts from irrigated fields (Fig. 8-1) and the runoff carries such pollutants to the nearest stream or lake. The **agricultural runoff** may also carry excess nitrates or other chemicals present in fertilizers, or in herbicides and insecticides from land being treated with persistent pesticides (a topic to be considered in a later section). In areas of extensive mining such as West Virginia, mine drainage can cause very harmful pollution in adjacent water supplies. Streams

Fig. 8-1. Irrigation in an agricultural field in Florida.

flowing out of mine shafts and runoff water that crosses slopes of rock removed from mines often become excessively acidic from dissolved chemicals.

Still another polluting by-product of our modern technology is **radioactive waste.** Perhaps the prime sources of such pollutants are research laboratories and hospitals that use radioisotopes extensively for tracing the metabolic pathway of materials in organisms and for a variety of diagnostic purposes in humans (localizing tumors, determining defects in normal circulatory anatomy, and determining blood volume). After passage through a patient, a waste radioisotope solution is still radioactive. Weekly collection and burial of this material in lead-lined containers is not generally feasible because of the need for special toilets, special handling, and other expensive requirements. The solutions containing these radioisotopes are merely flushed down the drain and thus enter the general sewer system, ending up eventually in some body of water. Though potentially hazardous in the future, radioactive waste from all sources today seems minor compared to other forms of pollution freely released into the environment.

Finally, one of the most common and currently controversial forms of water pollution is the process of **eutrophication.** This is the promotion of plant and animal growth in an aquatic ecosystem by adding substantial amounts of nutrients to the water. When eutrophication is accelerated by man's activities, pollution is rapid, for small unicellular algae and other aquatic plants have a phenomenal rate of increase under advantageous conditions, and can use up most of the free oxygen present in an overnourished body of water. Larger animals like fish then die from lack of oxygen. Three principal sources of excessive supplementary nutrients are runoff from stockyards, runoff from heavily fertilized farmland, and outflow from sewage plants that have incomplete sewage treatment and do not reclaim nutrient chemicals. A controversial source is many laundry detergents, which contain phosphates. Environmental scientists have worked to ban the growth-promoting phosphates from detergents, although some sanitary engineers and the major soap manufacturers claim that most commercial organic products (e.g., hand soaps, cleansers) contain phosphates anyway and that the removal of detergent phosphates alone would be useless. The chemicals currently used in non-phosphate detergents present a health hazard to children in the home and to adult users who may be sensitive to them. We have yet to strike the proper ecological balance in the inclusion or exclusion of phosphates in detergents, although their pollution-promoting tendency through eutrophication is well documented.

Air Pollution

Components

Gaseous wastes and particulate matter such as soot are the principal components of air pollution, but a surprising variety of substances pollute our atmosphere, especially around developed urban areas and manufacturing sites. Chemical pollutants present in significant quantities include carbon monoxide, a colorless and odorless gas. Carbon monoxide combines readily with hemoglobin in the red blood cells, and thus prevents the hemoglobin from carrying oxygen. Death from oxygen deficiency occurs if a person is exposed even to low concentrations of this gas. Sulfur oxides (especially sulfur dioxide), nitrogen oxides, and hydrocarbons are the principal components of "smog." Pollutants present in minor quantities include ozone and other oxidants, arsenic, asbestos, beryllium, fluorides, lead, organic and inorganic pesticides, and sulfides.

Sources of Air Pollution

In nature, air pollution arises principally from forest fires and volcanic eruptions. Generally, the infrequency with which these events happen and the short time they last insure that pollutants released into the atmosphere are soon dissipated by air movements. Since the advent of man as a technological animal, however, air pollution has become a much greater and more persistent feature of our world (Fig. 8-2). Today, the principal sources are processing industries and

Fig. 8-2. Air pollution over the city of Los Angeles (top) and spreading ninety miles east of Los Angeles up to 5,000 feet elevation in the mountains (bottom).

power-generating plants that burn coal and oil, and the internal combustion engine. Some cities have passed ordinances limiting the allowable amount of pollutants to be emitted from industrial plants, and state and federal standards are being established. An especially concerted effort by environmentalists, government, and automobile manufacturers has been made to reduce the emissions of the automobile internal combustion engine to an acceptable level. The ultimate solution to this vexing problem would be to switch to an alternative type of engine with less potential for pollution, one that uses steam or electric power instead of burning gasoline. Since California and other states have set deadlines in the mid-1970s for meeting minimal emission standards, Detroit technology is working particularly hard on this problem.

Environmentalists have been less successful in achieving the regulation of emissions by huge power plants. In the Four Corners area in the southwestern United States, where the borders of Arizona, New Mexico, Utah, and Colorado meet, a series of large power-generating plants has recently been built. The enormous amounts of air pollution released daily from these coal-burning plants are currently covering thousands of square miles. Conservationist groups and the Navajo Indian tribal council are attempting legal action to bring about the abatement of this air pollution.

Effects of
Air Pollution

The principal known effects of air pollution are, of course, on human health. In cities with a high incidence of air pollution, human longevity is decreased through a notably higher frequency of emphysema and other lung diseases. Of course effects are not restricted to people. Many species of flowers, shrubs, and trees are unable to thrive or even survive in cities such as Los Angeles. Commercial and amateur horticulturists in southern California who raised such flowers as orchids and bromeliads have seen disaster strike their greenhouses through smog damage to both blossoms and leaves, and have been forced to move or abandon their floral enterprises and avocations.

The damage from air pollution is not restricted to the immediate urban or factory area of the source. Smog moving out of the Los Angeles basin is damaging agricultural crops and killing mountain pine forests as far as 100 miles away. In late 1970 an aerial survey of the Angeles National Forest, which borders Los Angeles, showed that 261,000 Ponderosa pines had been damaged by smog. Not only are the pine community food web and other biological relationships being altered; the recreational and lumbering activities possible in such areas will undoubtedly change with the drastic rate of loss of the dominant tree species.

Air pollution may also cause major changes in weather and climate. The town of La Porte, Indiana, on the eastern side of the tip of Lake Michigan, has had an excessive run of bad weather for the last forty-five years. Total precipitation has increased more than 30 percent in forty years, while the number of hailstorms, days with hail, and total precipitation at La Porte greatly exceeds the records of nearby weather stations. The growth of air pollution in the Chicago-Gary industrial complex thirty miles west of La Porte is closely correlated with these trends; even the days of bad weather in La Porte usually correspond with days of bad air pollution in Chicago. The quantities of heat and water vapor in the pollution emitted by the Chicago factories apparently cause the formation of cumulus clouds, which then are blown across the tip of Lake Michigan, picking up additional moisture. At about the time these clouds reach La Porte, the particulate matter in the mixture of pollutants provides nuclei for condensation, and the result is precipitation.

The problem of air pollution is not confined to the outside environment, however. Smoking in closed areas like classrooms, conference rooms, airplane cabins, or cars causes high levels of particulate pollutants and gases such as carbon monoxide. In a January 1972 report to Congress, the U. S. Surgeon General announced evidence that the health hazard from such pollutants is not limited to smokers. Nonsmokers in a smoke-filled room may be exposed to harmful levels of carbon monoxide that are especially threatening to persons already suffering from chronic bronchopulmonary and coronary diseases. Carbon monoxide in such concentrations (20 to 80 parts per million) adversely affects human sight and hearing and hampers an auto driver's ability to respond to light and to judge distance. Higher concentrations of carbon monoxide cause death by interfering with the transport of oxygen in the blood. Of course, the smoker himself is subjected to far greater pollutant levels than is the nonsmoker. Vincent Schaefer stated in a 1969 article in the journal *BioScience* that "in the process of smoking, the individual insults his lungs with a concentration of at least ten million smoke particles per cubic centimeter. This is a concentration that is 10 to 100 times greater than is encountered in a very badly polluted urban area like Los Angeles or New York City." *

Solid Waste Pollution

Solid wastes (Fig. 8-3) in the United States are commonly disposed of by one of three methods: incineration, land-filling, or reclamation. **Incineration,** or burning of solid matter, is now considered undesirable because of its major contribution to air pollution. Although burning is still the principal method of disposal in some sections of the country, it is increasingly restricted to sparsely populated areas. **Land-filling** or **sanitary landfill** disposes of solid wastes by dumping them into a pit, natural canyon, marsh, or coastal estuary. As the depression is filled, the waste material is covered with soil. This is the commonest type of garbage and waste disposal system for towns and cities, because of its low cost, lack of processing trouble, and avoidance of air pollution. The city of Charleston, South Carolina, found that it cost about 65 cents a ton to dispose of garbage by using the landfill method in a marshy area on the coast. After clay was brought in to put on top of a 25-foot layer of waste, the land could be sold for other developments. Unfortunately, some coastal cities still find it eas-

* Vincent J. Schaefer, "Some effects of air pollution on our environment," *BioScience* 19 (1969): 896–897.

Fig. 8-3. Solid waste pollution outside one of our major western cities.

ier to dump their garbage and trash at sea, thus causing water pollution. This marine "disposal," with large-scale consequences for *all* areas around a sea, cannot be considered socially or ecologically responsible.

Reclamation is the environmentally beneficial way to avoid solid waste pollution and is rapidly gaining favor as new technological methods are developed to make it competitive economically with landfill. Reclamation is simply the reclaiming and recycling of waste materials. To take a single example, the largest reclamation problem in the United States is paper. Unfortunately, 50 percent of this paper waste is cardboard, and only 20 percent of the cardboard is recyclable under present methods. Among the more interesting methods of recycling, Atomic Energy Commission researchers have fed high-quality paper (onionskin and bone paper) experimentally to cattle; the cattle, whose digestive systems contain microbes capable of digesting cellulose, grew fat on the diet. Paper waste could also be used to grow yeast cultures, as for breweries. The major recycling of paper waste, though, is channeled into making new paper products.

Tin-coated steel cans used to be the commonest food storage container on the supermarket shelf; today aluminum cans, which are easily reclaimed, have captured a sizable percentage of the can industry's production. Unfortunately, all that glitters is not gold; nor will it rust. The cans that are not brought back for recycling but lie abandoned on roadsides are much more rust-resistant than the old-fashioned steel can. Steel cans now have resin coatings instead of tin; the resin can easily be removed during re-smelting, making it feasible to recycle steel cans. Because of their degradable properties if abandoned in nature, the new recyclable steel cans may be ecologically preferable to the less expensive aluminum cans.

Glass containers can obviously be directly recycled through re-use. Other imaginative ways of using glass include grinding it and using the granular material in insulation, vinyl floor tiles, building walls, and road surfaces. Plastics are one of the most challenging items to reclaim because they cannot be broken down in nature by biological action or weathering. They can be melted, but the resultant sticky mess is not readily disposable or recyclable. Fortunately, it has been found that specific impurities can be added to cause plastics to break down after a certain period of time. Manufacturers could adjust the composition of plastics for various articles according to the expected length of service of the particular item.

Finally, we might mention one dramatic solution to the problem of disposing of solid wastes. A former head of the Atomic Energy Commission, Glenn Seaborg, suggested breaking garbage into individual atoms with a hydrogen fusion torch. Unfortunately, the amount of resulting radiation would appear to make this idea impractical at present.

Pesticides and Pollution Problems

The term **pesticide** refers to any chemical substance used for the regulation of population growth in a species regarded as a "pest." Pesticides include **herbicides,** used for the control of herbaceous plants; **insecticides,** used for insect control; and **biocides,** general pesticides that may be used to kill all life. The principal uses of pesticides have been to kill plant or animal pests, to stop the spread of disease, and to protect crops, all perfectly laudable aims. Since the end of World War II, however, major problems have arisen from the development and overuse of certain pesticides. These have centered upon the increasing use of indestructible pesticides; their accumulation in the ecosystems of the world; increasing pest resistance to them; and their potential danger to humans and organisms in general.

Until World War II, the problem of persistent molecular types of pesticides did not exist. Before that time, naturally occurring compounds such as nicotine (extracted from tobacco) and lead arsenate were used as pesticides. But with the advance of chemical knowledge, chemists began to synthesize pesticide compounds *not* derived from natural sources. Among these were the chlorinated hydrocarbons, which include such insecticides as DDT (dichlorodiphenyltrichloroethane) and the DDT derivatives, DDE and DDD; dieldrin; chlordane; and the herbicides 2, 4-D and 2, 4, 5-T. Unlike naturally derived pesticides, these compounds are not broken down by biological action and they persist for many years in an unchanged state. Thus it was found that when DDT was sprayed on walls of houses and other living areas, malaria-carrying mosquitoes died even if they landed on the surface months after spraying. DDT aided in conquering malaria throughout the world and prevented typhus epidemics during World War II as well. Its use on agricultural crops (Fig. 8-4) seemed to promise untold benefits by increasing production.

Fig. 8-4. Spraying of pesticides on crops to kill specific pests has been instrumental in increasing modern agricultural production, but excess chemicals that drift in the air to adjacent wild areas can cause considerable harm to non-target organisms.

Then in 1946 it was first noticed that several fruit fly strains had become resistant to DDT. By 1948 eleven more species of flies had become tolerant. In 1958 seventy-eight additional insect species were resistant, and in 1969 at least 224 species of insects were found to have developed effective resistance to the lethal effect of DDT. This increasing insect resistance has become a classic example of rapid evolution observed in progress. In brief, the widespread use of DDT caused strong natural selection for genetic strains in an insect species that contain genes producing detoxifying enzymes, and against those genetic strains susceptible to DDT. There was also strong selection for pesticide-avoidance behavior, where genetic strains with behavioral patterns that kept the insect away from a pesticide tended to survive and reproduce more than those who caught full exposure to the chemical. In several tropical species of *Aedes* and *Culex* mosquitoes, the populations that in the 1940s and earlier were primarily house feeders on sleeping humans now will bite only outside houses, indicating that genotypes producing this behavioral pattern have survived to replace those that used to enter houses, alight on a DDT-sprayed wall, and die.

The Peruvian cotton disaster in the Cañete Valley in the 1950s clearly pointed up the result of the spraying that caused rapid selection of resistant insect genotypes. In this Peruvian coastal valley, major cotton production from its start in the 1920s until the late 1940s was aided by old-fashioned insecticides such as nicotine sulfate and calcium arsenate. The limited pest insect complex in the valley was kept under fair control. Then growers decided to employ the newest synthetic organic insecticides, including DDT, benzene hexachloride (BHC), and toxaphene. Excellent increases in cotton yield resulted as the modern pesticides appeared to decimate the insect populations. The new pesticides blanketed the valley. But after several years, some of the old pests had developed resistance to the insecticides and had become increasingly destructive. New pests appeared. The pests were immune to the organochlorine insecticides. By the 1955–56 season, the sprays had been increased greatly but insect resistance was general and the crop was now decimated, the yield being one of the lowest ever recorded for the area. To survive, the cotton growers had to abandon these insecticides and begin an integrated control program, using the older non-synthetic chemicals and bringing back natural biological control of the pests by encouraging their native enemies. Under this program, cotton yields increased greatly, the old pests decreased to their old levels, and the secondary pest outbreaks of the new insect species that had moved in soon disappeared.

If persistent pesticides were confined only to agricultural areas in developed nations, the matter would be important from an economic viewpoint and as an example of man's upsetting the natural balance to his own detriment, but it would not affect most of us directly. Unfortunately, persistent pesticides have two nasty features: they stay around for a long time and are easily spread. Aerial spraying results in such extensive vaporization that in tests over corn fields as little as 5 percent of the pesticide spray actually reaches the corn field. The rest drifts through the lower atmosphere to adjacent areas; even part of the pesticide residues in the sprayed field will wash off the leaves in the next rain and be carried out of the field. When pesticides reach a stream or river, whether by aerial drift or by rain runoff, they are usually absorbed into suspended dirt particles and carried by water movement to the oceans. In 1967, DDT was discovered in the body tissues of penguins and other wildlife in Antarctica, indicating that DDT was dispersing generally throughout the world, even to areas where no spraying had ever been done.

The persistent nature of molecules of DDT and its chlorinated hydrocarbon relatives, and their affinity for body fat, cause them to accumulate in the upper levels of natural food chains in all parts of the world. In the typical food-pyramid relationship, animals at each trophic level eat large numbers of organisms from lower levels. If these prey have any DDT in their tissues, it will be incorporated in the body tissues of the animals at the next level, and so on to the top carnivores. Hence birds of prey, such as the bald eagle or osprey, being at the top of their respective food chains, should receive the highest concentrations of DDT. As it turned out, this is exactly what happened; eagle and osprey populations began declining in the 1960s with corresponding increases in DDT concentrations in their bodies, and it was soon discovered that the reproductive success of these species had suddenly become almost zero. The cause was thin fragile eggshells, which easily broke under the parent's weight. In subsequent laboratory experiments DDT was found to interfere with hormonal balance, lowering the calcium ion content in the female bird's blood, which in turn lowered the calcium available for eggshell production. Since the initial discovery that DDT causes eggshell breakage in ospreys and bald eagles, similar devastating losses have been reported in populations of robins, brown pelicans, and many other birds.

Mammals as diverse as sea lions and bats have also shown dramatic reduction in reproductive capabilities in recent years. In Arizona, for instance, the populations of several of the 28 recorded bat species have decreased drastically. Between 1963 and 1969 one colony of Guano bats (*Tadarida brasilensis*) near the town of Morenci decreased from over 25 million individuals to only 30,000 individuals. These bats fly over agricultural fields at night to feed on flying insects, and their annual migratory route takes them over agriculturally developed areas of Sinaloa and Sonora, Mexico. With their long life spans (to 21 years), bats are particularly vulnerable to accumulating a lethal load of chlorinated hydrocarbons from the pest insects they eat. Large numbers of dead Guano bats, containing DDT and DDE in body fat, were found around the feeding range of the Morenci colony. E. L. Cockrum, a biologist at the University of Arizona who investigated this problem, has stated, "While the future of the southwestern Guano bats seems bleak and while the cause of the crisis, insecticide poisoning, cannot be proved beyond all doubt, one outcome can be agreed upon. Bats of the great Morenci maternity colony no longer destroy, as they once did, *40 tons* of insects nightly." *

Of course man, being a top predator in many food chains, has not escaped the flow of DDT through the world's ecosystems. Even Eskimos have been found to have 3.0 parts of DDT per million parts of tissue in their body fat, while in

---

* E. Lendell Cockrum, "Insecticides and Guano bats," *Journal of the Arizona Academy of Science*, vol. 5, no. 4 (1969), editorial page.

areas such as Hungary and Israel, with high use of chlorinated hydrocarbon insecticides, the concentrations in human
tissue are higher (12.4 ppm and 19.2 ppm, respectively). In
the U. S. population, 5 to 20 ppm is the common range of
DDT concentration. Unfortunately, it reaches its highest concentration in mother's milk, and such milk may actually be
unfit for infant consumption. DDT has also been shown to interfere with sex hormone balance (it mimics the action of the
female hormone estrogen) and cause infertility in female rats.
The same pattern of infertility caused by hormonal blockage
of ovulation was observed in American women and reported
by University of Washington scientists in April 1971.

Biological Control

To avoid the pollution problems inherent in the use of persistent pesticides, economic entomologists and ecologists have
suggested the use of organic phosphate compounds (e.g., parathion, malathion) or other biodegradable chemicals, combined with biological control methods.

Biological control is simply the suppression of reproduction of one type of organism by utilizing some feature of its
biology or physiology to destroy it or by use of another organism. The oldest known use of biological control dates to
several thousand years ago, when the Chinese placed bamboo
poles between orchard trees to allow predatory ants to raid
pest insects easily.

The principal biological control agencies used today are
parasites, predators, and microbial diseases. Natural parasites
of pest insects or plants, such as parasitic wasps, may be
mass-cultured in the laboratory and then released as needed
in crop areas. Predators such as ladybug beetles are sold by
the thousands (1 gallon at $6.50, equal to 125,000 beetles!) to
control scale insects and aphids. The most effective control is
offered by bacteria and viruses, though. These are species-
specific, killing only one particular pest, and do not accumulate in the environment like chemicals, merely joining the al-

ready existing microbe population. Thus far, insects have apparently failed to evolve resistance to these useful strains of microbial disease. The most effective biological agent in the Japanese beetle control program of the U. S. Department of Agriculture in the eastern United States is a viral disease that attacks the beetle grub underground.

The principal *disadvantages* of using microbes as biological control agents are fourfold.

1. Because of the specificity of most interspecific interactions of these types, one agent microbe is usually needed for each pest species.

2. Chemicals act much faster than microbial disease; so further damage may be done or movement to adjacent fields may occur after the microbes are released but before they are effective.

3. The microbes must be cultured in the laboratory in the same insect species that is acting as a pest in the field; so one must culture the host as well as the microbe.

4. Because of Food and Drug Administration limitations, there is not a single viral control organism being sold commercially for use by the general public on agricultural or horticultural pests. This last difficulty makes the earlier disadvantages almost academic, though we may anticipate some relaxation of the F. D. A. rulings in the future as the use of biological control methods becomes more imperative.

Other biological control agencies that are useful alternatives to pollution-producing pesticide chemicals are available. **Resistant varieties** of crop plants are being developed by plant geneticists who select variant genotypes with chemical defenses such as alkaloids or mechanical protection like thicker bark. **Male sterilization** has been a successful technique to eradicate or control the screwworm fly and several injurious fruit fly species. Male flies reared in large numbers in the laboratory are sterilized by radiation and released into wild populations weekly. If a sterile male mates with a virgin female, she will lay her eggs and they will fail to develop. The screwworm fly has been eradicated from cattle-raising areas on Caribbean islands and in Florida by such mass-release programs. **Organic attractant chemicals** that influence the chemo-sensory behavior of pest insects, such as sex attractants, can be synthesized in large quantities and used to attract and destroy large numbers of adults or at least confuse the sensory environment and so prevent matings. **Specific hormonal insecticides,** which upset hormonal balance within an insect when absorbed through its cuticle and cause reproductive failure or death, do not affect other species in the same area. Finally, **radiation signals** can be utilized to attract and destroy insects or to upset the biological clocks and seasonal cycles of pest species. Most night-flying adult insects are attracted to ultraviolet light, and electric grids or other trap devices coupled with ultraviolet light can be effective control devices for some species. One can change the photoperiod over truck gardens (valuable vegetable crop land near cities) with short periods of artificial lighting at night and make insect pests go into diapause or prevent normal egg-laying patterns.

The limitations of biological control as opposed to chemical control are its greater cost, more complex treatment procedure, and occasional uncontrolled reproduction of the biological agent. The generally greater cost arises from rearing the parasites, sterilized males, or other control agents in a laboratory. The man-hours involved in caring for the living organisms under tightly controlled conditions usually far exceed the manufacturing time required for a chemical product that could treat the same agricultural field. If repeated treatments with living material are needed in the field area, the complexity of operation in rearing and releasing biological control agents is considerably greater than spraying a pesticide from the air or ground. Occasionally control over the parasite or pathogen species is lost and it jumps to other, "good" species in the fauna of a treated area. This is more likely to happen where the agent species does not occur naturally, and it can occur even though the agent is species-specific on the pest species alone in other areas. We should also remember that many of the non-persistent, biodegradable pesticides may safely be used on crops. Thus the best control plan, which avoids the limitations of pollution-producing chemicals and the occasional lapses of biological control alone, is an integrated control program, using several control methods simultaneously in conjunction with a thorough study of the vulnerable periods in the pest's life cycle. The success of such a program in the cotton fields of the Cañete Valley of Peru after the disaster with chlorinated hydrocarbons is indicative of the effectiveness of this concept.

Summary

Pollution of the environment is simply the introduction of an undesirable change in a particular feature of concern to man or other organisms. Among current major problems in this area are water pollution (eutrophication, thermal changes, storm drainage, oil, vessel wastes, dredging, agricultural and irrigation runoff, and radioactive waste); air pollution; solid waste pollution; and pesticides of several types, especially the chlorinated hydrocarbon insecticides and herbicides. Biological control and integrated control programs are ways to handle pest problems without the use of persistent pesticides.

9
POPULATION GROWTH IN MAN

The Population Explosion: Nature of the Problem

The root of almost all the threats to natural communities and the ecology of our earth is the explosive growth of the human population. Man's burgeoning numbers are not restricted to the Asian and other less developed countries of the world. The United States now has some 208 million people, and crowding is becoming a fact of life even in such remote areas as Yellowstone and Yosemite National Parks. The inhabitants of the Los Angeles basin and of the New York metropolitan area have been familiar for years with the smog and other problems attending overpopulation in a small area. Now whole states, such as Oregon, have awakened to the dangers of unlimited population growth and are attempting to regulate or halt it. Special groups within the United Nations, as well as many private organizations such as the Population Reference Bureau, are attempting to diminish or reverse the precipitous worldwide rise in population.

Today's high growth rate is a relatively recent phenomenon, dating from about 1650 A.D., although there were several earlier surges in population growth. Man's primitive primate ancestors are believed to have been African forest species that lived alone or in small, loosely knit groups. With the development of bipedalism (walking on hind limbs alone), tool-making, and perhaps speech, early men began living on the open plains in family groups. About 600,000 years ago, Peking Man, Java Man, and similar *Homo erectus* forms moved into caves and other more permanent shelters, utilized fire, and made weapons. Man's survival rate was enhanced by these new cultural features, and this major **cultural revolution** set off the first real surge in world population growth.

Approximately 8,000 years ago, the second notable increase in rate of population growth occurred with the advent of the **agricultural revolution.** At this time in several major regions of the world man changed from a primitive, hunting-and-gathering level of existence involving every member of a nomadic group, to an agricultural society where only a part of the population could raise enough food to feed the whole society. A sedentary mode of existence, raising crops and livestock, presented fewer hazards to the average man and his family than the former migratory or wandering way of life. Food in the form of grains could be stored for times of scarcity and drought. The death rate consequently decreased and the live birth rate increased.

The third and greatest rise in man's population size began in the mid-seventeenth century and is still accelerating. This increase in growth rate was triggered by the **scientific-medical revolution** that started around 1650 A.D. Growth was further accelerated by social changes associated with industrialization. Medical knowledge and public health measures began lowering the death rate significantly at that time, and this trend has continued up to the present day. In highly developed countries such as Japan, the United States, and nations in Western Europe, the birth rate has also fallen, but not as drastically as the death rate. Thus their growth continues, though at a low rate in some countries. Technological advances in housing and transportation of food have made it possible for man to inhabit even remote polar or desert areas today, where previously population growth was limited by the lack of a sufficient natural supply of food or suitable living conditons.

In underdeveloped countries such as India and Pakistan, the medical and scientific advances that originated in Europe did not arrive until World War II. From 1940 to 1945, the Allies introduced public health practices such as malarial control and sanitation of public water supplies on a large scale, and the death rates in these countries fell. The high birth rates characteristic of these unindustrialized nations continued unabated. The gap between the birth rate and the death rate, then, has accelerated our population growth rate in all countries to the point where it is estimated that the world population will jump from our present 3.7 billion to 7.4 billion by the year 2000. The trend of the world's population growth since the time of Christ is shown in Figure 9-1.

Population control has, of course, been a problem for every species of animal or plant on this planet, but over time these populations maintain more or less constant population sizes below the carrying capacity of their environment. We have already looked at some of the regulating mechanisms involved (Chapter 5). These density-dependent and density-

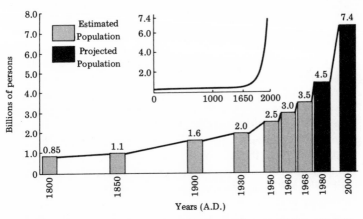

Fig. 9-1. The growth of the population of the world from 1 A.D. to 2000 A.D., with population estimates for the years 1800–2000 shown in detail.

independent factors have been found in all organisms whose ecology has been thoroughly investigated, and it would be peculiar indeed if they were lacking in one species, Man. Since the problem of a high rate of increase seems to be relatively recent in the history of man on earth, it is worth examining past and primitive societies to see how they were affected by population growth and how they controlled it. In this examination it will become evident why we have lost most of the natural or culturally instituted regulating factors that operated in primitive groups. Some were lost when civilization began in the agricultural revolution, and the great majority had disappeared by the time we entered the scientific-medical revolution.

Population Growth in Primitive Societies

The chief ecological and evolutionary facts that we found in considering population growth in plants and animals apply to man also: population stability is a prerequisite for survival, and selection operates against organisms in groups where population control is ineffective or absent. In primitive societies of the past and present, population-stability has been essential for survival. Since a hunting and gathering group requires a large territory to furnish what it needs all year, a low population density in the form of widely spaced groups is a necessity. Should a group exceed the carrying capacity of its area, individuals could survive by voluntarily emigrating to a new area, if they were unopposed by a neighboring group and if suitable land were available. Excess individuals could also fail to produce offspring or be eliminated from the group involuntarily by reason of famine, disease, or warfare. These last three factors were considered by Thomas Robert Malthus, an eighteenth-century Englishman, to be instrumental factors in controlling population growth. His famous 1798 and 1803 essays on the principles of human population growth were the first to warn of the dangers of overpopulation and its probable consequences for Man. In his writings, primitive societies provided a valuable base of comparison with industrial societies of his time.

Since strong selection would presumably occur against groups of individuals that did not have some form of population control, it is not surprising that man himself added cultural traits to control reproduction in his societies. Cultural evolution has produced an amazing variety of such checks to reproductive excess, and space permits only a partial list. Most societies have extensive marriage and reproductive taboo systems. The consecration of virginity is common to almost all modern human groups as well as many primitive groups. There is often punishment for out-of-wedlock sexual experience or for early motherhood in societies permitting premarital sexual activity. Frequently, primitive societies have minimum and maximum ages set by custom for motherhood or fatherhood. Required child spacing is not uncommon. In societies with this custom, reproductive contact by the couple is prohibited or restricted until a new child reaches a certain age. Widows are often forbidden to remarry for a period.

In some societies, celibacy is advocated as a high calling. In certain South Pacific societies and in servant classes in ancient civilizations, castration of males insured that celibacy would be observed. Certain African and other tribal groups practiced infibulation of young females as a pubertal initiation rite. Of course, this surgical removal of the clitoris removed much of the sensual pleasure associated with intercourse and hence perhaps reduced its frequency for those females. Prostitution and homosexuality were utilized in diverse groups as forms of sexual conduct that tended to reduce the reproductive contribution of the participants.

A very common practice in primitive groups was exposure of infants or other forms of infanticide. Interestingly, the Biblical book of Exodus describes how the Egyptian pharaohs at the time of Moses (approximately 1550 to 1447 B.C.) used exposure of male infants as a population-control measure against their Hebrew slave populations. Infanticide was com-

monly practiced by the Greeks and Romans at the height of
their civilizations, and it is probably universally characteristic of past and present-day primitive groups and rural cultures. Exposure of aged or sick persons who no longer contributed to the food-gathering capacity of the group was also a
common practice among North American Indian tribes and
other societies. Abortion, or killing of the fetus by mechanical
and chemical means, was practiced by most primitive groups
of peoples and is still common today, especially in rural peas-
ant cultures.

Sometimes physical combat within and between groups
for reasons unrelated to the normal warfare aim of acquiring
territory played a significant role in limiting population size.
The Jívaro Indians of eastern Ecuador, for example, spent
much of their lives in hunting other Jívaro enemies for the
non-territorial reasons of retaliation and revenge for injuries
suffered in previous raids. Cannibalism in some groups was a
form of warfare devoted partially to the aim of securing
human food. Certain societies used war and raids to obtain
enemy individuals for religious sacrifices. Records of the
Aztec civilization of central Mexico show that human sacrifice could be a significant factor in adding to the death rate
in a population. Human sacrifices were adopted by the Az-
tecs early in the fourteenth century and continued for about
two hundred years until the conquest of Mexico by Cortés in
1520. Captives were sacrificed at almost every festival. On
great occasions, such as the coronation of a king or the consecration of a new temple, appalling numbers of prisoners were
slaughtered on the altars. The *yearly* sacrifices throughout the
empire are estimated from excellent historical records to have
ranged from twenty thousand to over fifty thousand people.
At the dedication of the great temple of Huitzilopotchli in
1486, the ceremony included the sacrifice of some seventy
thousand captives!

We might close this consideration of early population-
regulating factors by mentioning that the practice of slavery
has often limited the subject population in harsh ways. In the
eighteenth and early nineteenth centuries, African slave traders and tribal raiding parties killed large numbers of Africans
while on expeditions to secure slaves for export to areas such

as America and the Caribbean. The exploiting groups of men in these and other periods of history had, of course, direct and absolute control over the later reproductive activities of those taken alive for slaves. In early civilizations as well as at least one twentieth-century society (India), slaves were sacrificially killed along with other members of the household when the head of a noble family was killed in battle or died of natural causes. The most common cultural rationales for this practice were that the departed soul needed companions to serve him in the next world, or that members of the household could hardly desire to continue living when their titular head was dead.

All these factors aided the three main Malthusian control mechanisms of famine, pestilence, and territorial warfare in limiting the size of the primitive human society. It is notable that the Malthusian factors are beyond the control of the individual and often beyond the control of his society. The culturally imposed factors that we have reviewed in these past few paragraphs were all voluntarily imposed by the societies themselves (or at least by segments of them). While often instituted ostensibly for other reasons, primarily related to mystical or nature-worship religious systems, these cultural factors exerted effective population control.

The great majority of these culturally instituted control measures are no longer morally acceptable to modern societies, and it is not likely that mankind will revert to the primitive type of religious structure in which they had their basis. Except for their historical interest, most do not offer any serious help for man's present problems. The chief exceptions are the social emphasis on female virginity (still current in our society), non-reproduction outside of marriage, and advancing the minimum ages for sexual reproduction within marriage. These could all contribute significantly to effective population control, in combination with other measures.

To summarize what we have learned, the population problem was essentially eliminated from early or primitive human groups by the same natural factors that control most animal populations, and by the limits placed by man himself through his cultural patterns. *Reproduction became a matter of community interest,* as a major part of the social patterns and adaptations enabling men to live communally. Before the advent of modern technology, environmental factors kept the population limited to areas with a large natural supply of plant and animal foods. Cultural evolution of social restrictions limited population size in a voluntary sense, though the society's rationale for these restrictive factors was often not directly associated with population control *per se.*

Population Growth in Modern Societies

The scientific-industrial revolution marked the beginning of a great upsurge in population growth (Fig. 9-1). As knowledge of medicine and social hygiene spread, more people lived after birth even if in "more misery," as Thomas Malthus cynically said in 1798. Along with this growth, the new revolution brought some degree of knowledge about birth control methods. With the concomitant change in motivation for smaller families engendered by industrialization, the birth rate in technologically advanced countries soon began to decline. To understand what occurred at this time and why, despite the hopes of some demographers, the same transition will not take place in currently underdeveloped major nations, let us review three basic demographic concepts.

1. $\text{Birth Rate} = \dfrac{\text{number of live births}}{1,000 \text{ members of population}}$

2. $\text{Death Rate} = \dfrac{\text{number of deaths}}{1,000 \text{ members of population}}$

3. $\text{Rate of Natural Increase} = \text{BR} - \text{DR}$

A birth rate of 50 live births annually per 1,000 population is considered very high. In 1971 several countries in Africa (Niger, Rwanda, and Swaziland) had the extraordinary birth rate of 52 per 1,000. A low birth rate today is around 15 per 1,000; in 1971 two European countries, Sweden and Luxembourg, had the world's lowest birth rate of 13.5 per 1,000.

Current death rates range between a maximum average of 30 deaths per 1,000 (Angola in middle Africa) and a minimum of 5 deaths per 1,000 (Singapore, Fiji, Taiwan, and the Ryukyu Islands). On a *worldwide basis,* the annual birth rate in January 1971 was 34 per 1,000 and the annual death rate was 14 per 1,000. This gives us an annual rate of increase of the world's population of 2.0 percent ($34 - 14 = 20$ per 1,000 growth rate, or 2.0 percent).

What does any rate of increase (say, 2 percent) mean in terms of adding more living bodies to the human population? Assuming no change in growth rate, the number of years required to double a population with a particular growth rate is as follows:

Rate of Increase (Percent)	Doubling Rate of Population (Years)	Example of Country or Region with Rate in 1971
0.1	700	East Germany
0.5	140	Denmark
1.0	70	Japan, United States (both 1.1 percent, 63 years)
1.5	47	Argentina
2.0	35	World, Namibia (Southwest Africa)
2.5	28	Afghanistan, Laos
3.0	24	Ghana, Iran
4.0	17.5	Costa Rica (3.8 percent, 19 years)
8.2	9	Kuwait

Historically, of course, growth rates have fluctuated considerably. Up to the year 1 A.D., the world's population increased at a rate of about 0.002 percent a year. By 1900–1925 the rate was approximately 1.0 percent, and today it is 2.0 percent. The most dramatic upsurge, as we have said, started around 1650 A.D. With our demographic points in mind, let us go back to that time now and look at the peculiar combination of circumstances in Europe that lowered the death rate and then lowered the birth rate, so that about two hundred years after the death rate began to decrease, the overall growth rate became relatively low.

The age-old limiting factors of famine and disease began to be alleviated in seventeenth-century Europe by technological developments in agriculture and food transportation and by medical advances that conquered most of the devastating epidemic and common childhood diseases. Progress in instituting public sanitation measures such as sewer systems and garbage collections reduced mortality factors. Through the next two centuries, these scientific and medical discoveries were exported to other parts of the world through missionaries, traders, and the colonies founded by leading European nations. With the drop in death rate at home and abroad, the rate of population growth rapidly increased.

In the population of western Europe, however, the birth rate began to decline starting shortly after 1800, following in a general way the declining death rate (Fig. 9-2). This diminution of the birth rate paralleling the lowering of the death rate has been called the **demographic transition.** It is thought that this decline in fertility was caused principally by the change in social attitudes towards children. With the progression from an agrarian society to an urban, industrial society, children became less of an economic asset and more of an economic burden. Children were useful workers on a farm, but in the city a father was the principal wage-earner, older children worked for very low wages, and young children prevented a mother from working. Under the crowded urban conditions and the socioeconomic pressures of industrial work, a small family became the most desirable state, and man was motivated to curb his birth rate by whatever means he could.

In the underdeveloped countries, the demographic situation at the mid-twentieth century showed uniformly higher birth rates than in pre-industrial Europe, continuing without any decrease, and a sharply decreasing death rate, the result of the introduction of modern health measures (Fig. 9-3). Instead of being invented and introduced over centuries as in Europe, purification of water supplies, vaccination campaigns, and malaria spraying campaigns were initiated almost

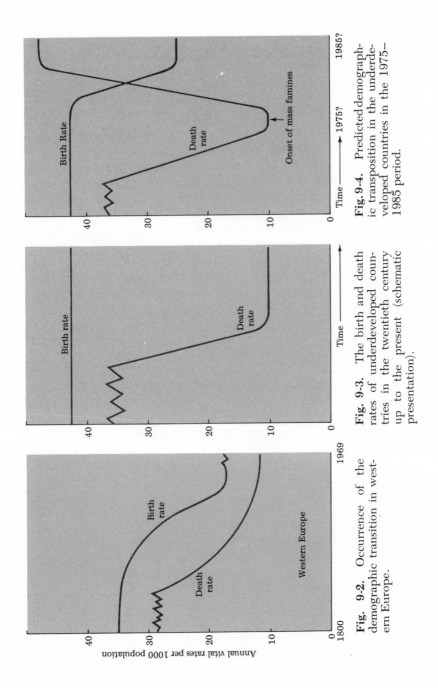

Fig. 9-2. Occurrence of the demographic transition in western Europe.

Fig. 9-3. The birth and death rates of underdeveloped countries in the twentieth century up to the present (schematic presentation).

Fig. 9-4. Predicted demographic transposition in the underdeveloped countries in the 1975–1985 period.

simultaneously in a few years' time. Thus today the demographic situation in these underdeveloped countries has been rapidly brought to a point that superficially resembles western Europe's population parameters around 1700–1800 A.D.

While one might expect to see a continuing parallel in population trends between Europe and underdeveloped countries, sociologists and demographers frequently question whether there *will* indeed be a "demographic transition" in the underdeveloped countries. That is, is it possible that the population problem will solve itself through a *natural* transition of motivation towards smaller families? Many population biologists think this will *not* occur, for the following reasons.

At the time of the demographic transition in Western Europe, the population was small enough so that industrialization and urbanization affected the social values of nearly everyone in those countries. The problem in India and other underdeveloped areas is that their populations are already so large that the majority of the people will simply not be affected by the current level of socioeconomic progress before food crises become severe. Thus biologists such as Paul R. Ehrlich in his book *The Population Bomb* and William and Paul Paddock in their book *Famine—1975!* have predicted that the death rate will greatly increase again within the next decade, without an earlier drop in the birth rate. While scores of millions die, the birth rate among the remaining populace will decrease because of malnutrition and the lack of desire to bring children into a starving society. Michael M. Sligh has suggested in a recent article that this will cause a **demographic transposition** effect in that the relative positions of the death rate and birth rate will be transposed, at least for a time (Fig. 9-4). This demographic transposition will have tragic immediate effects on the populations of many underdeveloped countries, but it may require tragedy on such an immense scale to shock the world into full adoption of population control and zero population growth.

It appears unlikely at this point that worldwide population growth will be curtailed by the same changes in economic and social values that led to the rise of the small family as a norm in Europe. Likewise, it seems that alternatives to the Malthusian parameters of war, famine, and pestilence will have to be sought. War as an overall population control factor will continue to be insignificant unless we have an atomic world war; in that event we would probably be wondering about our very survival as a species. The biological restraints that have always exercised some degree of population control, including famine and epidemic diseases, will undoubtedly continue to operate and, as has been mentioned, massive famines in the near future are predicted by some. Epidemic diseases caused by new mutant viruses may arise and sweep the world or parts of it at any time. In 1969 and early 1970 an extremely virulent virus called Lassa fever was discovered in northern Nigeria and proved so deadly that American researchers had to halt work on it. Fortunately, its spread in Nigeria abated spontaneously in March 1970. Dr. Hans Zinsser, in his book *Rats, Lice and History*, traced the history of epidemic diseases such as smallpox, influenza, and typhus and presented considerable evidence suggesting that infectious viral agents are constantly changing in character and pathogenic effect. In recent years we have become familiar with new flu viruses that sweep across the world and are replaced the next winter by new strains.

From even this brief review it is obvious that some means of voluntarily limiting population size would be far preferable to these disasters. Fortunately, a number of methods for population control are currently available; many of these are promoted as "family planning" methods, which can be used for timing conceptions in marriage. In the following pages we shall look at these products of the scientific-medical revolution and assess their relative merits for worldwide implementation and success as control measures.

Contraception and Family-Planning Programs

Contraceptive devices and methods have been designed to prevent conception by mechanical, chemical, hormonal, or "natural" means. Their economic cost and effectiveness in achieving the desired end vary widely.

Mechanical Contraceptives

These are devices that prevent conception by blocking passage of the sperm into the uterus or by preventing implantation of the fertilized egg in the uterine wall. The **condom** is a very thin latex sheath that fits tightly over the penis and prevents semen from entering the vagina at ejaculation. It requires no prescription and is widely sold (and distributed in the armed forces) as a means of preventing venereal disease. It is relatively inexpensive in the United States, but the cost is still prohibitive for general distribution in most underdeveloped countries. There are aesthetic and psychological disadvantages to its use; yet in the late 1960s it was estimated that 25 percent of all married couples in the United States used this method of contraception.

The **diaphragm** is a rubber cup with a spring steel rim that can be inserted in the vagina before intercourse to cover the cervical entrance to the womb, or uterus. The edges of the diaphragm are coated with a spermicidal agent to prevent sperm from slipping underneath the rim. It is removed several hours after intercourse. Available by prescription in the United States, the diaphragm has to be fitted (at a cost of about $15) by a doctor; the device itself costs about $2. The cost and relatively complicated routine of fitting and periodic insertion prevent its utilization in mass population control programs in the underdeveloped countries. The **cervical cap** is quite similar to the diaphragm and may be worn for three weeks at a time, with removal necessary only near and during the menstrual period. It is extremely effective. The principal disadvantage is the necessity of placing it correctly.

The **intrauterine device** (or **IUD**) is a plastic or metal object that may be inserted into the uterus cavity and left there to prevent conception as long as desired. IUDs are designed in various shapes. They probably act by dislodging the fertilized egg or by preventing its implantation in the uterine wall. It is also suggested that the presence of the foreign object in the uterus hastens the muscular movement of the oviducts and speeds the ovum to the uterus, preventing it from being fertilized en route. The failure rate of the IUD is among the lowest for all contraceptives: about one or two women out of a hundred using an IUD will conceive. The cost is minimal.

Chemical Contraceptives

These include sprays, foams, tablets, suppositories, creams, and jellies designed to kill or immobilize sperm before conception occurs. They are inserted into the vagina before intercourse. They are effective about 60 percent of the time, hence not very reliable for population control.

Hormonal Contraceptives

These contraceptives are the *most effective* in present use. They are female pills or injections to prevent ovulation by simulating the conditions of early pregnancy in the body. The steroid female hormones **estrogen** and **progestin** (a synthetic chemical similar to the natural hormone progesterone, which is produced by the ovaries) are administered either sequentially or in combined form for three weeks of the 28-day menstrual cycle. The pill method is simple, inexpensive, and virtually 100 percent effective. The only requirement is motivation to remember to take the pill once a day. About one woman in every four or five taking the pill experiences undesirable side effects. Male steroid hormonal pills are as yet unsatisfactory because of side effects.

"Natural" Contraceptive Methods

The **rhythm method,** or periodic abstention, is the only method of birth control approved by the Roman Catholic Church. Since the timing of ovulation (release of the mature egg by the ovary into the oviduct, where it can be fertilized) is usually 16 days before the menstrual period, one can abstain from intercourse from several days before ovulation until about a day after ovulation and avoid fertilization of the egg. Unfortunately, the timing of ovulation varies among women and even from month to month in the same woman; in fact, one out of six women has such an irregular cycle that the method will not work at all for her. The rhythm method has a notoriously high failure rate, both because of this irregularity of the cycle and because of the occasional lapse of discipline on the part of the participants.

Other "natural" contraceptive methods include **coitus interruptus, douching,** and **abstention** from intercourse altogether.

Overall, most of these contraceptive methods have been promoted on the premise that "family planning" was the goal to be reached. That is, using one or more of these procedures would allow a couple to decide how many children they would have rather than trusting to chance alone. So despite the high effectiveness of the mechanical, chemical, and hormonal devices, the use of contraceptives has proven successful to date solely as a population growth *depressant,* not a population *control.* The basic problem is to achieve an international *motivation* for small families of at most two children. There is no doubt that effective contraceptive *methods* are already available to stop population growth.

Abortion

If contraceptive methods fail and a woman conceives, the commonest method employed around the world to prevent the birth of an unwanted child is induced or therapeutic **abortion** (expulsion of the fetus from the uterine cavity). Up to about 12 weeks of fetal development, this can be done without much chance of injury to the mother. After about 16 weeks, however, the risks of death to the mother by hemorrhage become considerable. The medically approved method of abortion is dilation (of the cervix) and curettage (scraping) of the uterus; a physician working under sterile conditions can do a "D and C" with an early fetus with less risk than delivering a full-term pregnancy. Cruder forms of abortion are practiced in every nation in the world, and abortion represents the single greatest factor contributing to the death rate among pregnant women. In fact, one reason why abortion was made illegal in the nineteenth century was to protect the mother from its danger under the primitive medical conditions of that time.

In recent years there has been an international trend toward legalizing abortions, based on the premise that the decision whether to have a child should be left up to the individual, not society. The opponents of this premise state that the third entity involved, the unborn child, should be protected by society's laws from the unilateral act of abortion approved by the mother. While lawyers and religious groups differ on defining the point in development at which a fetus becomes a human person complete with a soul, opponents of abortion feel that it denies the child's right to be born. His parents had the right to decide whether to conceive him, but once conceived, his right to live should not be prejudiced. Obviously, the best solution lies in effective contraception, which avoids the supposed necessity of abortion.

Sterilization

Sterilization of the man or woman is 100 percent effective as a birth-control method, and has no side effects on sex life or normal physiology. Naturally, most sterilizations are obtained by couples who have completed their families and wish to avoid the complications of contraceptives. The operation in the male involves tying off or cutting the vas deferens tubes leading from the testes to the urethra tube in the penis; thus the ejaculate no longer contains sperm cells. This **vasectomy** operation through the scrotal sac wall takes about fifteen minutes and can be done very inexpensively under local anesthetic in a physician's office or field clinic.

An analogous operation, called a **salpingectomy,** can be done in the female. However, this involves special abdominal surgery under anesthesia, unless the operation on the fallopian tubes is done when they are accessible following the birth of a baby. In either the sterilized male or female, sperm and eggs continue to be produced regularly but eventually break down and are reabsorbed by the body or picked up by phagocytes (specialized white blood cells) from the blood. There is at least a 50 percent chance that either a vasectomy or a salpingectomy will be reversible.

In a third operation resulting in sterilization, a **hysterectomy,** the uterus itself is removed. This is rarely done for birth-control purposes alone but is a rather common operation in women experiencing menopause.

More severe sterilization operations include **castration** (removal of the testes) of the male, and **oöphorectomy** (removal of the ovaries) in the female. These operations result in detri-

mental hormone imbalance because the sex organs are endocrine glands producing hormones that control the secondary
sexual characteristics of an individual. Without these hormones, the body may experience serious alterations. Vasectomy and salpingectomy, of course, only prevent fertilization;
they do *not* prevent hormonal production or upset any other
normal bodily activity.

Male sterilization has proven a useful part of population
control programs in parts of India and other countries, but
western cultures have so far not readily accepted this simple
contraceptive measure. This is largely the result of ignorance
of the exact nature of the male operation and fears that a
man's sex life will end. Obviously, these fears are completely
unfounded. Vasectomies would seem to be an effective and
easy population-control measure to advocate among married
men who already have one or two children and do not wish a
larger family.

Prospects for the Future

The present impact of man's population growth on natural
communities, on the continued existence of other species, and
on his own biological and psychological character, all shout
in the loudest possible way the dangers of continued increase.
Imaginative proposals have been made to feed and house the
additional billions of humans soon to join our "standing crop"
of Man. These include using artificial symbioses between nitrogen-fixing bacteria and non-legume plants to utilize more
directly the vast reservoir of molecular nitrogen in the atmosphere, or increasing the production of food from the sea, or
perhaps artificially synthesizing protein foods from algal cultures on a massive scale. Trans-planetary migration of humans via spaceship has even been suggested to ease future
crowding on earth. Yet objective analyses of all these ideas
show that they are but proximate solutions that can only handle a minute fraction of our estimated future increases in

population. The ultimate solution to the crises we face between man and his earthly environment is, bluntly, *zero* population growth. Man has the choice of reaching agreement on the desirability of this goal and implementation of strategy to reach it, or continuing as he is with the consequences becoming now all too familiar to us.

Summary

Population growth in man has been caused primarily by a cultural revolution (600,000 B.C.), the agricultural revolution (6000 B.C.), and the scientific-industrial revolution that started about 1650 A.D. The last has caused the "population explosion" because of the sizable gap created between our birth rates and death rates around the world. Population growth in primitive hunting-and-gathering societies was prevented or minimized by famine, disease, war, and many culturally instituted behavioral patterns (e.g., infanticide and abortion). In modern societies medical advances and social hygiene lowered the death rate while the birth rate remained generally high. For the world in January 1971, the annual birth rate was 34 per 1,000 and the death rate 14 per 1,000, giving us an annual rate of increase of 2.0 percent, which will double the world's population every 35 years. It is doubtful that the demographic transition that reduced growth rates in European countries will take place in presently underdeveloped countries with large populations. Instead, a demographic transposition may appear in these countries because of deaths on a massive scale. True population control is possible if the people of the world develop the *motivation* to have small families (average of 2 children). The technological measures for voluntary achievement of the goal of zero population growth are available in the form of contraceptives, abortion, and sterilization techniques.

Additional Reading

The number of books and articles being published each year on environmental problems staggers the imagination *and* the bookshelves of libraries. While it may seem presumptuous to select a small list of these for suggested additional reading, your interest may have been aroused sufficiently so that you would like to pursue in more depth some of the topics we have touched upon in this book. The following offerings are grouped according to chapter.

1. POPULATIONS AND ECOLOGY (General Books)

Boughey, Arthur S. 1971. *Man and the Environment.* Macmillan, New York. 472 pp.

Ehrlich, Paul R., and Anne H. Ehrlich. 1972. *Population, Resources, Environment.* Second edition. W. H. Freeman, San Francisco. 509 pp.

Wagner, Richard H. 1971. *Environment and Man.* W. W. Norton, New York. 491 pp.

2 and 3. SOME BASIC PRINCIPLES OF ECOLOGY

Allee, W. C.., Alfred E. Emerson, Orlando Park, Thomas Park, and Karl P. Schmidt. 1949. *Principles of Animal Ecology.* W. B. Saunders, Philadelphia. 837 pp.

Kendeigh, S. Charles. 1961. *Animal Ecology.* Prentice-Hall, Englewood Cliffs. 468 pp.

Odum, Eugene P. 1971. *Fundamentals of Ecology.* Third edition. W. B. Saunders, Philadelphia. 574 pp.

Smith, Robert L. 1966. *Ecology and Field Biology.* Harper & Row, New York. 686 pp.

4. THE ORGANIZATION OF POPULATIONS

Andrewartha, H. G., and L. C. Birch. 1954. *The Distribution and Abundance of Animals.* University of Chicago Press, Chicago. 782 pp.

5. POPULATION GROWTH AND REGULATION

Slobodkin, Lawrence B. 1961. *Growth and Regulation of Animal Populations*. Holt, Rinehart and Winston, New York. 184 pp.

6. THE ECOLOGY OF COMMUNITIES

Shelford, Victor E. 1963. *The Ecology of North America*. University of Illinois Press, Urbana. 610 pp.

Whittaker, Robert H. 1970. *Communities and Ecosystems*. Macmillan, New York. 162 pp.

7. ENVIRONMENTAL ALTERATION

Ehrenfeld, David W. 1970. *Biological Conservation*. Holt, Rinehart and Winston, New York. 226 pp.

Owen, Oliver S. 1971. *Natural Resource Conservation: An Ecological Approach*. Macmillan, New York. 593 pp.

Weisberg, Barry. 1971. *Ecocide in Indochina: The Ecology of War*. Canfield Press, Harper & Row, San Francisco. 241 pp.

8. POLLUTION

Cox, George W., editor. 1969. *Readings in Conservation Ecology*. Appleton-Century-Crofts, New York. 595 pp.

Detwyler, Thomas R., editor. 1971. *Man's Impact on Environment*. McGraw-Hill, New York. 731 pp.

9. POPULATION GROWTH IN MAN

Ehrlich, Paul R. 1969. *The Population Bomb*. Sierra Club Books, San Francisco. 191 pp.

Emmel, Thomas C., and Michael M. Sligh. 1970. Human population problems. *Science Education*, 54:363–372.

Malthus, Thomas Robert. 1798. *On Population*. Reprinted edition (1960) by Modern Library, New York. 602 pp.

Zinsser, Hans. 1935. *Rats, Lice and History*. Bantam Books, New York. 228 pp.

Glossary

The definitions of terms in this glossary pertain specifically to the use of these words in ecology and population biology. Hence some terms that have other meanings outside these fields will be found to have rather restricted definitions here.

Abortion—expulsion of a fetus from the uterine cavity before normal birth.

Age Distribution—proportion of a population in each age class.

Aggressive Mimicry—a situation where one species mimics another species or an object in its environment in order to attract or deceive the prey species for the purpose of eating it.

Allopatric—occurring in different areas.

Arboreal—living in trees.

Autecology—the study of the ecology of the individual organism of a species.

Batesian Mimicry—a mimicry situation in which a harmless species (mimic) resembles a harmful species (model) and thus gains protection from predation.

Biogeochemical Cycle—the cyclical series of transformations of a chemical element through the organisms in a biotic community and their physical environment.

Biological Control—the suppression of reproduction of a pest organism by utilizing behavioral traits or other organisms rather than chemical means.

Biomass—the weight of all living organisms in a sample.

Biome—a major climax community type covering a wide area of a continent or the earth.

Biosphere—all living organisms on earth.

Biota—the flora and fauna of a region.

Biotic—relating to life; biological.

Biotic Potential—maximum possible growth rate of living things under ideal conditions.

Bulkhead Line—a legally set limit on commercial filling operations in a bay.

Carrying Capacity—the maximum population size that the environment can support without deterioration.

Carnivore—an animal that feeds on other animals.

Chaparral—a biome consisting of dense thickets of stiff or tough-leafed shrubs, found in areas with a Mediterranean climate.

Character Displacement—an outcome of competition in which two species living in the same area have evolved differences in morphology or other characteristics that lessen competition for food resources.

Clear-cutting—logging all trees in a forest area.

Climax Community—the terminal stage of ecological succession in an area.

Commensalism—a symbiotic relationship in which one species benefits and the other is neither benefited nor harmed.

Community—all the organisms of all species living in a particular area.

Competition—a struggle between individuals of the same or different species for food, space, mates, or any other limited resource.

Competitive Exclusion—a result of competition where one species is forced out of part of the available habitat by a more efficient species.

Contraception—the process of preventing conception (successful union of a sperm and egg cell).

Cryptic Coloration—coloration that causes an organism to resemble some inanimate object or background substrate.

Decomposers—organisms such as carrion beetles and fungi that feed upon and break down dead organic matter.

Demographic Transition—a decline in birth rate following a drop in death rate, as in the case of the population of Western Europe from 1650 to 1850.

Demographic Transposition—a predicted reversal of the present relative positions of the death and birth rates in major underdeveloped countries around 1975–85; or, any similar population trend when a country experiencing population growth reaches the point of being unable to supply the subsistence-level needs of a significant proportion of the population.

Density—the size of the population within a particular unit of space.

Desert—an arid biome characterized by little moisture, high diurnal temperatures, and low diversity of vegetation and animal life.

Dispersal—spreading or moving out from a point.

Dispersion—the internal distribution pattern of individuals in a population.

Disseminules—seeds, spores, eggs, or other non-adult stages of plants and animals that can be dispersed.

Dominance—the fact of being a major influence on numerical composition or internal energy dynamics in a community.

Dominant Species—a species of plant or animal that is particularly abundant or controls a major portion of the energy flow in a community.

Ecological Efficiency—the percent of available energy utilized by a trophic level from the next lowest level.

Ecological Pyramid—a triangular graphic form showing the sequence of diminishing numbers, biomass, or available energy as one goes up through the trophic levels.

Ecology—the study of the interrelationships between organisms and their environment.

Ecosystem—the biotic community and physical environment in an area.

Emigration—departure from one place to take up residence in another area.

Environment—the physical and biological characteristics of a certain region.

Environmental Resistance—all the limiting factors in the environment that are acting on a particular population.

Epiphylls—tiny plants such as mosses that grow on the surfaces of leaves of larger plants in tropical rain forests.

Epiphyte—a non-parasitic plant that grows upon other plants for physical support, deriving its required moisture chiefly from the air. Epiphytic plants include arboreal orchids, bromeliads, and many mosses and ferns.

Eutrophication—promotion of plant growth in an aquatic ecosystem by rapidly adding substantial amounts of nutrients. Available oxygen is used up by the plants and substantial fish kills may result.

Evolution—a change in gene frequency in a population, usually involving a visible change in the species' characteristics.

Extinction—an outcome of competition and natural selection in which the species or population dies out completely.

Food Chain—the transfer of food energy from green plants (ultimately from the sun) through a series of species.

Food Web—the complex interlocking patterns of food chains in a biotic community.

Gause's Principle—two species cannot occupy the same niche simultaneously.

Grassland—a treeless, grassy plains biome found in central parts of temperate North America, Eurasia, and Australia.

Growth Form or Curve—the manner and speed of population increase.

Habitat—the physical place where an organism lives.

Herbivores—animals that eat plants.

Home Range—physical area of an individual's normal activity.

Host—an organism that is fed upon by another organism.

Immigration—one-way movement into a new area of residence from neighboring areas.

Infanticide—killing a human infant after birth.

Laterite—a hard, impermeable, reddish crust of soil formed by water leaching exposed soils in cleared areas of tropical rain forests.

Leaching—dissolving out of soluble materials (such as salts and minerals) by water percolating through soil, especially in areas of heavy rainfall.

Migration—periodic departure and return of individuals to and from a population area.

Morphology—the form and structure of animals and plants.

Mortality—death rate.

Mullerian Mimicry—a situation in which all potential prey species in a mimicry complex are harmful and share a common warning color pattern and behavior.

Mutualism—a symbiotic relationship where both species benefit.

Natality—birth rate.

Niche—the unique occupation or way of life of a plant or animal species: where it lives and what it does in the community.

Nitrogen-fixing Bacteria—bacteria with the ability to convert inorganic N_2 into forms, especially nitrates, that are immediately usable by plants.

Oscillations—periodic fluctuations in population size.

Parasite—an organism that feeds on another organism (its host), generally without killing it.

Parasitism—a symbiotic relationship where one species (the host) is harmed but not killed immediately and the other species feeding on it (the parasite) is benefited.

Periodism—a particular temporal sequence of activity.

Pesticide—a chemical used to kill species regarded as pests.

Pollution—the introduction of an undesirable change in some aspect of the environment.

Population—an aggregation of organisms of the same species living in the same area.

Primary Production—the energy accumulated and stored by plants through photosynthesis.

Predator—an organism that kills and eats another organism.

Producers—organisms that convert light energy from the sun into chemical-bond energy.

Productivity—the production of organic matter per unit of area in a community over a particular time interval, usually a year.

Saprophyte—a plant, such as a fungus or mushroom, that feeds on dead and decaying matter.

Savanna—tropical grassland biome with scattered trees.

Sere—the complex series of changes in an area, from the initial condition to the climax community.

Social Hierarchy—a series of dominance-subordination relationships in a group (= "pecking order").

Standing Crop—the number of individuals or total biomass present in a community at one particular time.

Stratification—vertical layering of a plant or aquatic community.

Substrate—the substance or base on which an organism grows.

Succession—the replacement of one community by another.

Survivorship—the percentage of individuals in a population still living at various times after birth.

Symbiosis—the living together in intimate association of two diverse types of organisms.

Sympatric—occurring in the same area.

Taiga—the northern coniferous forest biome, found south of the Arctic Circle.

Temperate Deciduous Forest—the broadleaved forest biome north and south of the equatorial tropics.

Territoriality—the behavior of defending an area against intrusion by other individuals.

Trophic Level—a feeding level. Organisms having the same general source of energy or nutrition are said to be in the same trophic level.

Tropical Deciduous Forest—a tropical biome with well-developed broadleaved forest and seasonal loss of leaves.

Tropical Rain Forest—the most complex biome on earth, characterized by great species diversity, high rainfall all year, and warm temperatures. The broadleaved forest remains green throughout the year.

Tundra—the treeless plains biome of northern arctic regions and high alpine mountaintops.

Turbidity—cloudiness of water, from the presence of suspended sediment or small organisms such as algae.

Vagility—a species' inherent ability to move.

Warning Coloration—bright coloration advertising the fact that a potential prey species is harmful (distasteful, poisonous, irritating, etc.).

INDEX

Explanations of terms that appear in figure captions or are illustrated by photographs are identified by *italicized* numbers.

Abortion, 172, 175. *See also* Contraceptives
Activity cycles, 7, *9*
Adaptation, 6, 11, 61, 74, 75
  in dispersal, 74, 75, 77
  in feeding, 60
  See also Coevolution; Coloration; Mimicry; Natural selection
Adrenal glands, 91
Aedes, 150
Africa, 30, 51, 52, 69, *114*
Age distribution, 77, 81. *See also* Survivorship
Agent Orange, 127, *128. See also* Herbicides
Aggregation, 77, 78
Aggression, 68
Aggressive mimicry, 49. *See also* Mimicry
Agricultural revolution, 158, 160
Agriculture, 33, 52, 54, 89, 100, 103–104, 140, *149,* 150, 151, 158
  clearing, 124–126, 129, 135, 144
  crop resistance to pests, 154
  irrigation, 100–101
  rotation of crops, 21
  slash-and-burn, 126
  See also Domestication; Gathering; Grazing; Meat; Pesticides; Soil
"Air plants." *See* Epiphytic plants
Air pollution, 141–143
  carbon monoxide, 141, 144, 145
  effects of, *143–145*
  nitrogen oxides, 141

smog, 141, *142,* 143
sulfur oxides, 141
Alaska, *134*
Alcid. *See* Bird
Aleutian Islands, 1
Alfalfa, 16
Algae, 15, 16, 17, 18, 26, 51, 79, 140
Alligators, 66
Alouatta villosa, 67, *68*
Aluminum
  cans, 147
  in soil, 124
Amazon Basin, 124
Ambush bug. *See* Insect
American redstart. *See* Bird
Amino acids, 17, 18. *See also* Protein
Ammonia, 17, 18. *See also* Nitrogen
Amphibian
  frog, 50, *51,* 119
  predatory, 42
Andes, *130*
Andrewartha, H. G., 88
Angeles National Forest, 144
Annual plants, 85, 93
Anolis frenatus. See Reptile, lizard
Antarctica, 151
Antelope, 52, 69, 103
Antibiotics, 65
Ant. *See* Insect
Aquatic community. *See* Aquatic ecosystem; Community
Aquatic ecosystem, 29, 34, 35, 38, 101, *119*
Arboreal orchids. *See* Epiphytic plants

183

Arboreal vine snake. *See* Reptile
Arctic mammals, 93, 98
  fox, *94, 95*
Arizona, 143, 152
  University of, 152
Arsenate, 148. *See also* Pesticide
Artificial selection, 52
Ascension Island, 71, *72, 73*
Aswan Dam, 101
Atmosphere
  as reservoir, 14, 15, 16, 18
  temperature of, 22, 23
Atomic energy, 23
Atomic Energy Commission, 147
Australia, 88, *111*, 112, 115
Autecology, 3
Automobile industry, solid waste pollution, *146. See also* Emission standards
Autotroph, *113. See also* Photosynthesis

Baboon, 69, *70*
Bacteria, 14, 16, 17, 18, 25, 27, 28, 39, 55, 57, 59, 90, 107, 153. *See also* Decomposer; Denitrifying bacteria; Nitrogen-fixing bacteria; Saprophyte
Balanus. See Barnacles
Bamboo, 127
Banana. *See* Cultivation
Bark beetle. *See* Insect
Barley. *See* Cultivation
Barnacles, 59, 60, 138
Basiliscus basiliscus. See Reptile, lizard
Bass. *See* Fish
Batesian mimicry, 45, *48. See also* Coloration; Mimicry
Beans. *See* Cultivation
Bear, 29, 109
Beavers, 89
Bedbug. *See* Ectoparasite
Bee. *See* Insect
Beetle. *See* Insect
Behavior, 74
  dispersal, 74, 77
  in mimicry, 45, 49
  See also Emigration; Immigration; Migration
Benzene hexachloride (BHC), 150. *See also* Pesticides
Big Cypress Swamp, 133
Bill size. *See* Bird; Character displacement; Competition
Binomial system of nomenclature, 110
Biocides, 148. *See also* Agriculture; Pesticides; Pollution
Biogeochemical cycles, 7, 12–24, 37–38, 99. *See also* Erosion; Leaching
Biological clocks, 155

Biological control, 151, *153–156*
  sex attractants, 155
  sterilization, 154, 155
Biomass, 78, 79, 103
Biome, 107, *108*, 109–119, 120, 121. *See also* Chaparral; Climax; Desert; Ecosystem; Grassland; Taiga; Temperate deciduous forest; Tropical deciduous forest; Tropical rain forest; Tropical savanna; Tundra
Biotic community. *See* Community
Biotic potential, 64, 77, 83, *84*, 86, 88, 92, 97
  maximum, 84
Birch, L. C., 88
Bird, 20, 45, 51, 66, 68, 89, 93, 97, *108*
  alcid, 44
  American redstart, *44*
  bald eagle, 151
  bill size, 60, 61
  blue tit, *43*
  brown pelican, 152
  cattle egret, 49, 51
  ducks, 74, *134*
  European woodcock, *43*
  fledging, 83
  geese, 74, *134*
  hawk, 40, 100
  honey-guide, 52
  Ivory-bill Woodpecker, 3
  long-billed curlew, *43*
  migratory, 74, 75, *76*, 129, *130*
  murres, 138
  nest site, 67
  nesting, 89
  Old World cattle egret, 49, 51
  osprey, 151
  owl, 100
  parrot, 115, *116*
  penguin, 44, 151
  poor-will, *46*
  predatory, 40, 42
  purple sunbird, *53*
  razorbills, 138
  red-necked grebe, *43*
  ring-necked pheasant, 89
  robins, 89, 152
  sea, 19
  sharp-shinned hawk, 41
  snowy owl, *94, 95*
  waterfowl, 75, *76*, 138
  white-throated sparrow, *43*
  Whooping Crane, 3
  woodpecker, 31
  yellow-throated vireo, *43*
  See also Chicken; Flyway; Pecking order; Turkey
Birth defects, 127
Birth rate. *See* Natality

Bladderwort, 39
Blue-green algae, 18
Blue tit, *43*
Bobcat. *See* Canadian lynx
Bombing, *126–129*. *See also* Defoliation
Bones, phosphorus from, 19, 20
Boston, 84
Braconid wasp. *See* Insect
Brazil, 71, *72, 73*
Bream. *See* Fish
Bromeliads, *118*. *See also* Epiphytic plants
Buffalo, 40
Bulkhead lines. *See* Landfill
Bumblebee. *See* Insect
Bunch grasses. *See* Grasses
Butterfly, 30, 75
   checkerspot, *53*
   Hamadryas, 46
   Heliconius, 30, 48
   Monarch, 45, *48*
   viceroy, 45, 48
   See also Mimicry

CO$_2$. *See* Carbon dioxide
Cactus, *113*
Caddisfly, 27. *See also* Insect
Calcium, 152
California, *102, 106*, 111, 131, 143
   Mojave Desert, 3
Canada, 93, *95*
Canadian lynx, 93, 94
Cañete Valley (Peru), 150, 156
Cannibalism, 39, 162
Capparis aphylla, 53
Caprimulgidae. *See* Bird, poor-will
Carbohydrates, 14, 16
Carbon cycle, 13–16, 21–22, 37. *See also* Carbon dioxide; Fossil fuel
Carbon dioxide, 14, 15, 16, 22, 23, *113*. *See also* Carbon cycle
Carbon monoxide. *See* Air pollution
Carbonification, 15
Cardiac glycosides, 45
Caribbean, islands of, 1, *73*, 154, 163
Caribbean Sea, 133
Caribou, *108*, 135
Carnivores, 16, 18, 25, 28, 32, 34, 35, 37, 39. *See also* Consumer; Efficiency; Predation
Carolina "chameleon," 10
Carpenter ant. *See* Insect
Carpenter bee. *See* Insect
Carrying capacity, *86–87*, 89, 90, 97, 104, 119, *159*. *See also* Population
Cassava. *See* Cultivation
Castes, 69
Castration, 161, 173. *See also* Sterilization

Cattle. *See* Grazing
Cattle egret. *See* Bird
Cedar Bog Lake (Minnesota), 35
Celestial clues, 72
Celibacy, 161
Cellulose, 147
Cercaria. *See* Fluke
Chaparral, *111*–112. *See also* Climax
Character displacement, 59, 61, 62
Checkerspot butterfly. *See* Butterfly
Chelonia mydas. *See* Green turtle
Chemical energy, 24, 26, 28, 29
Chicken, 52, 68
China, 124
Chinese liver fluke. *See* Endoparasite
Chloride. *See* Salt
Chlorinated hydrocarbons. *See* DDT
Chlorophyll, 13, 21, 33. *See also* Photosynthesis
Cholera. *See* Disease organisms
Chthamalus. *See* Barnacles
Cicada. *See* Insect
Clear-cutting, 131–*132*, 135. *See also* Lumbering
Climate, 88, 89
   changed by pollution, 144
   See also Density-independent factors
Climax, 104, *105*, 107–119, 121, 123, 135
   chaparral, *111*–112
   desert, *113–114*
   grassland, 112
   taiga, 109, *110*
   temperate deciduous forest, 109–*110*
   tropical deciduous forest, 115
   tropical rain forest, 115–119, 126
      importance, 120
   tropical savanna, *114*–115
   tundra, *108*–109
   See also Biome; Communities; Succession
Clonorchis sinensis. *See* Fluke
Clover, 16
Clumped dispersion, 64, 65, 77. *See* Dispersion
Coal, 143. *See* Carbon cycle; Fossil fuel; Mining
Cockroach. *See* Insect
Cockrum, E. Lendell, 152
Coelenterates
   Hydra, 83
Coevolution, 11, 43
Colombia, 124, 125
Colonial species, 77. *See also* Social organization
Colony, 69
Colorado, 46, 53, *108, 110*
Coloration, 42, 45, *46*, 49, *50*, 61
   eye lines, *43*, 44
   facial patches, *44*

Coloration (*continued*)
  See also Cryptic coloration; Mimicry; Repelling coloration; Warning coloration
Combustion, 15, 16. *See also* Air pollution
Combustion engine, 143
Commensalism, 49, 51, 55, 61. *See also* Symbiosis
Communities, 3, 11, 38
  aquatic, 100
  climax formations, *107–119*
  differentiation, *99–100*
  dominance, *101–103*
  ecology of, *99–120*
  horizontal differentiation, 100
  importance of climax community, *119*
  lake, *100–101*
  minor, 100
  productivity, *103–104*
  succession, *104–107*
  temporal differentiation, 100
  terrestrial, 100, 119
  vertical differentiation, 100
Competition, 34, 38, 57, 58, 59, 60, 61, 66, 67, 75, 77, 90
  effect on biotic potential, 84
  See also Extinction
Competitive exclusion, 59, 60, 61
Concentration, 74
Condom. *See* Contraceptives, mechanical
Connell, J. H., 59
Conservation of matter and energy, 24
Conservationists, 133
Consumer, 34, 35. *See also* Carnivore; Efficiency; Herbivore
Contraceptives
  chemical, 171
  hormonal, 171
  mechanical, 170
  "natural" methods, 171–172
  See also Abortion; Sterilization
Convergence, 48
Corn, 21, 27, 52. *See also* Cultivation
Corps of Engineers, 133, *134*
Costa Rica, *30, 46, 50, 68, 116, 125*, 126
Cotton. *See* Cultivation
Coyotes, 89
Craterization. *See* Bombing
Creosote bush, 65
Cross-Florida Barge Canal, 133, *134*
Crowding, 91, 166. *See also* Density
Crude density, 78, 79. *See also* Density
Cryptic coloration, 45, *46*. *See also* Coloration
Culex, 150
Cultivation, 124, 125
  banana, 126

  barley, 52
  beans, 52
  cassava, 126
  corn, 21, 27, 52
  cotton, 21, 150, 151
  irrigation, 100, 101
  legumes, 16, 17, 18, 21, 55
  papaya, 126
  potato, 52
  rice, 18, 52
  rotation of crops, 21
  rye, 52
  squash, 52
  sugar cane, 126
  tobacco, 52, 158
  wheat, 52
  See also Agriculture; Pesticides
Current
  Equatorial, 72
  underwater, 20
Cuzco (Peru), *130*
Cycles, 12. *See also* Biogeochemical cycles

Dams, 100
Danaus plexippus. See Butterfly, Monarch
Darlingtonia californica, 40. See also Pitcher plant
DDT, 1, 89, 148, 150, 151, 152, 153, 156
  DDD, 148
  DDE, 148
Death, 15, 16, 18, 19, 20, 137. *See also* Decomposer; Mortality; Saprophyte
Death rate. *See* Mortality
Decay organisms, 15, 136. *See also* Bacteria; Decomposer; Saprophyte
Deciduous forest. *See* Biome; Temperate deciduous forest; Tropical deciduous forest
Decomposer, 13, 14, 16, 18, 29, 30, 32, 33, 34, 37. *See also* Bacteria; Saprophyte
Deer, 69
Defoliant chemicals. *See* Herbicides
Defoliation, *126–129*, 135. *See also* Bombing
Deforestation, 21
Demographic transition, 166, *167*, 168
Demography, 81
Dendrobates. See Amphibian, frog
Denitrifying bacteria, 17, 18. *See also* Bacteria
Density, 64, 77, 78, 79, *85*, 87–92, *96*, 97
  crude density, 78, 79, 97
  dependent factors, 87, 88, *89–92*, 94, 97, *159*

independent factors, 87, *88–89*, 97, *159*
oscillations, 93, *94*, 98
See also Crowding; Interspecific competition; Population
Department of Agriculture, 132, 154
Desalinization, 124
Desert, 34, 67, 113–114, 135
agricultural inroads, 124, 125, 126
See also Biome; Climax
Detergents, 138, 140
Detroit, 143
Dew, *113*, 114
Diapause, 92, 93, 155
Diaphragm. *See* Contraceptives, mechanical
Dichlorophenoxyacetic acid, 127. *See also* Herbicides
Differential reproduction, 5, 6, 11. *See also* Adaptation; Natural selection
Differentiation, 100
horizontal, 100, 120
temporal, 100, 120
vertical, 100, 120
Diffusion, 15
Digestion, 18
Dionaea muscipula, 39, 40. *See also* Venus' Fly-trap
Disease, 90, 148, 166, 175
flu, 169
influenza, 169
Lassa fever, 169
smallpox, 169
typhoid, 136, 137, 169
See also Malaria; Malthus; Viruses
Disease organisms, 136, 137
Dispersal, 6, 7, 42, 64, 71, 74, 75, 77. *See also* Distribution; Emigration; Immigration; Migration
Dispersion, 64, 65, 71, 77, 79, 100
clumped, 64, 65, 66
random, 64
uniform, 64, 65
See also Social organization
Disseminules, 75
Diversity, 4, 121
DNA, 19
Domestication, 52, 54
Dominance, 68
in a community, 101–103, 120
farmland community, 103
Dormancy. *See* Diapause
Downhill transport. *See* Erosion; Leaching; Runoff
Dredge-and-fill, 129, *139*
"Drip tip," *118*, 119
Drosera, 39, 40
Drosophila. *See* Insect, fruitfly
Drought, 89, *111*

Dutch elm disease, 89

Earthquakes, 131
Earthworm, 89
Ecological density, 79. *See also* Density
Ecological efficiency. *See* Efficiency
Ecological niche. *See* Niche
Ecological pyramid, 35–37. *See also* Pyramid
Ecology, 1, 2, 11
Ecosystem, 3, *4*, 5, 6, 11, *15*, 19
man's effect on, 42
See also Climax; Community; Energy flow; Stratification
Ectoparasite, 55. *See also* Parasitism
Eelgrass, 19, 28
Efficiency, 25, 29, 32, 33, *34*, *35*, 37, 67, 107
in parasitism, 55
See also Food chain; Pyramid
Electric power, 135
Electrification, 18. *See also* Lightning
Electromagnetic radiation. *See* Sunlight
Element flow. *See* Biogeochemical cycles
Elk, 69
Elm, 89
Emigration, 71, 77, 78, 90, 91
emigrants, 79
See also Dispersal
Emission standards, 143
Endocrine system, 91
Endoparasite, 55. *See also* Fluke; Parasitism
Energy flow, 13, 24, 25, 29, 32, 33, 34, 36, 37, 38, 49, 99, 121. *See also* Efficiency; Food chain; Pyramid; Thermodynamics
England, 138
Entropy, 25
Environmental alteration, 121. *See also* Man; Pollution
Environmental resistance, *84*, *85*, *86*, *87*, 97. *See also* Carrying capacity
Enzymes, 39
Epiphytic plants, 51, *118*, 119
Equatorial current, 72
Erosion, 18, 19, 20, 21, 101, 124, 127
glacial, 100
See also Flooding; Leaching
Eskimos, 152
Esox americanus. *See* Fish, pickerel
Estivation, 92
Estrogen, 153, 171
Euphydryas anicia. *See* Butterfly, checkerspot
European woodcock. *See* Bird
Eutrophication, 140, 141. *See also* Pollution
Everglades National Park, 66, 133

Evolution, 5, 6, 38, 150, 158. *See also* Adaptation; Coevolution; Coloration; Mutation
Evolutionary orderliness, 5, 11
Excrement, 19, 20
Excretion, 20
Exodus, 161
Exponential growth curve, *84–85*, 97. *See also* Growth form
Extinction, 3, 42, 57, 58, 59, 61, 69, 89, 152. *See also* Competition; Predation
Eye lines. *See* Coloration

Facial patches. *See* Coloration
Family planning, *169–175*. *See also* Abortion; Contraceptives; Sterilization
Famine, 163, 166, 168, 169, 175
Farmland community, 103
Feininger, Tomas, 124, 125
Ferns, 104
Fertility. *See* Natality
Fertilizer, 21, *139*. *See also* Agriculture
Fire, 122, 123, 127, 135
Firefly. *See* Insect
Fish, 52, 93, 138
  bass, 26, 27, 28
  bream, 26, 27, 28
  as host, 55, 56
  migratory, 20
  mullet, 27, 28
  pickerel, *43*
  predatory, 42
  salmon, 20, 135
  spawning areas, 129
  steelhead, 20
  striped bass, 84
  swordfish, 1
Flea. *See* Ectoparasite
Flooding, 89, *133*. *See also* Erosion
Florida, 23, 26, 27, 33, 34, 49, 122, 129, 131, 133, *139*, 154
  phosphate mining in, 21
Flower, 49, 52, 53, 88
  bromeliads, 143
  orchids, 143
  roses, *85, 86*
Fluke, 55
  life cycle, *56*
  See also Endoparasite
Flyway, 74, 75, *76, 130*. *See also* Bird; Migration
Food chain, 26, 28, 35, 109, 151. *See also* Food web
Food plant, 45, 88
Food supply, 67. *See also* Agriculture; Crops

Food web, 27, *28*, 37, 99, 107, 109, 119, 144
Foraging area, 7. *See also* Territory
Forest fire. *See* Fire
Forest succession, *105. See also* Succession; Temperate deciduous forest
Fossil bones, 19, 20
Fossil fuel, 15, 16, 21, 23
  consumption of, 22
  See also Carbon cycle
Foxes, 89
France, 138
Freshwater marsh, energy flow in, 32
Frog. *See* Amphibian
Fuel. *See* Fossil fuel
Fungus, 17, 18, 27, 30, 31, 51, 52, 97, 119
  hyphae, *52*
  lassoing, 39
  root, 126
Fur-bearing mammals, 109. *See also* Bear; Martens; Weasels
Fusion, 147

Gas, 15, 16. *See also* Fossil fuel
Gaseous cycle, 14, 37
Gathering, 54
Gause, G. F., 57. *See also* Gause's Principle
Gause's Principle, 57, 62
Gazelle, 115
Gecko, 40. *See also* Reptile, lizard
Geographic barriers, 63
Geologic subsidence, 20
Geologic time, 19
Geologic upheavals, 20
Geometrid moth. *See* Insect
Giraffes, 115
Glacial erosion, 100
Glass, 147
Glucose, 24, *113*
Goats, 52. *See also* Grazing
Grasses, *108*, 109, 112
Grassland, 112, *114. See also* Biome; Climax formations
Grazing, 112, 131
  cattle, 51, 52, 103, 147, 154
  goats, 52
  pigs, 27, 52
  sheep, 52
  See also Agriculture; Meat
Great Plains, 112. *See also* Grassland
"Greenhouse effect," 22, *23*
Green plants, 14, 16, 24, 26, 34
  eel grass, 19, 28
  See also Crops; Food chain; Photosynthesis; Producer; Sunlight
Green turtle, 71, *72, 73*, 74

Growth form, 64, 77, *84–87*
  J-shaped growth curve, 84–85
  S-shaped growth curve, *86–87*
Guano, 19, 20
Guano bat, 152

Habitat, 6, 11, 75, 77, 79, 89, 99, 100
  modification of, 66
  See also Competition; Dispersal;
    Niche
Hamadryas. See Butterfly
Hardwood forests, *110,* 123. *See also*
    Temperate deciduous forest
Hawk. *See* Bird
Heat
  dissipation of energy, 24, 26, 29, 37
  See also Energy flow; Food chain;
    Greenhouse effect; Temperature
Heliconius. See Butterfly
Hemiptera See Insect, "true bug"
Hemoglobin, 141
Herbaceous plants, *114*
Herbicides, 126, *139,* 148
  Agent Orange, 127, *128*
  2, 4-D (dichlorophenoxyacetic acid),
    127, *128,* 148
  2, 4, 5-T (trichlorophenoxyacetic
    acid), 127, *128,* 148
  See also Agriculture; Pesticides; Pol-
    lution
Herbivore, 14, 18, 25, 28, 29, 30, 32,
    33, 34, 35, 37, 39, *108,* 113, 115.
    See also Consumer; Efficiency; Pyr-
    amid
Hibernation, 92
Home range, 67. *See also* Territoriality
Homo sapiens. See Man
Honey badger, 52
Honey-guide. *See* Bird
Horizontal differentiation, 100, 120. *See*
    also Communities; Differentiation
Hormone, 91
Horticulturists, 143
Host organism, 16, 49, 51, 54, 55, 56,
    91, 154
  tree, 79
  See also Commensalism; Mutualism;
    Parasitism; Symbiosis
Howler monkey, 67, *68*
Hudson Bay Company, 93, *94*
Hungary, 153
Hunting, 54, 135, 150
Hydra, 82, 83
  survivorship curve, *82*
Hydroelectricity, 135, 137
Hydrogen cycle, 13, 14, 37
Hyperparasitism, 55
Hyphae. *See* Fungus
Hysterectomy. *See* Sterilization

Immigration, 71, 77
  immigrants, 79
  See also Dispersal
Incineration, 145. *See also* Solid Waste
    pollution
India, 53, 124, *159,* 163, 167, 174
Indiana, 144
Indians
  Aztec, 162
  Jivaro, 162
  North American, 162
  Plains, 40
  South American, 50, 126
Indochina, 127
Industrialization, 158
Industrial-scientific revolution, 164, 175
Infanticide, 161, 175
Infibulation, 161
Infrared radiation, 22, 23, 24. *See also*
    Heat; Sunlight
Inorganic form of elements, 13, 14
Insect, 39, 40, 45, 88, 93, 119, 153, 154,
    155
  ambush bug, 49
  ant, 69, 93
  aphid, 153
  army ant, 115, *116*
  bark beetle, 31
  bee, 52, 66, 69
  beetle, 29, 31, 45, 50, 153, 154
  braconid wasp, 54
  bumblebee, 49
  caddisfly, 26, 27, 28
  carpenter ant, 29, 31
  carpenter bee, 31
  cicada, *96,* 97
  cockroach, 3, 49
  firefly, 49
  fruitfly, 82
  geometrid moth, 45
  katydid, 45
  long-horned beetle, *50*
  mealybug, 79
  midge, 26, 28
  mosquito, *108,* 129, 148, 150
  moth, 50
  social, 69
  soil insect, 79
  sphinx moth, 54
  termite, 29, 31, 69, 93
  thrips, *85, 86,* 87, 88
  "true bugs," 49
  walking stick, 45, 46
  wasp, 49, 69, 97, 153
    growth pattern, 85
  water beetle, 27, 28
  See also Butterfly; Parasitism
Insecticides, 148, 150, 153. *See also*
    Agriculture; Pesticides; Pollution

Insolation. *See* Sunlight
Interaction, 42. *See also* Coevolution; Competition; Predation; Symbiosis
Interspecific competition, 57, 62. *See also* Competition
Intraspecific competition, 57, 61, 90, 97. *See also* Competition; Density-dependent factors
Intrauterine device (IUD). *See* Contraceptive, mechanical
Ireland, 124
Irondequoit Bay, 137
Irrigation. *See* Agriculture; Cultivation
Irrigation pollution. *See* Pollution, irrigation
Israel, 153
Ivory-bill Woodpecker. *See* Bird

Japan, 124, 158
Java Man, 158. *See also* Evolution

Kangaroos, 112
Katydid. *See* Insect
Kenya, 70, 103

Lake communities, *100–101*
Lake Mendota (Wisconsin), 35
Lake Michigan, 144
Lake Ontario, 138
Landfill, 131
Land-filling, 145. *See also* Solid waste pollution
La Porte (Indiana), 144
Lassa fever, 169
Lassoing fungus, 39
Laterization. *See* Soil
Leaching, 18, 124, *139*. *See also* Erosion
Leaf-drop, 92, 93
Legume, 16, 17, 18, 21, 55. *See also* Agriculture; Cultivation; Nitrogen cycle
Lemming, 74, *94, 95, 96, 108*
Lemmus trimucronatus. See Lemming
Lianas, 119
Lice. *See* Ectoparasite
Lichen, 51, 104, *108*, 109
Life cycle, 74
  turtle, 74
Life span. *See* Survivorship
Light
  through CO_2, 22
  energy input, 13, 15, 25
  See also Greenhouse effect; Sunlight
Lightning, 17, 18
Limestone, 16. *See also* Carbon cycle
Limpets, 138
Lincoln, Frederick, 74
Linnaeus, 110
Litter, 65

Liver fluke. *See* Endoparasite; Fluke
Locust, 91
Logging. *See* Lumbering
Long-billed curlew. *See* Bird
Longevity, 81. *See also* Mortality; Survivorship
Longleaf pine. *See* Trees
Los Angeles, *142*, 143, 145, 157
Lumbering, 122
  clearcutting, 89, 131, 144
  See also Fire; Trees
Lung diseases, 143, 145
Lynx. *See* Canadian lynx

Mabuya m. mabouya. See Reptile, lizard
Malaria, 27, 148, *159*, 166. *See also* Insect; Mosquito; Parasite
Malathion. *See* Organic phosphate compounds
Malthus, Thomas Robert, 160, 163, 164, 167
Mammals, predatory, 42
Man, 63
  cause of extinction, 112
  effect on biogeochemical cycles, 21, 37
  effect on ecosystem, 42, 99, 119
  effect on environment, 121
  effect on habitat, 89
  evolution of, 158
  health, 143
  migration, 129
  mortality, 81
  natality, 81
  pollution, 136
  population, 64, 81, 99, 122, 126, 157–175, *159*
  as predator, 40, 41, 52, 152
  survivorship, *82*, 83
  urbanization, 129
  See also Agriculture; Artificial selection; Domestication; Technology; Urbanization
Manduca quinquemaculatus. See Insect, sphinx moth
Mangrove swamps, 127, *128*
Marine organisms, 17, 18, 19, 20. *See also* Aquatic community; Fish
Marriage, 161
Marsh, 101
Marsupials, 112, 115
Martens, 109
Mature community. *See* Climax
Meat, production of, 52. *See also* Grazing
Medicine, 158
Mercury. *See* Pollution
Metabolic orderliness, 7, 11, 137. *See also* Orderliness

Metabolism, 13, 36, 92. *See also* Estivation; Hibernation
Mexico, 152
Mice, 94
Microbes, 154
Midge. *See* Insect
Migration, 20, 71, *72, 73,* 74, 75, 77, 89, *95, 108,* 109, 152
   man, 129
   trans-planetary, 174
   See also Dispersal
Migratory fish, 20
Milkweed, 45, *50. See also* Food plant
Mimicry, 45, *48. See also* Aggressive mimicry; Batesian mimicry; Coloration; Mullerian mimicry
Mining, 21, *139. See also* Fossil fuel; Leaching
Minks, 89
Minnesota, 35
Miracidium. *See* Fluke
Modification of habitat, 66. *See also* Dispersion, clumped
Mojave Desert, 3, *4*
Moles, 97
Monkey, Howler, 67
Moose, 135
Mortality, 64, 66, 77, 78, 80, *81,* 83, 84, 91, 97
   of man, 81, 158, 165, 166, 168
Moses, 161
Mosquitos, 150
Moss, 104, 109, 119
Moth. *See* Insect
Mullerian mimicry, 45, *48. See also* Mimicry
Mullet, 27, 28. *See also* Fish
Mushrooms, 27
Musk ox, *108*
Muskrats, 89
Mutation, 138
Mutualism, 49, 51, 52, 53, 54, 55, 61. *See also* Symbiosis

Natality, 42, 64, 77, 78, *80–81,* 84, 97
   in man, 158, 165, 166, 168
National forests, 132, 135
Natural barriers, 75, 77. *See also* Dispersal; Geographical barriers
Natural selection, 6, 11, 42, 150, 161
Nectar. *See* Flower
Nectarinia asiatica. See Bird, purple sunbird
Nematode worms, 39
Neotropics, 48
Nest site, 7, *9,* 67. *See also* Bird; Competition; Niche
New York, *111,* 137, 145, 157

Niche, 6, *8,* 11, 57, 62. *See also* Gause's Principle
Nicotine, 148. *See also* Pesticides
Nitrates. *See* Nitrogen cycle
Nitrogen cycle, 14, 16, *17,* 18, 19, 21, 37, 55. *See also* Erosion; Leaching; Legume; Nitrogen-fixing bacteria
Nitrogen-fixing bacteria, 16, 17, 18, 55. *See also* Bacteria
North Carolina, 40, *95*
Numenius americanus. See Bird, long-billed curlew
Nutrients, 101, 104, 107. *See* Biogeochemical cycles; Food web
Nymph, *96*

Ocean, 17, 18
   floor, 20
   See also Current; Fish; Water Pollution
Odum, Howard T., 33. *See also* Silver Springs, Florida
Oil, 143. *See also* Carbon cycle; Fossil fuel; Oil spill
Oil spill, 1, 138. *See also* Water pollution
Oklawaha River, *134*
Olfactory clues, 72
Omnivore, 14
Oöphorectomy. *See* Sterilization
Orange tree, 79
Orderliness, 5
   evolutionary, 5, 11
   metabolic, 7, 11
   spatial, 6, 11
   temporal, 7, 11
Oregon, 157
Organic compounds, 14, 16, 24, 27, 29, 124. *See also* Carbohydrates; Soil
Organic phosphate compounds, 153
Osa Peninsula, *116*
Overcrowding, 67, 71, 74, *96*
Oviposition, 72
Oxybelis aeneus. See Reptile, arboreal vine snake
Oxygen cycle, 13, 14, 37
Oysters, 83
   survivorship, *82,* 83

Pacific Flyway, 74–76, 130
Pakistan, *159*
Panama Canal, 1
Papaya. *See* Cultivation
Paper, reclamation of, 146
Paramecium aurelia, 57–59. *See also* Protozoa
Paramecium caudatum, 57–59. *See also* Protozoa

Parasitism, 13, 27, 49, 54–56, 61, 90, 129
  in banana, 126
  in biological control, 153, 155
  in biotic potential, 84
  See also Ectoparasite; Endoparasite;
    Food chain; Hyperparasitism; Sym-
    biosis
Parathion. *See* Organic phosphate com-
    pounds
Paratyphoid. *See* Disease organisms
Parus caerulens. See Bird, blue tit
Pathogens, 90, *95. See also* Bacteria;
    Pesticide; Viruses
Peat. *See* Carbon cycle; Fossil fuel
Pecking orders, 68. *See also* Social hier-
    archy
Peking Man, 158. *See also* Evolution
Penguin. *See* Bird
Perennial plants, 92
Perfection of cycling, 14
Periodism, 7, 11, 92, 97
  diurnal, 7
  lunar, 7
  nocturnal, 7
Permafrost, *108,* 109
Peru, 130, 150, 156
Pesticide, 10, 12, 89, *148–153,* 156
  biocides, 148
  biodegradable, 153, 155
  dispersal of, 151
  herbicides, 148
  immunity to, 150
  insecticides, 148, 150
  See also Agriculture; Pollution
Pestilence, 163, 168
Phosphate. *See* Detergent; Phosphorus;
    Water pollution
Phosphorus, 19, 21
  cycle, 19, *20*
  See also Detergent; Water pollution
Photoperiod, 88
Photosynthesis, 13, 14, 15, 20, 21, 22,
    24, 28, 32, 33, 35, 51, 101, 109,
    110, 113. See also Algae; Chloro-
    phyll; Efficiency; Producer; Sun-
    light
Phytoplankton. *See* Plankton
Pickerel. *See* Fish
Pig, 27, 52. *See also* Agriculture
Pine forest, *102,* 111, 122. *See also*
    Taiga
Pinus ponderosa. See Ponderosa pines
Pioneer community, 107
Pioneer organism. *See* Succession
Pitcher plants, 39, *40*
Pituitary gland, 91
Plains Indians. *See* Indians
Plankton, 7, 15, 20, 88, 101, 138
  phytoplankton, 19

Plants. *See* Green plants
Plastics, 147
Podiceps griseigena. See Bird, red-
    necked grebe
Polar ice caps, 23
Pollen. *See* Flower
Pollination. *See* Flower
Pollution, 64, *136–156*
  air, 133, 141–143, 156
  eutrophication, 140, 141, 156
  irrigation, 139
  mercury, 1, 12
  noise, 133
  oil, 138, *156*
  pesticides, 148–153, 156
  radioactive waste, 140, 156
  silt, *139*
  solid waste, 145–147, 156
  thermal, 137, 156
  vessel, *139,* 156
  water, 136–141, 145, 156
Ponderosa pines, *102,* 144
Poor-will. *See* Birds
Population, 38, 54, 57, 64, 66, 68, 69,
    71, 73, 74, 75
  definition of, 3, 75
  density, 78, 79
  ecology, 3, 11
  explosion, 157–160
  growth, 78, 80
  human, 1, 3, 11, 64
  measurement of, 79
  overcrowding, 39
  positive and negative growth, 80
  predatory regulation, 40
  regulation of, 74, 75, 87–92
  stability, 160
  See also Carrying capacity; Competi-
    tion; Growth form; Man; Parasit-
    ism; Population biology; Predation
Population biology, 63, 64
Population growth, 80, *86,* 88, 157–175
  control, 162, 163
  major factors, 80
  man, 157–175
  negative, 80
  positive, 80
  rate, 84, *85, 159*
  See also Contraceptives; Mortality;
    Natality; Survivorship
Potato. *See* Cultivation
Potential energy. *See* Chemical energy;
    Food chain
Power, 100
Prairie dog, 91
Predation, 20, 27, 35, 38, 39, 40, 42, 43,
    44, 45, 49, 51, 61, 73, 74, 90, 91,
    94, 96, 109
  in biological control, 153

in biotic potential, 84
mortality, 81
in plants, 39, *40*
spiders, 64
See also Coloration
Prey, 39. *See also* Predation
Primary consumer. *See* Herbivore
Primary succession, *106*, 107. *See also* Succession
Producer, 13, 28, 29, 30, 32, 34, 35, 37. *See also* Efficiency; Green plants; Photosynthesis
Productivity, 36
in a community, 103, 104
Prophylaxis. *See* Disease organisms
Protective coloration. *See* Cryptic coloration
Protein, 39
synthesis, 16, 17, 18
Protoplasm, 19, 20
Protozoa, 57, 58, 59, 89. *See also Paramecium*
Public works projects, *132–135*
Purple sunbird. *See* Bird
Pyramid
of biomass, 36
of energy, 36
of numbers, 35
See also Food web

Rabbits, 89
Radiation, 1, 147, 154, 155. *See also* Pollution
Radioactive waste, 140
Radioisotopes. *See* Radioactive waste; Pollution
Rain, 3, 18, 88, 89, 115, 121, 124, *132*. *See also* Biome; Desert; Erosion; Leaching
Rampart Canyon Dam, *134*
Random dispersion, 64, 77. *See also* Dispersion
Ratel. *See* Honey badger
Reclamation, 145, *146*. *See also* Solid waste pollution
Recreation, 131
Recycling in sedimentary cycles, 19, 20
Redia. *See* Fluke
Red-necked grebe. *See* Bird
Relative abundance, index of, 79, 97
Repelling coloration, 45. *See also* Coloration; Mimicry
Reproduction, 103
in clumped dispersion, 66, 77
man, 161
in population growth, 80
potential, 56
rate, 90
success, 60, 152

turtles, 71, 73
See also Differential reproduction; Natality; Societies
Reptile
aboreal vine snake, *43*
lizard, 10, 45
predatory, 42
Reservoir
of elements, 14, 15, 19, 20, 21
water 101, *134*
Respiration, 13–16, 24, 26, 29
Rhythm method. *See* Contraceptive, "natural" methods
Rice, 18, 52. *See also* Cultivation
River Styx, *134*
Robin. *See* Bird
Rocky Mountains, 91
Rodents, 100, 112. *See also* Lemming
Roman Catholic Church, attitude toward birth control, 171
Rookery, *9*. *See also* Bird
Root system, 13, 16, *17*, 18, 19
Roses. *See* Flowers
Rotation. *See* Cultivation
Roundworms, 27. *See also* Parasite
Runoff, 19. *See also* Erosion; Leaching; Watershed
Rye, 52. *See* Cultivation

S-shaped growth curve, *86–87*
Saigon, 127
Saigon River, *128*
Salmon. *See* Fish
Salpingectomy. *See* Sterilization
Salt, on roads, 137, 138
San Francisco Bay, 84, 129
Sanitary landfill. *See* Landfilling
Sanitation, *159*
Saprophyte, 13, 27. *See also* Decomposer
Savanna, 103, *114*, 115. *See also* Biome
Schaefer, Vincent, 145
Scientific-medical revolution, 158, 160
Scolopax rusticola. See Bird, European woodcock
Scotland, 59
Screwworm fly, 154
Sea birds. *See* Bird
Sea level. *See* Greenhouse effect
Seaborg, Glenn, 147
Seasons, 74
abundance of food, 74
effect on population, *86*, 88, 92
See also Periodicity; Population
Secondary pest, 151
Secondary succession, 107
Sediment, 17, 18, 19, 20, 37, 101, 132
Sedimentary cycle, 19, 37

Seral stages, 104, 121. *See also* Succession

Sere. *See* Seral stages

Setophaga ruticilia. See Bird, American redstart

Sewage, 137, 140, 166

Sharp-shinned hawk. *See* Bird

Sheep. *See* Grazing

Shrews, 97

Shrubs, 107, 109, *111*, 112, 114

Sierra Nevada Mountains, *106*

Sigmoid growth curve, *86–87*, 97

Silica, 124

Silt pollution. *See* Pollution, silt

Silver Springs (Florida), 26, 27, 33, 34, 35

Slash-and-burn agriculture, 126

Slavery, 162, 163

Sligh, Michael M., 168

Smog, 130, 141, *142*, 143, 157

Snail, 55, 56, 129

Snake. *See* Reptile

Snowmelt, *132*

Snowshoe hare, 93, *94*

Social attraction, 77

Social hierarchies, 67–68, 77. *See also* Pecking order; Social organization

Social interaction, 66

Social organization, 67, 69, 75, 77. *See also* Dispersion

Societies, 67, 69. *See also* Social organization

Soil, 16, 18, 29
  laterization, 124
  phosphorus in, 19
  topsoil, 124
  See also Agriculture; Erosion; Leaching

Solar energy. *See* Sunlight

Solid waste pollution, *145–147*
  incineration, 145
  land-filling, 145
  reclamation, 145
  See also Pollution

South American Indians. *See* Indians

South Atlantic, *72*

South Carolina, 145

Soviet Union, 124

Spatial orderliness, 6, 11. *See also* Orderliness

Specialization, 40, 61, 73. *See also* Bill size; Bird; Character displacement

Species, development of, 6. *See also* Evolution

Specific density, 79

Sphinx moth. *See* Insect

Spiders, predation, 64

Sporocyst. *See* Fluke

Squash, 52. *See also* Cultivation

Stability, 5, 28, 74, 121
  in predation, 42
  See also Density-dependent factors; Population

Standing crop, 103, 120

Steelhead. *See* Fish

Sterile individuals in social organization, 69

Sterilization
  hysterectomy, 173, 174
  salpingectomy, 173, 174
  vasectomy, 173, 174
  See also Biological control; Contraceptives; Family planning

Stockyards, 140

Storm drains. *See* Pollution, water

Stratification, 7, *8, 9,* 11
  in succession, 105
  thermal, 101

Streams, 19

Stress, 91, *96*

Striped bass. *See* Fish

Strontium-90, 1. *See also* Radiation

Subordination, 68. *See also* Social organization

Subsidence, geological, 20

Substrate, 104, 107

Suburban development, 129

Succession, 104–107, 121
  climax, 104
  forest, *105*
  primary, 107
  secondary, 107, 126
  seral stages, 104
  See also Communities

Sugar cane. *See* Cultivation

Sulfur oxides. *See* Air pollution

Sundews, 39, *40*

Sunflower, 53

Sunlight, 3, 20, 21, 22, 23, 25, 26, 28, 29, 32, 33, 34, 88, 100

Survival, 6, 34, 39, 66, 69, 160. *See also* Adaptation; Natural selection; Societies

Survivorship
  curves, *82*
  definition, 81
  effect on population growth, 78, 80

Sweden, 110

Swordfish. *See* Fish

Symbiosis, 38, 49, 52, 55, 61. *See also* Commensalism; Mutualism; Parasitism

Tadarida brasilensis. See Guano bat

Taiga, 109, *110. See also* Biome; Climax formations; Pine forest

Tampa Bay, 129

Tank plants, *118*
Tapeworm. *See* Endoparasite
Tapirs, 115, *118*
Taproot, 123
Technology, 122
Temperate deciduous forest, 6, 109, 110. *See also* Biome; Fire; Lumbering
Temperate zone, 34, 103, *110*
Temperature, 88
  of earth, 22
  of ocean, 21
Temporal differentiation. *See* Differentiation
Temporal orderliness, 7, 11. *See also* Orderliness
Terminal bud. *See* Trees, longleaf pine
Termites. *See* Insect
Terrestrial ecosystem, 17, 18, 19, 38, 100, 119, 122, 129
Terrestrial reservoirs of nutrients, 20. *See also* Reservoirs
Territoriality, 67, 77. *See also* Social organization
Territory, 67–68. *See also* Foraging area; Territoriality
Tetraopes. See Insect, beetle
Texas, 122
Thecadactylus rapidcaudus. See Reptile, lizard
Thermal pollution. *See* Pollution
Thermal stratification. *See* Stratification
Thermodynamics, Laws of, 24, 29, 37
Thrips imaginis. See Insect, thrip
Ticks, 27 55. *See also* Ectoparasite; Parasitism
Tide, effect on barnacles, 59
Timber, 131
Timberline, *108*
Tin cans, 147
Tobacco, 52. *See also* Cigarette smoking; Cultivation
Top carnivore, 29, 151. *See also* Carnivore
Topsoil. *See* Soil
Torrey Canyon, 138, 139
Toxaphene, 150. *See also* Pesticides
Trees
  acacias, 114, 115
  birch, 109
  fir, 109
  longleaf pine, 122, *123*
  palm, 114
  pine, *102*, 109
  spruce, 109
  willow, 109
Trichlorophenoxyacetic, 127. *See also* Herbicides
Trophic level, 28, *30*, 37. *See also*

Carnivore; Decomposer; Herbivore; Producer; Pyramid
Tropical deciduous forest, 115, *116.* *See also* Biome; Climax
Tropical rain forest, *4*, 5, 7, *8*, *30*, *46*, *50*, 99, 125, 127, 135
  agricultural inroads, 124
  as a biome, 115–119
  See also Biome
Tropical savanna, *114*–115. *See also* Biome; Climax
Truck gardens, 155
"True bugs." *See* Insect
Tundra, *108*–109. *See also* Biome; Climax
Turbidity, 101. *See also* Sedimentation; Water pollution
Turkey (bird), 52
Turtle grass, 72
Turtles, Green, 71
Typhoid. *See* Disease organisms

Ultraviolet light, 155
Uniform dispersion, 64, 65, 77. *See also* Dispersion
United Arab Republic, 101
United Nations Population Reference Bureau, 157
Uplifting, 100
Upwelling, 101
Urbanization, *129–131*, *142*, 157, 166, 167. *See also* Man
Ursus. See Bear
U.S. Army Corps of Engineers. *See* Corps of Engineers
U.S. Fish and Wildlife Service, 74
U.S. Forest Service, 122, 132
U.S. Surgeon General, 144

Vagility, 75, 77. *See also* Dispersal
Vasectomy. *See* Sterilization
Venus' Fly-trap, 39, 40
Vertical differentiation, 100. *See also* Communities; Differentiation
Vessel pollution. *See* Pollution
Viceroy butterfly. *See* Butterfly
Victoria Island, *95*
Vietnam, 127, *128*, 135
Vireo flavifrons. See Bird, yellow-throated vireo
Virginia, 122
Viruses, 90, 153, 154
Volcanism, 17

Walking stick. *See* Insect
Warfare, 163, 168, 169, 175
Warming coloration, *50*. *See also* Coloration
Washington, University of, 153

Wasp. *See* Insect
Water
  in atmosphere, 22
  in photosynthesis, 14
  See also Desalinization
Water beetle. *See* Insect
Water hyacinth, 3
Water pollution, 136–141, *146*. *See also*
    Pollution
Watershed, 131
Water supplies, 139
Weasels, 109
Weather. *See* Density-independent fac-
    tors
Weeds, 107
West Virginia, *139*
Wheat, 52

White-throated sparrow. *See* Bird
Whooping Crane. *See* Bird
Wildlife preservation, 131
Wisconsin, 35, 89
Wolves, *94*. *See also* Predation
Woodpecker. *See* Bird

Yeast, 147
Yellowstone National Park, 157
Yellow-throated vireo. *See* Bird
Yosemite National Park, 157
Yukon River, *134,* 135

Zero population growth, 175
Zinnser, Hans, 169
Zonotrichia albicollis. *See* Bird, white-
    throated sparrow